CW01650372

Blac

Polic

Q&A 2016

Blackstone's
Police Investigators'
Q&A
2016

Paul Connor

OXFORD
UNIVERSITY PRESS

OXFORD
UNIVERSITY PRESS

Great Clarendon Street, Oxford, OX2 6DP,
United Kingdom

Oxford University Press is a department of the University of Oxford.
It furthers the University's objective of excellence in research, scholarship,
and education by publishing worldwide. Oxford is a registered trade mark of
Oxford University Press in the UK and in certain other countries

First published in 2015

Impression: 1

Published in the United States of America by Oxford University Press
198 Madison Avenue, New York, NY 10016, United States of America

British Library Cataloguing in Publication Data
Data available

ISBN 978–0–19–874570–9

Printed in Great Britain by
Clays Ltd, St Ives plc

Contents

Introduction

On 14 January 2003 the Association of Chief Police Officers approved the 'Initial Crime Investigators' Development Programme' (ICIDP) as a successor to the 'National Foundation Course in Criminal Investigation'. Since then, the ICIDP has been split into three distinct phases with Phase 1 culminating in 'Trainee Investigators' sitting the National Investigators' Examination. The first National Investigators' Examination (NIE) took place in March 2003 and the examination has been held every three months since that time.

The aim of this book is to assist Trainee Investigators who are studying and revising for the NIE.

Every answer is followed by a paragraph reference to *Blackstone's Police Investigators' Manual*. This means that once you have attempted a question and looked at an answer, the Manual can immediately be referred to for help and clarification.

Each question and answer has the same unique number. This should ensure that there is no confusion as to which question is linked to which answer. For example, Question 2.1 is linked to Answer 2.1.

At the back of the book you will find a checklist. This has been designed to help you keep track of your progress when answering the multiple-choice questions. If you fill in the checklist after attempting a question, you will be able to check how many you got right on the first attempt and will know immediately which questions need to be looked at a second time.

I have included chapters on studying and revising for the NIE and taking the NIE to assist students in their efforts to pass the examination.

I know how hard students have to work to pass the NIE and I applaud your efforts. I sincerely hope that this book will help you in your study and contribute to your successful performance in your forthcoming examination.

Acknowledgements

The primary purpose of this book is to provide advice and direction for students taking the National Investigators' Examination and to enable them to test their knowledge against multiple-choice questions based on the *Police Investigators' Manual*.

I could not have accomplished this task without the assistance of many officers from West Midlands Police, West Mercia Constabulary and Essex Police. I wish to thank all the officers who have provided me with feedback about their examination experiences.

Thanks must also go to Peter Daniell, Lucy Alexander and all the team at Oxford University Press for their continued professional support of my work.

Most of all I would like to thank my wife, Kate, whose encouragement, patience and understanding are the reason these words are in print.

Studying and Revising for the NIE

Before beginning, plan carefully.
Cicero (106BC–43BC)

Before any methods of studying or revising for the National Investigators' Examination are suggested, it is vital that students understand that there are no shortcuts to success. Attaining a pass in the NIE will be achieved by many hours of study and revision and not by the use of any time- and effort-saving device or formula.

The primary cause of failing the examination is a lack of study and revision, so logically the first and most critical question a student should ask is, 'How much should I study and revise?' This question must then be subdivided and addressed from the dual points of, 'How much time should I study and revise for?' and 'How much of the content of the Manual and the Workbook should I study and revise?'

'How much time should I study and revise for?'

I have carried out a number of surveys with Trainee Investigators in order to establish what time period a *successful* student will revise for. As you might expect, answers to the question 'How much time did you study/revise for?' generate a varied response ranging from a low of 60 hours to a high of 400 hours. I advise you to set yourself a *minimum* 120-hour study/revision target for your 2016 examination as 120 hours is the average time spent studying/revising by the respondents to the surveys.

Having set the target of 120 hours' study/revision, the next factor to consider is over what time period students should study/revise. The standard approach by police forces taking part in the ICIDP process is to provide students with the *Police Investigators' Manual* and accompanying Workbook a minimum of 14 weeks prior to their examination. This has resulted in many forces distributing the Manual and Workbook to students on their 'Induction Day', usually held on or near to that 14-week period. Therefore, students may understandably set a 14-week period over which they will study/revise for a total of 120 hours, giving an approximate daily target of just under 75 minutes a day or an approximate weekly target of just under 8½ hours (these figures are a guide).

It is not suggested that students slavishly adhere to a regime of 75 minutes per day/8½ hours per week as this may not suit the study/revision style of the individual concerned (a facet of study/revision covered later in this chapter). The daily/weekly figure is an indication of the task that lies ahead for NIE students.

Depending on your study/revision style and general approach to the NIE, it may prove advantageous to obtain the Manual and Workbook at the first available opportunity. There is no logical reason why individuals who have been accepted onto the ICIDP should not be provided with the Manual and Workbook, subject to their availability, before the study/revision period begins. Obtaining the Manual and Workbook 17 weeks in advance of the NIE rather than 14 will be an advantage; that extra three weeks can make all the difference as it allows students to spread their study/revision over a greater period of time. I assure you that study/revising for the NIE has proved to be a demanding test for students in the past; this is just as much the case today. Many NIE students have reported the difficulty of balancing study/revision for the exam against the heavy workload of a detective, not to mention individual social and family commitments. To counter these pressures and to provide time for study/revision, it is not uncommon for students to take annual leave prior to the exam. This decision, whilst commendable, can have drawbacks. The majority of students making the decision to study/revise during annual leave will arrange for that leave to take place either 1 or 2 weeks in advance of the NIE. The temptation to leave study/revision until that time is significant. The problem is that by leaving study/revision until this late stage there is no margin for error; how will the student deal with their leave being cancelled or having to utilise the leave for some other purpose unimagined at the time when they took this decision? The second issue is that there is a great amount of work to do to prepare adequately for the NIE and 1 or 2 weeks might not be enough; how will the student deal with the fact that they underestimated the time it will take to study/revise or that when they begin to study/revise the task of reading and answering questions for the best part of 8 hours a day is beyond them? My advice is not to take this chance. Taking annual leave before the exam will undoubtedly help with study but students should begin studying/revising at the first available opportunity, i.e. start when first in possession of the Manual and Workbook.

Starting to study/revise at the first opportunity is vital; putting study/revision off makes the task so much harder. To further illustrate this point, students should recall how much time per day/week they would have to study/revise if provided with the Manual and Workbook 14 weeks prior to the NIE. Now consider a hypothetical student who decides not to study/revise until 5 weeks prior to the NIE. Aiming for 120 hours of study/revision, that student will have to study/revise for approximately 310 minutes per day/24 hours per week to catch up with the amount of work required.

Setting aside so much time each day is a challenging activity to say the least and places additional unnecessary pressure on the student. Of course, that target is beyond many people and so a lesser target is set. In turn, that means less study/revision is done and obviously that increases the chance of a lower mark and potential failure.

Having set a target of how many hours' study/revision should be undertaken, the next issue is how that time should be split from the period of initial possession of the Manual and Workbook to taking the NIE.

In the '14-Week Study and Revision Programme' section I have set out a detailed approach to this task. ***This might not suit everybody as we all have our own study/ revision methods and styles***. If this is the case the student should consider some of the following general observations with regard to study/revision.

Taking the 14-week period as an example, the student will be aware that the overall study/revision target is 120 hours. This target can then be split into a daily target or a weekly target. It has already been suggested that students may not wish to study/ revise for 75 minutes per day but if this suits the individual then there is no reason not to take this approach. Indeed, many of the successful students who participated in the NIE surveys chose to study study/revise for 1 to 2 hours per day. One of the advantages of this approach is that the study/revision target is broken down into achievable portions. Understandably, many students state that they find it difficult to study/revise for any longer than 2 hours at a time as the material they are reading is sometimes difficult to learn and their concentration suffers as a direct result. I would recommend that whatever time you set aside for study/revision, you should take a 5-minute break every hour to give your mind a chance to rest. Some students may choose to study/revise for more lengthy periods of time, perhaps up to 8 hours in one sitting. There is nothing wrong with this approach either as the methods for studying/revising for the NIE are as individual as the student taking the exam. If this method suits your individual style then do not change it for the sake of change.

Students may wish to use a mixture of the two methods. For example, a student may have adopted a study/revision pattern of 30 minutes per day/3 hours 30 minutes per week for the first 10 weeks and then in the last four weeks the amount of time devoted to the process is increased to approximately 3 hours per day/21 hours per week to bring the required study/revision period up to the desired 120-hour mark. This method has been favoured by many of the students who took part in the NIE surveys. The concept of this approach is that as the date of the NIE gets closer students should be looking to 'peak' with their knowledge base. The ideal situation is that the high point of that peak will be the taking of the NIE.

Regardless of the method a student decides to employ for study/revision purposes I would recommend that when an opportunity arises to study/revise, they take it. I would go so far as to say even 10 minutes spent reading the Manual is of value and for this reason I would encourage students to take their Manual and Workbook to work as well as reading it at home. When the opportunity to read the Manual and/or Workbook arises it should not be dismissed. Workplace opportunities may be limited with the pressures placed on Trainee Investigators but they may prove advantageous to some students. For example, a student dealing with a suspect for an offence of burglary may take 10 minutes to read the section on burglary before interviewing the suspect and equating the law to the circumstances surrounding the incident they are dealing with.

Students should be aware that time spent in study/revision is time well spent. Whilst it can never be an absolute guarantee of a pass in the NIE, investing the necessary hours of study/revision certainly lays the foundation for success.

'How much of the content of the Manual and the Workbook should I study/revise?'

The multiple-choice questions that students will answer in the NIE are based solely on the content of the *Police Investigators' Manual*.

Police Officers taking the NIE
Your syllabus is contained in Parts 1 to 4 of the *Police Investigators' Manual*
DO NOT STUDY PARTS 5 AND 6!

Parts 5 and 6 of the *Police Investigators' Manual* relate to a separate examination taken by officers from the National Crime Agency and Immigration Enforcement.

The *Police Investigators' Workbook* is designed as a study aid to help students understand the law in practice and to provide examples of such. On that basis, students might consider that the Workbook is unnecessary and omit it from their study/revision; I would suggest that they should not. It should be used as an additional means of understanding the law contained within the Manual and not ignored. However, as the questions within the NIE are not based on material within the Workbook, there is no need for students to study/revise the Workbook with the intensity required when examining the Manual.

As has already been stated, the questions in the NIE are based on the content of the Manual alone. Even so, the syllabus is considerable in size and it may be tempting for a Trainee Investigator to consider methods of cutting down on the content they will have to examine. One approach often considered is that students can cut out certain sections that they deal with regularly in the workplace because of that workplace knowledge; this would be a mistake. The fact that a student deals with thefts, burglaries and assaults on a daily basis will not, alone, provide them with the requisite knowledge on those subjects in order to answer questions correctly in the

NIE. The practical application of the law and the theoretical application of the law, whilst related, are not always the same. Students should not treat these areas with contempt purely because of their workplace familiarity with the subject. Conversely, students may look at certain sections and consider that the likelihood of dealing with such an incident in the workplace is insignificant and therefore so is the requirement to know the subject for the purposes of the exam. Do not think that this is the case. Purely because an offence is not an everyday occurrence in a student's workplace does not mean that it is never committed or that it is unimportant; if it is included in the syllabus it is as testable as the crimes that make up 95% of a CID officer's daily routine.

Having examined the issues surrounding 'How much should I study/revise', I will now turn to some methods of studying/revising.

Methods of studying/revising

The prospect of studying and revising from the *Police Investigators' Manual* can be an overwhelming one for students. Many have not taken a police examination since their initial training and this can, in some cases, be in excess of 10 years prior to taking the NIE. Even students familiar with the format of multiple-choice examinations, as their initial training period was not that long ago or perhaps because they have taken the Sergeants' or Inspectors' examination at some time, find the task daunting. One of the primary difficulties faced by all students, regardless of their experience, is deciding on an approach to studying and revising from the Manual; having set the time they will study and revise for, how will they go about it?

Perhaps the most important point to make at this stage is that nobody is expecting the student to remember, word for word, the whole of the *Police Investigators' Manual*. I would go so far as to say that this task is impossible. The task for the student is to retain enough information from their study and revision in order to pass the NIE; whether the student gets 99% or 55% is irrelevant as a pass is a pass (although the pass mark for the NIE is given as 55%, it is a 'rounded-down' figure from 55.71%).

There are no absolute rules when it comes to these methods as all students differ in the way they absorb and retain information. However, I am often asked about alternative systems by students seeking to maximise the benefit of the time they will invest in the task. One method of approaching your study/revision is advanced in the '14-Week Study and Revision Programme' section but there are several other approaches that may be preferable to you. Next are several tried and tested methods used by students who have taken and passed the NIE (they are in no order of popularity or effectiveness).

1. Reading through the text of the Manual in order (beginning to end)

Many students favour this method because it is simple and effective. Students will read and re-read the same text continually, a task that can become tiresome and heighten the danger of 'scanning' the text rather than actually reading it and taking in the detail. To counter this I suggest students consciously slow down their reading speed; take more time reading the definitions and 'Keynote' explanations of the law in action. It is far better to take time and therefore ensure comprehension rather than race through the text in an effort to finish reading the Manual as soon as possible.

2. Reading through the text and 'highlighting' relevant points and words

A version of method 1, this method naturally draws the attention of the student to important elements of legislation highlighted by that student. Used correctly, this method can make referring to the Manual a speedier process. However, students should not overuse the 'highlighter' as the end result is often half or whole pages of the Manual highlighted with no discernible relevant points as the page turns into a mass of bright pink, yellow, blue or green.

3. Begin from the student's perceived weakest area

For example, a student may consider their weakest area to be 'Sexual Offences' or 'Evidence' and start by reading and re-reading that particular section. One of the advantages of this method is that by dealing with the difficult from the outset, the task will become easier as the student progresses to areas of strength, such as 'Property Offences'. A disadvantage is that in beginning with an area of weakness, the student may become demoralised at an early stage of the process.

4. Begin from the student's perceived strongest area

This is the exact opposite of method 3 with the opposite advantage and disadvantage, i.e. starting from an area of strength will boost the confidence of the student at an early point but leaving the difficult area(s) until last may demoralise the student in the run-up to the NIE.

> I would raise a note of caution with regard to methods 3 and 4. These methods operate on the student's perceived areas of weakness or strength and the student is sometimes incorrect as to their ability. For example, a student may believe that 'Property Offences' is an area of strength when in fact this is not the case and on closer examination of the text it is an area of weakness, and vice versa. Students should be aware of the detrimental effect this may have.

5. *Read a section in the Manual, make short notes from that section and then study/revise from the short notes*

Another popular choice with students, this method condenses the Manual into smaller, more manageable portions and allows the student to draw their own attention to significant points. Making notes from the text sometimes helps to cement knowledge in the mind of the student as the exercise involves reading the text, making a mental decision on relevant points, writing down those points and then re-reading them. I would not recommend a total abandonment of the Manual after the notes have been written as there is always the danger that in making the notes, a student may inadvertently miss out a vital part of a definition or explanation or incorrectly note it down. I would also urge students not to use notes made by another person as notes are a very individual exercise—what I think is important or what I need to remember may not be the same for you.

6. *Reading the Manual from cover to cover (to understand the nature and difficulty of the task of studying/revising), constantly re-reading the Manual and taking part in study/revision sessions with another student(s)*

Some students have been successful by meeting with a fellow student or students and testing each other on their knowledge of the Manual. The element of competition can act as a spur for students to work hard and answer more questions correctly than their colleague(s). It also enables students to discuss difficulties with certain areas of law and help each other to understand those areas; one student's weak area is another's strong area. It is not always possible to meet with a fellow student but this should not preclude the use of this method as there is nothing wrong with students asking their tutor or work colleagues to test them.

7. *Split the Manual into the four component sections and set aside a time period in which to study each section*

An example of this method is the student who sets aside 12 weeks to study/revise and splits those 12 weeks into four 3-week sections. Each 3-week section is devoted to one section of the Manual, for example 'Sexual Offences'. The student will study/revise according to his/her own preferred method. This method is successful as the Manual can sometimes be a barrier to effective study/revision because of its size. Breaking it down into component sections can lower that barrier. The drawback with this method is that some sections are far larger than others, for example, 'Evidence' is at least three times longer than any of the other sections of the Manual and may, as a consequence, require considerably more time to deal with effectively. However, there is no reason why the student could not alter the split of the study/revision period to reflect this and any other factors that affect the student's study/revision programme.

8. Read the whole book and make crammer cards on offences. Alternate between reading the crammer cards and reading the Manual

A version of method 5 but instead of notes, the student will study/revise from cards with the very basic details of the chosen offences written on those cards. Using cards in this manner can really help with study/revision as the student will only have the card to concentrate on rather than a full page of A4 from the Manual or notes that they have written. As with method 5, students should not exclusively use the cards they have written because they may miss out certain details from the Manual in the process.

Whatever method a student employs, I would recommend that some form of testing knowledge, e.g. answering multiple-choice questions, follows study/revision from the Manual. I have known many students whose knowledge of the Manual was certainly good enough to pass the NIE; however, they did not test that knowledge by answering questions. The result of this is that in the NIE, the student who has not practised multiple-choice questions can become disorientated by the complexity of the questions and the choice put before them. The result of this has, in many cases, been failure.

Apart from this book and the multiple-choice questions in the Workbook, a further study aid should be considered—a mock examination. Blackstone's have published a National Investigators' Mock Examination (written by David Pinfield) which follows the format of the examination both in the type and style of questions and the broad areas that will be questioned. Many students who took part in my surveys reported that they would take the mock examination 2 to 3 weeks in advance of the real examination. This would highlight areas of weakness and give the TI the time to rectify the gap in their knowledge. Some forces will offer TIs the opportunity to take the mock examination under examination conditions—if such an offer is made I strongly suggest the offer be taken as practising in such conditions can only assist TIs in becoming more familiar with the examination process.

Do not

Having examined alternative study/revision methods it is also advisable to mention methods that students should not employ in their study/revision.

1. Do not use any other legal textbooks to study/revise from

Although students may be tempted to utilise other legal textbooks (aside from the Manual) to enhance their knowledge, there is a high risk that such a method will only confuse the student. The law is not always black and white, it is sometimes grey and, accordingly, different legal textbooks will often have different interpretations of the law. This might be a bonus if the student was answering essay-type questions where the answer is expected to discuss different opinions but it is an obstruction to answering a multiple-choice exam question, as only one answer from the four choices is right. If the student reads from other texts there is a strong chance that when answering questions in the NIE they will feel that two or three of the options could be correct. In addition, questions in the NIE are often worded to mirror the text of the Manual. If the student has read from other sources then their ability to recognise the correct option will be adversely affected.

2. Do not use the 'Police National Legal Database' (PNLD) as a primary study/revision tool

This facility is an excellent professional tool for police officers to use in the workplace. However, like using other legal texts it may conflict with the Manual and confuse rather than enlighten the student. The further difficulty with the PNLD is that it is constantly updated with new law and procedures and this new law may contradict the law that is written in the Manual. There is a possibility that the law that was correct when your Manual was printed has since been superseded by a new Act of Parliament or by a case law decision and is now no longer correct. Whilst it is desirable to maintain your professional knowledge by keeping up to date with legal developments, this can have a negative effect on your study/revision. Students then ask, 'What should I answer if this question comes up in the exam?' The answer to that question is that you answer according to the Manual regardless of whether it is right or wrong.

On that last point, students are often concerned about changes in the law where the Manual is inconsistent with those changes. This is also a concern for the examiners who construct the examination. If the examiners are aware of a contradiction in the law, it is unlikely that a multiple-choice question relating to that law will be set in the NIE, in order to avoid confusion. However, there is always the possibility that such questions may be set inadvertently (as has occurred in several promotion examinations) and hence my previous advice.

3. Do not answer multiple-choice questions ONLY

I have known several students who have told me that their learning style meant that answering multiple-choice questions was the way they preferred to learn and that they had never looked at the Manual. One student (who used this method) came out of the NIE and told me that she had ticked every question she had guessed; she had 65 ticks and failed the examination. I think that makes my point.

In conclusion, if the student has a study/revision method or pattern that they find works for them then my advice is simple; use it. Every student is different and will learn in a different way and at a different pace. One fact I am sure of is that 99.9% of students get the result their efforts deserve; students must study and revise to succeed.

Taking the NIE

In order to pass the NIE, students will have to spend many hours studying and revising to expand their knowledge of the law. This preparation for the examination is an absolute necessity; without it students invite failure. I am sure any hard work will not be wasted but in order to maximise the benefit of any study/revision students carry out, they should also know how that knowledge will be tested.

Students need to understand exactly what they will be doing when they sit the examination. This is a small but nevertheless vitally important part of preparation. Becoming familiar with the technicalities of a multiple-choice question (MCQ) examination is part of a professional and ordered approach to the task; in addition, it will increase the student's confidence regarding the examination.

The aim is for students to sit down at the time of the examination knowing what their target is and how they will achieve it. The only unknown factor should be the precise content of the examination; everything else should be recognisable to the student. This chapter will deal with the examination format so that the process should not catch students unaware.

Do not underestimate the danger of ignoring this part of preparation as in doing so students run the risk of panic setting in at the beginning of or during the examination. This could have a devastating effect on performance. I am not trying to train students as question writers, but I believe just a little time invested in this task will serve students well. I know very few people who have no nerves before sitting such an examination; students can reduce those nerves and therefore improve performance by becoming accustomed to the MCQ examination format.

The standard MCQ style

Before we look at differing styles of MCQs, students need to familiarise themselves with some terms relating to the subject that they may be unfamiliar with. This section is only for information.

Look at the following question:

You have arranged that WILSON, a suspect for robbery, will attend your station along with his solicitor. WILSON arrives with his solicitor and you arrest him for the offence. After the custody officer has completed the custody record and before you interview WILSON, his solicitor presents a pre-prepared statement written by WILSON that relates to the robbery. WILSON's solicitor suggests that his client does not need to be interviewed by the police as the statement represents all his client is willing to say.	STEM
As the interviewing officer, what action will you take?	LEAD-IN
A Inform the solicitor that any statement made by WILSON to the solicitor is subject to legal privilege and as a result it cannot be introduced to the investigation. **B** Point out to the solicitor that the contents of the statement will be considered but that the decision to interview rests with the police. **C** Confirm that the statement represents all WILSON wants to say. If that is the case then he may not be questioned about the robbery unless it is to clear up any ambiguity. **D** WILSON and his solicitor should sign and date the statement. You should seize the statement and treat it as if it were a 'written statement under caution' by the defendant.	OPTIONS

The terms used in the shaded column are the only technical MCQ terms used in this chapter.

Individual forces should draw the attention of an NIE candidate to the National Investigators' Examination section of the College of Policing website where a copy of the 'NIE Rules and Syllabus' can be examined/downloaded (www.college.police.uk). There is a great deal of important and useful information contained in the 'NIE Rules and Syllabus' document. But for now, I want to concentrate on the style of the questions in the NIE. The guide illustrates a typical example of the style of MCQ that students will face when they take the examination. Next is a further example:

BREEN plans an armed robbery on a security van that regularly picks up cash at a local bank. He enlists the help of FISH and TODD, who agree to actually carry out the armed robbery while BREEN waits for them at a rendezvous point. BREEN has no intention of taking part in the commission of the armed robbery itself. Unknown to BREEN, the security company has been 'tipped off' about the robbery and changes the day of collection so that the security van does not arrive at the bank. FISH and TODD leave empty-handed.

Does BREEN commit statutory conspiracy contrary to s. 1 of the Criminal Law Act 1977?

A No, BREEN has no intention of taking part in the actual armed robbery itself.

B Yes, BREEN commits the offence as soon as he plans the robbery and before he enlists the help of FISH and TODD.

C No, the commission of the offence is impossible because the security van would never arrive at the bank.

D Yes, BREEN has agreed on a course of conduct that will involve the commission of an offence.

The correct answer is D. BREEN does not have to take part in the offence to be guilty of conspiracy as he has agreed on a course of conduct that will involve the commission of an offence by one or more parties to the agreement, making answer A incorrect. Answer B is incorrect as at this stage BREEN is only planning the offence and is the only person involved; you need at least two parties to commit statutory conspiracy. Answer C is incorrect as you can conspire to commit the impossible under s. 1(1)(b) of the Criminal Law Act 1977.

Although this is the typical style of examination question, there are some MCQs that do not conform to the previous archetypal layout. These different MCQs are responsible for one of the most common misconceptions about the NIE and indeed any type of police promotion examination: that the question style is complex and detailed. This is not the case. The content might be somewhat difficult and that is reasonable; after all, students would not expect the examination to be easy. However, the style of question students will face in the NIE is exactly as the two examples I have just given. In other words, a 'stem' giving you the facts of the question, the 'lead-in' directing you to the area of law to be tested and finally four clear 'options' that are viable alternative solutions to the problem.

MCQ styles that are not used in the NIE

There are a number of valid ways of compiling MCQs. Some of them are excluded from the standard best practice for question setting in the NIE.

MCQs where the answer options are effectively presented in two stages (as in the following PARKER example) are generally excluded and students will not come across this style of question in the NIE.

This type of question can be presented in a way that does fall within the NIE style. An example of the two-stage approach and how that question could be amended to fit within the NIE style is in the following AGNEW example.

PARKER breaks into a warehouse intending to steal anything of value that he can find. He forces a door and gets into the warehouse but finds nothing during his search. Frustrated at his lack of success, PARKER damages a toilet inside the warehouse before he leaves.

What offences does PARKER commit?

(i) Burglary contrary to s. 9(1)(a) of the Theft Act 1968.
(ii) Burglary contrary to s. 9(1)(b) of the Theft Act 1968.
(iii) Attempted theft contrary to s. 1 of the Criminal Attempts Act 1981.
(iv) Criminal damage contrary to s. 1(1) of the Criminal Damage Act 1971.

A (i), (ii) and (iv) only.
B (ii) and (iii) only.
C (i) and (iv) only.
D (ii), (iii) and (iv) only.

MCQs using roman numerals as options are not contained in the examination. They unnecessarily complicate matters and are very confusing for the student. Not only does this type of MCQ test students' knowledge of the law but also it tests their ability to select the correct option. Mistakes are easily made when students are under pressure and it is possible that the correct answer is known but the wrong option is picked because of the complicated layout of the question. Students will be relieved to know that this style of question is out of favour with NIE examiners. In case you were wondering, the answer to the previous question is C.

Also removed from the examination are questions that follow the style shown here:

In which, if either, of the following cases has an offence of 'obstruct police' contrary to s. 89 of the Police Act 1996, been committed?

(i) STEVENS is caught in a speed trap. After he is given a speeding ticket he doubles back and drives 200 metres away from the speed trap. He holds out a homemade sign that states, 'All drivers slow down—Police speed trap ahead!' warning drivers about to commit a speeding offence of the speed trap.

(ii) INGLETON is stopped and questioned by PC CONNOLLY who believes INGLETON may have seen the direction that an armed robber has run off in. INGLETON refuses to answer any of the questions put to him by the officer.

A (i) only.
B (ii) only.
C Both.
D Neither.

Once more, a complicated type of question because it effectively asks the student to answer two questions at once and, again, I can state that this style of question will not be in the examination. The answer to this question is A.

What students may see in the examination is a version of the last style of question, an example of which follows (I have put the (i), (ii), 'Both' and 'Neither' options by the side to illustrate my point):

AGNEW and CLARKE decide to break into a house. AGNEW is in possession of a screwdriver to force the window and CLARKE is in possession of a knuckle-duster just in case the occupier causes any trouble. CLARKE knows about the screwdriver but AGNEW has no idea that CLARKE has a knuckle-duster with him. The two men break into the house but are arrested while inside searching for property.

Who, if anyone, is guilty of aggravated burglary (contrary to s. 10 of the Theft Act 1968)?

A AGNEW alone commits aggravated burglary. ((i) only)
B CLARKE alone commits aggravated burglary. ((ii) only)
C CLARKE and AGNEW commit the offence. (Both)
D The offence of aggravated burglary has not been committed by either of the men. (Neither)

The answer to this question is B.

Questions with longer sets of facts take longer to process

The next point I want to make relates to the length of the MCQ. This is important as it links to a central element of the examination time.

It is plain that not all MCQs will be of exactly the same length. The unwritten rule is that the MCQ should not be more than 250 words long. There is no lower limit but to test a student's knowledge and so that the question makes sense and is written following the correct style, it is unlikely that the MCQ will be less than 50 words long. For example the six questions in this chapter range from 103 to 210 words long, with an average of 144 words per question.

So why is this relevant? It is relevant because students have to know how long it takes to read a question, consider the facts, come to a conclusion and mark their answer on the question paper. Students have 120 minutes to complete the 80-question NIE, that's an average of 90 seconds per question. It might not sound a long time but it is certainly long enough to deal with each question in the examination. The time it takes to consider the facts and come to a decision is what many students worry about but the main factor affecting how long it takes to answer a question is a student's reading time.

It is important not to worry if it is taking a little longer than 90 seconds to answer each question, as it is likely that students will be able to make up for lost time as the examination progresses. A strict 90 seconds per question approach will probably work against students rather than for them as answering questions is not an exact science.

Some questions will be easy, others will not. However, regardless of the difficulty of the question, the one factor that will impact on time is the length of the MCQ.

Examine the following question and time how long it takes to answer it:

The Crime and Disorder Act 1998 took existing offences and then set out circumstances under which those offences would be deemed to be 'aggravated'.

Which of the following offences is covered by that legislation?

A Riot, contrary to s. 1 of the Public Order Act 1986.

B Violent disorder, contrary to s. 2 of the Public Order Act 1986.

C Affray, contrary to s. 3 of the Public Order Act 1986.

D Fear or provocation of violence, contrary to s. 4 of the Public Order Act 1986.

This question has 76 words in it. You, like many other students, will have started to consider the answer as you were reading through the MCQ, but how long did it take you to actually deal with the question in its entirety? The following table shows the results from a sample of 10 police officers:

Allocated time per question	= 90 seconds
Read time (how long it took just to read the MCQ)	= 15 seconds
Consideration of question and marking the answer	= 21 seconds
Total time to answer question	= 36 seconds
Spare time (to make up for previous/carry on to next MCQ)	= 54 seconds

It is important to bear in mind that these are averages and you may have taken more time or maybe even less to answer this question. The point is that this length of question gives you one of two things: the chance to catch up on your time if you are behind your average of 90 seconds per question schedule or, alternatively, the chance to bank time for when you meet the more lengthy and complex MCQs. The answer to the question is D.

Now examine the following question and time how long it takes you to answer it:

MARSTON is part of a religious commune. UNWIN believes that MARSTON is in danger as the commune will ask MARSTON to turn all her property over to them. UNWIN decides that she will return MARSTON to her parents' home by whatever means are necessary. UNWIN visits the commune and finds MARSTON. She asks MARSTON to walk with her while they discuss her situation and MARSTON agrees. MARSTON refuses to return with UNWIN who then lies to MARSTON, stating that MARSTON's mother is seriously ill and that she must come with her. MARSTON agrees and begins walking with UNWIN. Several minutes later, MARSTON asks for proof of her mother's illness from UNWIN who, at this point, physically drags MARSTON along for several metres before she lets her go.

At what point, if at all, does UNWIN first commit the offence of kidnap?

A When UNWIN initially begins walking with MARSTON intending to return her by whatever means necessary.

B When she lies to MARSTON about her mother and MARSTON walks with her for several minutes.

C When UNWIN uses physical force to drag MARSTON for several metres.

D UNWIN does not commit the offence because she has a lawful excuse to carry away MARSTON.

This question contains 203 words. Let us examine how our 10 police officers fared with the question:

Allocated time per question	= 90 seconds
Read time (how long it took just to read the MCQ)	= 51 seconds
Consideration of question and marking the answer	= 20 seconds
Total time to answer question	= 71 seconds
Spare time (to make up for previous/carry on to next MCQ)	= 19 seconds

Our 10 candidates managed to complete the question in less than 90 seconds but this may not be the case under examination conditions. There is always that question that takes longer than average, either because it is complicated or perhaps because you find it difficult. You must be prepared for this to happen and do not panic if you spend longer than 90 seconds on a particular question. Do not let this play on your mind during the examination. Deal with the question and move on. It may be worth taking a more measured approach to reading the question so ensuring that you do not have to repeatedly read through the elements of it in order to make sense of the answer options. This question is part of the section on Child Abduction, Kidnap and False Imprisonment and a full answer is included in the relevant answers section.

Binary questions

Answer the following question:

TWIST is arrested for an offence of theft by PC YOUSEF. PC YOUSEF is escorting TWIST to her police vehicle when PHILBIN approaches the officer and points an imitation pistol at her. Intending to make the officer release TWIST, PHILBIN tells PC YOUSEF that unless she releases TWIST, he will shoot her. PC YOUSEF tells PHILBIN that she knows the pistol is a fake and ignores his demand.

With regard to the offence under s. 17(1) of the Firearms Act 1968 only, which of the following statements is correct?

A The fact that an imitation firearm is used is immaterial; PHILBIN has committed the offence.

B The person using the weapon must be the person under arrest; therefore PHILBIN does not commit the offence.

C As PC YOUSEF does not believe that the imitation firearm is real, the offence is not committed.

D PHILBIN does not commit the offence because the term 'firearm' under s. 17 does not include imitation firearms.

Normally, the standard MCQ asks one question of a candidate, i.e. which of the following four options is correct? I call this style of question the 'binary question' because it is one question that is a combination of two questions:

1. Do you know what s. 17(1) of the Firearms Act 1968 is?
2. If you do, which of the following options is correct?

This style of MCQ is still acceptable and may be included in your examination. If you find yourself dealing with such a question and you know that you do not know what s. 17(1) of the Firearms Act 1968 is, what can you do? The only option is to synthesise an answer using the information contained in the stem and/or the lead-in and the options. For example:

The stem tells you that TWIST has been arrested and, intending to make PC YOUSEF release TWIST, PHILBIN is using a firearm—it has to be using a firearm to resist arrest.

Of course, if you did not know anything about firearms law then you would have found this question all the more difficult. Even if you did know, then you would have to know more about the section to accurately answer the question. However, working out the subject matter from the question content might help you eliminate one or even two of the options and therefore give you a better chance of obtaining a correct answer. The answer to this question is A.

Having considered the question styles that will and will not present themselves to the student taking the NIE, we should turn to some other important issues to consider with regard to the examination.

Verification questions

The NIE contains 80 MCQs but students are only marked from 70; the remaining 10 MCQs are verification questions. Usually, verification questions are placed into the examination randomly, i.e. not all 10 are placed at the beginning, middle or end of the examination (although in rare cases that can sometimes occur).

It is necessary to test verification questions in order to assess their suitability for future examinations. The fact that these questions are not marked may tempt students to guess which questions within the NIE are the verification questions and pay less attention to them as a result. I would strongly advise against this course of action. As the verification questions are usually placed randomly in the examination it is very difficult to decide accurately whether a question is a verification question or not. If a student guesses incorrectly then they may lose a mark from a question that counts towards the result and this must be discouraged. It is a far better policy to treat every single question as a question that counts rather than guessing whether it is a verification question.

Pass mark

The pass mark for the NIE has been set at 55%. However, this precise mark is unattainable due to the fact that only 70 questions from the 80 that students answer are marked (see 'verification questions' in the previous section). The actual pass park for the exam is 55.71%. This means that a student can pass the examination if they answer 39 of the 70 marked questions correctly. It is important to know what is required to pass the examination as this gives the student a target to aim for. The actual target to guarantee a pass is to get 49 questions right out of 80. Getting 49 questions right would mean that a student would pass the NIE even if they had answered all 10 of the verification questions correctly within those 49 correct answers (49/80 – 10 = 39 = 55.71% = Pass). Research shows that the average student loses 5 questions to the verification process so it is vital that students do not rely on luck to get them through the NIE. The further away from the target of 49 correct questions the student is, the greater the chance of failure.

Begin immediately

When the examiner informs you that you may be begin, *do not* read through all the questions before you start the examination. Start answering the questions straight away. Reading through questions is suitable for essay-type examinations but any student taking this course of action in the NIE will squander a large proportion of the examination time. Apart from wasting time, it will be of no benefit to the student as, by the time they have read question 80, they will most certainly have forgotten question 1. I know of several occasions when this approach has been taken and each resulted in failure for the student involved.

Do not change your answers

Research has shown that more students change correct answers to incorrect answers than incorrect answers to correct answers. In other words, a student's first answer is often correct. Unless the student is checking their answers and realises they have made an error or misunderstood the question, it is better to stick with the original answer.

Do not miss questions out

During the NIE it is almost inevitable that the student will come across a question that causes them some difficulty. This will probably be because the question is complicated and/or the student has some knowledge, but not quite enough, to answer the question. A student may invest 90+ seconds trying to answer this question before deciding to leave it to the end of the examination. Invariably, the student will mark the question paper next to the question but will not mark an answer on the answer sheet. I would advise that the student should answer the question, even if it is their best guess. This is because, when the student returns to the question at the end of the examination, they will still have to read the question again to familiarise themselves with the circumstances. This eats into any time the student has to check their answer paper. If the student runs out of time then at least there is a mark against that question rather than a blank space that will receive no mark. The other danger of leaving a gap in the answer paper is that such an action can accidentally lead to the student filling in the wrong answer boxes to a question. This is an easy mistake to make when answering MCQs and can lead to failure purely because of the student's error.

Do not be an 'administration failure'

Perhaps the worst reason for failing the exam is making some type of error that could have easily been avoided. The student has prepared for the NIE by investing time and effort in their study and revision only to ruin their chances of success by a lack of consideration of the very basic detail surrounding the examination. There are several possible ways that students can become what I term 'administration failures'; some thought should be given to the following factors to ensure that you do not fall into this category.

1. Do you know the venue for your examination?

Find out where your examination is going to be held and make sure that you have considered how you will need to get there, i.e. your route and mode of transport.

2. Give yourself plenty of time to get to the examination venue

Regardless of whether you are familiar with the venue for the examination or not, you should ensure that you will arrive in plenty of time. The NIE is held at various test centres across the country and you will be told that you must be at the test centre 30 minutes before the examination begins. You will be allowed into the examination room 15 minutes before the NIE begins and you cannot afford to be late. The examination invigilators are under strict instructions (which they will adhere to regardless of the reason for being late) that students arriving after this time will not be allowed into the examination room. If necessary, carry out a 'dry run' to the venue at the same time as you will need to on the day of the examination. Whatever time it takes to get to the venue, I suggest you add an hour to it and you have your start time. The last thing that a student needs is to be refused access because they are late. Even if the student arrives close to the cut-off time because of traffic congestion they will be flustered and not in the best frame of mind to sit the examination. It is far better to be at the venue early and relaxed.

3. Use your Warrant Card as a ruler in the examination

As you answer each question, place your Warrant Card underneath the A, B, C and D box that relates to that question. This will prevent you from accidentally placing your answer against the wrong question number. It will not add any significant time to the time it takes to answer the questions.

> *I am a strong believer in luck and I find the harder I work the more I have of it.*
> Benjamin Franklin (1706–90)

The 14-Week Study and Revision Programme

The origins of this programme can be found in 2004 when I was assisting a student who had failed her first attempt at the National Investigators' Examination (scoring 28.6% in the process). The student was extremely upset and naturally concerned that a second failure would mean removal from the CID and that her previous efforts had gone unrewarded. Unlike some trainers and supervisors, I have always been aware of the pressure that this examination brings, but this student's predicament highlighted the fact that the stakes in the NIE can be high and that failure and, ultimately, removal from the ICIDP has the potential to be extremely damaging to the student concerned. This is particularly true when the student genuinely wants to pass and is willing to work but simply does not know how to go about it.

When I questioned the student, the reason for this failure became obvious to me. Although the student had done some study and revision (although not enough in my opinion) it had been carried out in a very haphazard fashion. This factor was far more to blame for the student's failure than the lack of study and revision. The student was flitting from one subject to the next using no apparent logical methodology in the process. The student lacked one of the central elements required for success in any examination: an ordered approach.

An ordered approach

An ordered approach is essential from the outset. That order is obtained by being able to answer three questions:

1. What do I need to study/revise for this examination (what is the syllabus)?
2. How much time (in total) do I have to study/revise it?
3. How will I organise 1 and 2?

Many students, not only the 28.6% failure mentioned previously, have a disordered approach because they do not have an answer to question 3. This has a negative effect on study/revision and damages morale, both of which can be fatal or at least damaging to their result. I realised that I was going to have to provide my student with an answer to question 3 because she could not find it herself and would inevitably fail again. My aim, therefore, was to provide a straightforward study/revision programme that ensured my student revised the whole syllabus in time for her next examination and would present her with an improved chance of success. I achieved that aim. My student passed on her second attempt with a mark of 78.5%. The student later told me that she had increased the amount of study/revision carried out (something else I told her to do) but had benefited immensely from the programme I had created as it provided an ordered framework into which the student's study/revision efforts were placed.

I decided that rather than wait for future students to fail before the programme was made available, I would provide it to them at the outset, when it is most required. The programme was provided to West Midlands officers in December 2005 (sitting the NIE in March 2006) and proved to be invaluable (West Midlands Police achieved a 100% pass-rate in this exam). It was then provided to West Midlands and Essex officers sitting the June and September 2006 NIE. From December 2005, over 200 officers field-tested the programme achieving an unparalleled degree of success. The programme was introduced to this Q&A in the 2007 edition. The programme has not remained static since that time as there have been many changes in the syllabus and the way the Manual is constructed along with consequent alterations in the amount of time devoted to study by successful NIE candidates.

I am not saying that you must use this programme or that it guarantees success (any such claim would be unwarranted). What I am asking you to consider is that over 200 of your peers have found it extremely beneficial along with thousands of others who have used it on a national basis for the exams held between 2007 and 2015 and, based on that fact, you might consider whether it could be of use to you. Alternatively, if you have a method that works for you, stick with it; do not change just for the sake of change.

Should you choose to follow this programme, please remember the following points:

- You will probably need a larger version of the Study/Revision Log. If you do, you can create your own in a variety of ways (enlarging and photocopying the example given, using MSWord or Excel to create your own log or even just using lined paper with columns drawn in).
- The programme targets 120 hours study/revision because research suggests that figure is a realistic overall target to aim for.
- Just because the programme starts approximately 14 weeks before the examination does not mean that you should leave your study/revision until the start date—you can begin studying/revising at any time and the sooner the better!

- Once you start the programme, stick with it. You must follow my instructions and do not worry whether or not my methodology works—it does.
- Be disciplined in your approach and keep an accurate record of your study/revision time.

Following the programme—week 1 example

In the first week of the programme you are asked to study/revise State of Mind, Criminal Conduct, Incomplete Offences, Issues in Evidence and Offences Against the Administration of Justice and Public Interest (all from the 'Evidence' section of the *Police Investigators' Manual*). It might seem a lot to ask you to get through but several of these subjects are over and done with relatively quickly as far as chapters in the Manual are concerned.

For the whole week do nothing else but study/revise the material contained in these pages!

Some of these subjects have corresponding sections in the *Police Investigators' Workbook*. Where that is the case you could take the following approach:

1. Begin your study by answering two or three multiple-choice questions on 'State of Mind and Criminal Conduct' contained in this book or in the Workbook (it does not matter if you have no knowledge whatsoever of the subject you are being tested on—your best guess will be fine).
2. When you have answered the multiple-choice questions read the sections on 'State of Mind and Criminal Conduct' contained in the Manual (once only).
3. After you have read the 'State of Mind and Criminal Conduct' sections in the Manual, complete the Workbook section on 'State of Mind and Criminal Conduct'.
   To get the most out of the Workbook you must *try to complete any written exercises you are asked to. If you do not know the answer to a question, do not worry as all of the exercises have an explanation. Do not fall into the trap of telling yourself, 'I know that' when you do not and then not bother writing anything down in the space provided. Practising self-deception with regard to the level of your knowledge might make you feel secure when you are reading the Workbook but it will not help you to learn. Being honest with yourself about your own knowledge level will be far more beneficial in terms of passing the NIE.*
4. Attempt the 'Recall Questions' at the end of the 'State of Mind and Criminal Conduct' section.
5. When you are satisfied with your answers, return to the Manual and read the sections on 'State of Mind and Criminal Conduct' for the second time.
6. When you have finished reading the 'State of Mind and Criminal Conduct' sections for the second time, return to questions you answered at the beginning of this process and make a second attempt at them. When you have finished, check your answers.

Be prepared to perform badly at first but do not give up because of this performance; it is quite normal. Your knowledge and ability will steadily increase as you move through the stages and if you follow the previous instructions I am confident that you will finish the process with a good level of knowledge. Remember that this process will provide you with a good *foundation* of knowledge but in order to maintain that level you should briefly revisit the subject from time to time.

Repeat these steps with the other material you are asked to cover in that week.

You will see that some weeks demand that you cover more material than in others, particularly with reference to Evidence. This is intentional as the programme aims to make your knowledge base stronger in some areas than others.

The Manual contains subjects with no corresponding section in the Workbook. For these sections you should use the multiple choice questions from this Q&A to check your knowledge of the subjects.

Answer Questions—Read Manual Material—Answer Questions (2nd attempt)

If you cannot find any questions on the subject:

Read It—Read It Again—Read It Again

You only finish when the week actually ends, not when you have done everything once. If you have completed all of the questions you can find, finished all of the exercises and questions in the Workbook, answered all of the questions in this Q&A and obviously know the subject backwards, fine. Read it again and again and again, no matter how boring you think it is or how well you think you know it!

Should I take a break?

I have included a flexible option to include a one-week break (for those taking the examination in March 2016 this break can be extended by a further 2 weeks over the Christmas period—if you only want one week rather than two, shave a couple of days off either side of the potential break period). Whenever you are taking the NIE, the choice of whether to take that break is yours. However, if you do take that break then I will presume that you need to so do not study/revise during this time. If you ceaselessly push yourself when you need to stop then you are in danger of 'burning out' before you actually sit your examination. Taking the examination in this condition is highly likely to result in failure. Imagine you are in a gym lifting a weight with your arm. You will lift it so many times before you stop and rest, but after the rest you can complete more repetitions of the exercise. If you do not stop lifting the weight and keep pushing, you will end up injured and unable to move your arm and unable to complete the exercise. Your mind is exactly the same. Give your mind a total break from the difficult exercises you are asking it to complete on a daily basis and when you return to your study/revision you will do so refreshed and better able to deal with the final push to the examination. Of course you might decide to keep going or maybe only take two or three days' rest—how you manage this process is your preference.

Keeping track

Each day you should enter the amount of time you have worked for in your Study/ Revision Log. This includes '0' minutes when you have not managed to study/revise.

The log does not demand that you rigidly complete (for example) exactly 75 minutes a day, every day, but exists so that you can see where you are in terms of hitting your 120-hour target and how far ahead or behind your schedule you are. Some days you will pass the target, some days you will not, but the log will not lie about your commitment to the process. By regularly filling the log in and being honest about the amount of time you have spent studying/revising, you can create internal pressure on yourself to get ahead or catch up. I recommend that you put this somewhere in your home where you will see it every day; do not put it inside a cupboard so you can hide away from your lack of study/revision. If you are married, have a partner, have children, place it somewhere where they can see it and get them to remind you of how you are doing to create external pressure to maintain the pace. Getting ahead of schedule allows you to pick a day or days off when you will be too busy to study because of work or social commitments.

If you reach your 120 hours target before the last day of the study/revision programme, well done BUT DON'T STOP. The finishing post is passed when you sit down to take your examination, not when you have completed 120 hours' study/ revision.

Start dates

Your study/revision programme start date depends on when you are sitting the NIE.

Examination Date	Start Date
1st March 2016	9th November 2015
7th June 2016	29th February 2016
6th September 2016	30th May 2016
29th November 2016	22nd August 2016

How does it work?

The following plan covers everything contained inside the *Police Investigators' Manual* and a final 2 weeks where you choose what you will do.

When approaching the plan, begin by thinking that you are not going to take a break at all and that you will follow the 14-week programme as it is set out here.

WEEK 1 Evidence State of Mind; Criminal Conduct; Incomplete Offences; Issues in Evidence; Offences against the Administration of Justice and Public Interest
WEEK 2 Evidence Entry, Search and Seizure/PACE Code B; Bail
WEEK 3 Evidence Disclosure of Evidence; The Regulation of Investigatory Powers Act 2000
WEEK 4 Evidence Detention and Treatment of Persons by Police Officers/Code C
WEEK 5 Evidence Interviews/Code C/Code E/Code F
WEEK 6 Evidence Identification/Code D

WEEK 7 **Sexual Offences** The whole section
WEEK 8 **Property Offences** Theft; Burglary; Aggravated Burglary; Robbery; Blackmail
WEEK 9 **Property Offences** Fraud; Handling Stolen Goods; Buying Scrap Metal for Cash; Proceeds of Crime; Criminal Damage
WEEK 10 **Assaults, Drugs, Firearms and Gun Crime** Homicide; Non-fatal Offences Against the Person; Child Abduction; False Imprisonment; Kidnapping; Cybercrime
WEEK 11 **Assaults, Drugs, Firearms and Gun Crime** Public Order Act 1986 Offences; Racially, Religiously Aggravated and Homophobic Offences; Misuse of Drugs; Firearms and Gun Crime; Terrorism and Associated Offences
WEEK 12 **Sexual Offences** The whole section
WEEK 13 AND WEEK 14 **Final Revision** Candidate choice on subject matter

Of course you may ask why the 'Sexual Offences' section is covered at the mid-way point and also towards the end of the study/revision process. The reason is because it is approximately 40 pages in length and is worth an average of 12 marks in each NIE. That is a fantastic potential return for such a small section and you should seriously expect to get most, if not all, of those questions right. You do that and you will already have 17.14% towards your 55% objective.

If you are not taking a break then the plan is straightforward but what if you want to have a break for a week? Simple, you use that mid-way (week 7) 'Sexual Offences' week for the break and take it out of the equation. You now have a 13-week plan with the option to introduce that one-week break into it **at a time that suits you.**

Those of you who are taking the NIE in March 2016 will notice that the programme starts earlier than you might expect. This is because I have made a presumption and built in a potential 2015/2016 Christmas/New Year study/revision break of two weeks. Of course, if you want to study/revise over Christmas you may, but I consider this to be not only difficult but also unpleasant and wonder if you will actually accomplish much in this time. The choice, as ever, is yours.

Study/Revision log (time)

The last part of the study/revision programme is your daily log. You *MUST* ensure that this is filled in every day, regardless of the fact that you may not have completed any study/revision (for those days enter '0' minutes). The whole idea is that you can see how on or off-target you are with your study/revision and make sure that you are not falling behind.

I have set you an overall target of 120 hours or 7,200 minutes study/revision. What I want you to do is convert that into an average daily target from the day you begin the study/revision process (eliminating any break period you have decided that you will take). For example, say that I am taking the NIE on 1 March 2016 and decide to begin on 9 November 2015. That gives me 113 days. I have decided to take 2 weeks off from 23 December so I actually have 99 days to revise. 7,200 divided by 99 = 72.72 which I will round up to 75 minutes each day. My 'Study/Revision Log' will look as follows:

Start date	9 November 2015
My 'Total Target' is:	7,200 minutes (120 hrs)
My 'Daily Target' is:	75 minutes (1 hr 15 mins)
My 'Weekly Target' is:	525 minutes (8 hrs 45 mins)
The latest I will complete my study/revision by is:	29 February 2016

Date	Study/Revision schedule (mins)	'Today I studied/revised for'	My running total	+ or –
9/11/15	75			
10/11/15	150			
11/11/15	225			
12/11/15	300			
13/11/15	375			
14/11/15	450			
15/11/15	525			
16/11/15	600			
17/11/15	675			
18/11/15	750			

Every day I fill this log in so that by 18 November 2015, my log might look as follows:

Start date	9 November 2015
My 'Total Target' is:	7,200 minutes (120 hrs)
My 'Daily Target' is:	75 minutes (1 hr 15 mins)
My 'Weekly Target' is:	525 minutes (8 hrs 45 mins)
The latest I will complete my study/revision by is:	29 February 2016

Date	Study/Revision schedule (mins)	'Today I studied/revised for'	My running total	+ or –
9/11/15	75	120	120	+45
10/11/15	150	0	120	–30
11/11/15	225	60	180	–45
12/11/15	300	30	210	–90
13/11/15	375	240	450	+75
14/11/15	450	0	450	Level
15/11/15	525	120	570	+45
16/11/15	600	60	630	+30
17/11/15	675	20	650	–25
18/11/15	750	120	770	+20

I have said before that I do not expect anyone to do exactly whatever their daily figures work out at—I would be astonished if someone did. It is a *guide* at the end of the day, please remember that.

This is a very disciplined and organised approach to the management of time and so if it is not your style and it is actually a barrier to learning then the last thing you should do is force yourself to fill in such a log. However, you should recall that an ill-disciplined and disorganised approach can have disastrous consequences. You might not like it but if the log pricks your conscience and makes you do the work it could make all the difference.

To summarise, you need to:

- adopt an ordered approach to your study/revision by understanding what you have to study/revise and how long you have to do the study/revision and then organise yourself to accomplish these tasks;
- choose a study/revision method that works for you;
- be meticulous in your study/revision;
- show discipline and do not attempt self-deception; you will pay for it in the long run.

And remember, the only place that success comes before work is in a dictionary.

PART ONE

Evidence

1 State of Mind, Criminal Conduct and Incomplete Offences

QUESTIONS

Question 1.1

LLOYD is involved in an argument with GOUGH at a bowling alley. LLOYD picks up a 14 lb bowling ball and throws it at GOUGH, intending to cause him an injury. GOUGH ducks and the bowling ball hits DOOGAN, causing her an injury. The ball then drops onto a table smashing several glasses in the process.

Considering the doctrine of transferred *mens rea*, which of the following statements is correct?

A LLOYD would only be liable for the injury to DOOGAN.
B LLOYD would only be liable for the damage to the glasses.
C LLOYD would be liable for the injury to DOOGAN and the damage to the glasses.
D LLOYD would not be liable for the injury to DOOGAN or the damage to the glasses.

Question 1.2

When considering *mens rea*, offences may fall into the categories of specific and basic intent. The distinction between such offences is important when considering defences.

Which of the following comments is correct?

A An offence of maliciously wounding or inflicting grievous bodily harm (contrary to s. 20 of the Offences Against the Person Act 1861) would be a crime of 'specific' intent.

B An offence of burglary (contrary to s. 9(1)(a) of the Theft Act 1968) would be a crime of 'basic' intent.

C An offence of murder (contrary to common law) would be a crime of 'basic' intent.

D An offence of burglary (contrary to s. 9(1)(b) of the Theft Act 1968) would be a crime of 'basic' intent.

Question 1.3

MASTERS is evicted from her home and moves in with her next-door neighbour OXFORD. The two are unrelated. OXFORD is housebound and extremely ill and needs constant attention otherwise she will die. MASTERS tells OXFORD that she will look after her and that OXFORD can dismiss the full-time nurse OXFORD has employed to perform this duty; OXFORD agrees. MASTERS looks after OXFORD for 6 months but then becomes bored by the constant care OXFORD requires. MASTERS totally ignores OXFORD for over 4 days and as a result, OXFORD dies.

Would MASTERS be criminally liable for her omission to act?

A No, MASTERS is under no duty to act under a statute, a public office or under the terms of a contract.

B Yes, MASTERS has taken it upon herself to carry out a duty and has then failed to do so.

C No, MASTERS must have some sort of relationship with OXFORD such as a parent with a child.

D Yes, MASTERS has created a dangerous situation and has taken no action to counteract the danger she created.

Question 1.4

MEREDITH assaults PERK by pushing her through a glass window. This causes several deep cuts to PERK's wrists. PERK manages to escape and seek medical attention at a hospital where she is left waiting for some 4 hours before being told that her injuries are not life-threatening as long as she has a blood transfusion. PERK is a Jehovah's Witness and refuses to have the transfusion because of her religious beliefs. As a result of her refusal to have the transfusion, PERK dies from the injuries. Apart from the initial waiting period, hospital staff carried out their duties carefully.

Which of the following is correct with regard to MEREDITH's criminal liability?

A MEREDITH is liable for PERK's death, as defendants must take their victims as they find them. PERK's refusal to have the blood transfusion on religious grounds would not affect MEREDITH's liability.

B MEREDITH is not liable for PERK's death as her refusal to have a blood transfusion breaks the causal link between the assault and PERK's death.

C MEREDITH would not be liable for PERK's death because the negligent treatment PERK received on her arrival at the hospital would be classed as an 'intervening act', breaking the causal link.

D MEREDITH is liable for the death of PERK as under no circumstances could negligent medical treatment ever break the chain of causation from MEREDITH's assault to PERK's death.

Question 1.5

BULL is homeless and breaks into an abandoned house looking for shelter. He goes upstairs into the back bedroom and lies down on a mattress. BULL lights a cigarette and then falls asleep. He wakes up several minutes later to find that the mattress is on fire. BULL does not put out the fire; instead he gets up and goes into another room and goes to sleep. The mattress continues to burn, causing serious damage to the bedroom. The only reason BULL survives is because of the rapid attendance of the fire brigade.

Which of the following comments is correct regarding BULL's criminal liability?

A BULL is not liable as a defendant can only be punished for his/her positive conduct; an omission cannot be punished by criminal law.

B BULL is liable for the criminal damage as he has created a dangerous situation and has a duty to act.

C Unless BULL is under a duty to act under a statute, a contract or because of a public office, he will not be liable for an omission to act.

D BULL is not liable, as criminal law will only punish an omission if the defendant has taken it upon him/herself to carry out a duty and then fails to do so.

Question 1.6

During an argument in a pub, McCLEOD attacks RUMLEY causing him serious brain damage. RUMLEY is already suffering from a serious stomach ulcer when McCLEOD attacks him. RUMLEY is taken to hospital but the brain damage caused in the assault prevents doctors from operating on the stomach ulcer, which eventually ruptures and kills RUMLEY.

What is McCLEOD's criminal liability in these circumstances?

A McCLEOD will not be liable for the death of RUMLEY as it is the lack of medical treatment that is the cause of RUMLEY's death.

B McCLEOD has no liability for the death of RUMLEY as the ultimate and actual cause of death was an untreated ulcer.

C McCLEOD would be liable for manslaughter, as his criminal conduct has made a significant contribution to RUMLEY's death.

D McCLEOD would not be liable for RUMLEY's death, as the ruptured ulcer would be viewed as an intervening act.

Question 1.7

PYE agrees to accompany his friend BASRAN to an isolated farm where BASRAN intends to steal the farm owner's car. PYE is fully aware of BASRAN's intention and has agreed to act as a 'look out' while BASRAN steals the car. PALFREY, the owner of the car, confronts them as BASRAN is breaking into the car. Unexpectedly, BASRAN produces a knife and stabs PALFREY, causing her a serious injury. PYE had no idea that BASRAN was carrying a knife and only accompanied BASRAN in order to steal the car.

Considering the law relating to principals and accessories, would PYE be liable with regard to the wounding against PALFREY?

A PYE is an accessory present at the scene of a crime when it is committed. His presence may amount to encouragement that would support a charge of aiding, abetting, counselling or procuring the wounding offence.

B PYE is an accessory who has helped in the commission of an offence. A court will treat him in the same way as the principal offender (BASRAN) for the wounding of PALFREY.

C PYE did not physically assist BASRAN in the wounding of PALFREY. Unless this element forms part of the offence, PYE can never be liable as an accessory to the wounding offence.

D Although PYE and BASRAN are part of a joint enterprise, BASRAN has gone beyond what had been agreed. As such, PYE could not be held liable for the consequences of such an 'unauthorised' act by BASRAN.

Question 1.8

A travel company employs LUCAS and KIRK as coach staff; amongst other duties, the two sell refreshments to customers travelling by coach. LUCAS suggests to KIRK that they make their own sandwiches and sell these to people using the coach instead of the sandwiches supplied by the travel firm. KIRK agrees to the suggestion.

Would this constitute an offence of conspiracy to defraud (contrary to common law)?

A No, because this offence involves deceiving another into acting in a way that is contrary to his/her duty.

B Yes, but you must show that the defendants were dishonest.

C No, at least three people must be involved in the conspiracy.

D Yes, but only as long as you prove that the end result would amount to the commission of an offence.

Question 1.9

McEVOY is due to be a contestant on a 'live' general knowledge TV show. When McEVOY takes part in the show his wife will be watching at home. Before the show begins husband and wife devise a plan so that when McEVOY is asked a question by the host of the show, McEVOY's wife will send him a text message via his mobile phone that will contain the correct answer. If all goes according to plan, the two will win up to £50,000.

Does this amount to a statutory conspiracy (contrary to s. 1 of the Criminal Law Act 1977)?

A Yes, the two have agreed on a course of conduct that will amount to the commission of an offence.

B No, McEVOY cannot commit statutory conspiracy if the only other party to the agreement is his wife.

C No, for there to be a conspiracy there must be an agreement with at least three people involved.

D Yes, unless the plan is later abandoned by the two.

Question 1.10

WISEDALE plans to falsely imprison a schoolboy and sexually assault him. He plans to gain access to a local school and commit the offence in the school toilets. WISEDALE buys a rucksack and places a kitchen knife, some rope and masking tape into the rucksack. He gains entry to the school and hides in the toilets waiting for his chance to commit the offence. The school caretaker catches him before the offence is committed.

Considering the law relating to attempts under s. 1 of the Criminal Attempts Act 1981, at what stage, if at all, does WISEDALE commit the offence of attempted false imprisonment?

A When he plans to gain access to the school and commit the offence in the toilets.

B When he buys the rucksack and places the kitchen knife, rope and masking tape into the rucksack.

C When he gains entry to the school and hides in the toilets waiting for a chance to commit the offence.

D The offence of attempted false imprisonment is not made out in these circumstances.

Question 1.11

KRAY arranges to handle a container load of electrical goods stolen in the course of a robbery. Unknown to KRAY, the container full of goods has been intercepted by the police who arrest the driver, return the contents to the rightful owner and substitute a container full of boxes containing old newspapers for the original container. A police officer drives the substituted container to the arranged meeting point and KRAY arrives shortly after, driving a large goods vehicle. KRAY backs the goods vehicle up to the container, opens the container doors and begins to load the worthless boxes into his goods vehicle when he is arrested.

Does KRAY attempt to handle stolen goods in these circumstances?

A No, in these circumstances the goods have ceased to be stolen and as the goods are not stolen the offence cannot be committed.

B Yes, although it is physically impossible to handle goods that are not stolen, this impossibility would not preclude such a charge under the Criminal Attempts Act 1981.

C No, this offence does not exist and would be a legal impossibility.

D Yes, but the prosecution would have to show that KRAY intended to dispose of the goods in order to show he had 'embarked on the crime proper'.

Question 1.12

SUTTON is a drug dealer and regularly supplies BOND with heroin. SUTTON visits BOND at her home address and sells her £200 worth of heroin before leaving. Several hours after SUTTON has left, BOND prepares the heroin for injection, applies a tourniquet to her arm and injects all of the heroin. She dies several minutes later of an overdose.

With regard to the chain of causation and intervening acts, which of the following comments is correct?

A SUTTON supplied BOND with the heroin and is therefore the direct cause of her death and would be liable for her murder.

B BOND exercised her free will and has brought about her own death by injecting the heroin; SUTTON is not liable for her death.

C Although SUTTON is not the direct cause of BOND's death, the fact that he supplied her with the heroin makes him guilty of her manslaughter.

D Even if SUTTON actually prepared the heroin and injected BOND with it, bringing about her death, he would not commit an offence.

Question 1.13

TI GARRETT and TI DESULT are discussing a case where a number of offenders have been charged as accessories to the primary offence. The officers make a number of comments in respect of the law surrounding principals and accessories.

Which is the only comment to show a correct understanding of the law?

A TI GARRETT states that if an accessory 'aids, abets, counsels or procures' an indictable offence then their sentence is punishable by a term of imprisonment that will be half the length of a principal offender.

B TI DESULT states that when an accessory is charged, it must be made clear on the charge what form the accessory has taken, i.e. have they aided, abetted, counselled or procured the offence?

C TI GARRETT states that, generally speaking, aiding or abetting an offence will usually involve the presence of the accessory at the scene of the offence.

D TI DESULT states that if you are trying to show that a defendant procured an offence there is no need to show a causal link between the conduct of the accessory and the offence.

Question 1.14

LATIF approaches ENLY in a street intending to rob him. LATIF holds a knife towards ENLY and tells ENLY that unless he hands over his wallet he will be stabbed. ENLY panics in the face of such a violent threat and turns away from LATIF and runs across a nearby road to escape. As ENLY does so he is hit by a car and is seriously injured as a consequence.

Is LATIF responsible for the serious injury received by ENLY?

A Yes, as ENLY's reaction is one that could reasonably be anticipated from any victim in such a situation.

B No, the car striking ENLY would be interpreted as an intervening act, breaking the chain of causation.

C Yes, but LATIF could not be held accountable for the death of ENLY should he die from the serious injury.

D No, as ENLY's reaction is one carried out entirely of his own volition.

Question 1.15

TI GERMAIN is investigating an offence of s. 18 wounding/grievous bodily harm (contrary to the Offences Against the Person Act 1861) and has the offender, MANLEY, in custody. The offence took place in a pub and involved MANLEY picking up a glass, smashing it on a bar and shouting loudly *'I'm going to cut you to ribbons!'*, driving the glass a dozen times into the face of the victim. This has resulted in wounds requiring hundreds of stitches and reconstructive surgery. TI GERMAIN interviews MANLEY who states that he did not intend to wound the victim of the offence. After the interview, TI GERMAIN speaks to her supervisor about the offence and in particular the need to prove that MANLEY intended to cause the wounds/ grievous bodily harm.

Considering the mental element of 'intent', which of the following comments is correct?

A The intention required to prove a s. 18 wounding is defined by statute.

B Even though MANLEY denies the offence, a court could infer the necessary intent.

C The only way to prove intent for such an offence is by obtaining a confession from MANLEY.

D Whether to infer intent from the defendant's actions is a question of law to be decided by the magistrates or judge as appropriate.

Question 1.16

DC OGRILL is assisting in an enquiry into an incident where a self-employed boiler engineer botched a routine boiler service leading to an escape of carbon monoxide gas; that leak killed a family of four who owned the house where the boiler was situated. As a result of those deaths the possibility of prosecuting the boiler engineer for manslaughter (by gross negligence) is being considered by the enquiry team.

Thinking only about the mental element of 'negligence', which of the following statements is correct?

A Negligence is concerned with the defendant's compliance with the standards of reasonableness of ordinary people.

B Negligence is similar to strict liability as there is little to prove beyond the act itself and the state of mind of the defendant is immaterial.

C Negligence involves a subjective element, i.e. the standards of the defendant are important.

D It is the conduct of the defendant which is all important when considering negligence.

Question 1.17

Companies which are 'legally incorporated' have a legal personality of their own, that is they can own property, employ people and bring law suits: they can therefore commit offences, giving us the concept of 'corporate liability'.

Considering companies and 'corporate liability', which of the following comments is true?

A Legally incorporated companies can only be prosecuted for offences of strict liability.

B A legally incorporated company cannot be convicted as an accessory to an offence, i.e. it cannot aid, abet, counsel or procure the commission of an offence.

C There are occasions where the courts will accept that the knowledge of certain employees will be extended to the company.

D Companies cannot be prosecuted for offences that require a state of mind, i.e. *mens rea*.

Question 1.18

PINTER is a paedophile who wants to carry out a sexual assault against his next-door neighbour's 11-year-old child. He plans to kidnap her when she is playing in a nearby park and take her to his lock-up garage where the assault will be committed. PINTER's problem is that he only has one arm and does not think he will be able to restrain the child. He approaches SANDY (who PINTER thinks would be interested in these types of offence if asked to join in) and asks him to help out in the kidnap and sexual assault. PINTER believes that his request will encourage SANDY to commit the offences and if he says 'Yes' the two men will commit the offences. SANDY is utterly horrified by PINTER's suggestion and refuses to have anything to do with PINTER's suggested plan.

With regard to offences under ss. 44 to 46 of the Serious Crime Act 2007 (encouraging or assisting crime), which of the following comments is correct?

A An offence has not been committed as PINTER's encouragement did not have the effect that he desired (that SANDY would join the venture).

B To prove encouragement, PINTER would need to approach SANDY or another person on a second occasion.

C PINTER has not committed an offence as he would need to intend that his act will encourage or assist the commission of an offence (he only believes that it will).

D PINTER has committed the offence in these circumstances.

Question 1.19

ARUN (aged 14 years) has a 'crush' on FLATLEY (aged 25 years) who is ARUN's school teacher. ARUN watches the car park of the school where FLATLEY has parked his car and when FLATLEY appears and is just about to open the door of his car ARUN intercepts him. ARUN strikes up a conversation with FLATLEY about a lesson she took part in that day but all the while she is intending to persuade him to let her have oral sex with him (FLATLEY's penis to her mouth). Moments into the conversation, ARUN states '*I'd do anything for you, absolutely anything*'. FLATLEY quickly becomes concerned about the tone of the conversation when ARUN states, '*Take me back to your place and I'll give you a "blow-job"*'. FLATLEY tells ARUN that this is not going to happen and he immediately returns to the school to report the incident.

At what point, if at all, does ARUN commit the offence of encouraging or assisting an offence (contrary to s. 44 of the Serious Crime 2007)?

A When she initially strikes up the conversation with FLATLEY.

B When she tells FLATLEY she would do anything for him.

C When she asks FLATLEY to take her back to his home for oral sex.

D ARUN does not commit the offence in these circumstances.

Question 1.20

In order to prove the *actus reus* (criminal conduct) of an offence, the prosecution are required to prove two elements.

What are those two elements?

A That the defendant's conduct was voluntary and that he/she realised the consequences of his/her actions.

B That the defendant brought about a consequence as a result of his/her actions and that this consequence was a realistic possibility when the act took place.

C That the defendant's conduct was voluntary and that it occurred while the defendant still had the requisite *mens rea*.

D That the defendant knew what was likely to occur and he/she had the requisite *mens rea* for the act at the time of the offence.

Question 1.21

TI CARTER is dealing with SPARROW who has been arrested in connection with an incident that occurred at a public house. It appears that HARDWARE had a disagreement with SPARROW who lost his temper with HARDWARE. SPARROW picked up a wooden chair and threw it at HARDWARE intending to cause grievous bodily harm to HARDWARE but the chair missed HARDWARE and hit GROUCOTT in the face causing her a broken jaw and very serious facial cuts. The chair fell to the floor and in the process smashed a vase standing on the floor.

Considering the doctrine of transferred *mens rea*, which of the following statements is correct?

A SPARROW is not liable for any offences in relation to HARDWARE.

B SPARROW is only liable for the injury received by GROUCOTT.

C SPARROW is liable for the attempted s. 18 (Offences Against the Person Act 1861) against HARDWARE and a s. 18 (Offences Against the Person Act 1861) against GROUCOTT only.

D SPARROW is liable for the attempted s. 18 (Offences Against the Person Act 1861) against HARDWARE, a s. 20 (Offences Against the Person Act 1861) against GROUCOTT and the criminal damage to the vase (s. 1 of the Criminal Damage Act 1971).

Question 1.22

MINACK and LORIMER agree to carry out a burglary at a house owned by OXFORD; the house is in the middle of a row of houses and the two men agree that they will gain access to the house via a service road at the rear of the premises. MINACK leads the way but makes a mistake when he chooses the house to be broken into, accidentally selecting a house belonging to ATHERTON who is a neighbour of OXFORD. MINACK and LORIMER enter the house and as they do so they are confronted by ATHERTON. MINACK produces a knife and stabs ATHERTON causing him serious injury in the process. LORIMER did not know that MINACK had a knife with him.

Considering the law in relation to joint enterprise, which of the following comments is correct?

A LORIMER is liable for the burglary at ATHERTON's house and for the injury to ATHERTON.

B LORIMER is only liable for the burglary at ATHERTON's house.

C LORIMER is only liable for the injury received by ATHERTON.

D LORIMER is not liable for the burglary or the injury to ATHERTON.

Question 1.23

BULLMAN wishes to commit a robbery at a supermarket. He originally intended to commit the offence alone, but realises that to escape capture he needs somebody to act as his getaway driver. He approaches FLINTOFF and suggests that he assists him as the getaway driver; FLINTOFF does not want to get involved in the offence and refuses BULLMAN's request.

In relation to offences under the Criminal Attempts Act 1981 alone, which of the following statements is correct?

A BULLMAN is guilty of attempting to conspire with FLINTOFF.

B BULLMAN is guilty of attempting to counsel FLINTOFF to commit the offence.

C BULLMAN commits no offence under this legislation.

D BULLMAN is guilty of attempting to procure the commission of an offence.

Question 1.24

PATAVAN and CRADDOCK are chatting in a pub. PATAVAN tells CRADDOCK that he is having a hard time meeting all of his monthly bills and that he is extremely short of cash. CRADDOCK informs PATAVAN that a nearby jeweller's shop has a problem with its CCTV and alarm system and that neither will be working for the rest of the week. CRADDOCK encourages PATAVAN to go into the jeweller's shop and steal as much jewellery as he can. CRADDOCK believes that his advice will assist PATAVAN to commit the offence but does not actually believe PATAVAN will commit the offence as he has a very timid nature. PATAVAN tells CRADDOCK he will commit the offence of theft and leaves the pub and makes his way to the jeweller's intending to commit the offence of theft. However, he has a change of heart during the journey and decides not to commit any offence.

Considering the offences associated with encouraging or assisting an offence (under s. 45 of the Serious Crime Act 2007), which of the following comments is correct?

A No offence under this legislation has been committed as PATAVAN did not actually commit the offence of theft from the jeweller's shop.

B The offence is committed when CRADDOCK provides information about the jeweller's shop believing it will assist PATAVAN to commit an offence.

C No offence is committed because CRADDOCK does not believe that PATAVAN will commit the offence.

D The offence is committed when PATAVAN tells CRADDOCK that he will commit the offence of theft.

ANSWERS

Answer 1.1

Answer **A** — The doctrine of transferred *mens rea* only operates if the crime remains the same. In *R* v *Latimer* (1886) 17 QBD 359, the defendant lashed out with his belt at one person but missed, striking a third party instead. As it was proved that the defendant had the required *mens rea* when he swung the belt, the court held that the same *mens rea* could support a charge of wounding against any other victim injured by the same act. Therefore, LLOYD is liable for the assault on DOOGAN, making answers B and D incorrect. If the nature of the offence changes, then the doctrine will not operate. LLOYD's *mens rea* to injure will not transfer into the *mens rea* for an offence of criminal damage, making answer C incorrect.

Investigators' Manual, para. 1.1.12

Answer 1.2

Answer **D** — A crime of 'specific' intent is only committed where the defendant is shown to have had a particular intention to bring about a specific consequence at the time of the criminal act. Answers B and C are examples of such offences—they are not 'basic' intent offences and these answers are therefore incorrect. Answer A is incorrect as the offence of maliciously wounding or inflicting grievous bodily harm (contrary to s. 20 of the Offences Against the Person Act 1861) is a crime of 'basic' intent, not 'specific' intent. Answer D (burglary contrary to s. 9(1)(b) of the Theft Act 1968) simply requires proof that the person entered the building/part of a building as a trespasser and that he/she went on to commit one of the prohibited acts and, as such, this is an offence of basic intent.

Investigators' Manual, para. 1.1.2

Answer 1.3

Answer **B** — Criminal liability usually arises as a result of a defendant's action. However, in some cases a defendant can be criminally liable because of an omission or a failure to act. The section on omissions gives specific examples of when such a liability may arise, one of those being when a defendant has taken it upon him-/herself to carry out a duty and then fails to do so (*R* v *Stone* [1977] QB 354). Although answers A, C and D all relate to criminal liability via omissions, they are still incorrect.

MASTERS is liable for her inaction. Answer D is incorrect as the creation of a dangerous situation involves the doing of some act and then a failure to prevent the harm in question occurring. MASTERS has not 'done' an act.

Investigators' Manual, para. 1.2.4

Answer 1.4

Answer **A** — This question relates to the 'but for' test applied to the principles surrounding the causation. The simple way to deal with this question is to ask, 'But for MEREDITH's actions, would PERK have died?' The answer is 'No'. The next step is to ask if there has been an intervening act that breaks the chain of causation. Again the answer is 'No'. Defendants must take their victims as they find them, so refusing a blood transfusion on religious grounds will not break the chain of causation (*R* v *Blaue* [1975] 1 WLR 1411), making answer B incorrect. Negligent treatment has to be grossly negligent to break the chain of causation, making answer C incorrect. Answer D is incorrect because although negligent medical treatment will not normally break the chain of causation, there are exceptions where this has been the case (*R* v *Jordan* (1956) 40 Cr App R 152).

Investigators' Manual, paras 1.2.5, 1.2.6

Answer 1.5

Answer **B** — Criminal conduct is generally associated with the actions of the defendant; however, there are certain circumstances where an omission will attract criminal liability, making answer A incorrect. Such a duty can arise from a number of circumstances including where the defendant is under a duty to act under a statute (answer C), where the defendant has taken it upon him/herself to carry out a duty and then fails to do so (answer D), where the defendant is in a parental relationship with a child or young person or where the defendant creates a situation of danger (answer B and based on the case of *R* v *Miller* [1983] 2 AC 161). This makes answers C and D incorrect.

Investigators' Manual, para. 1.2.4

Answer 1.6

Answer **C** — There must be a causal link (or chain of causation) between the act of the defendant and the consequences; this is generally called the 'but for' test, e.g. if McCLEOD had not assaulted RUMLEY would he have died? The answer must be 'No'.

If the assault had not taken place then the ulcer could have been operated on and RUMLEY may have lived. This question is based on the circumstances in the case of *R* v *McKechnie* [1992] Crim LR 194, where the court held that the defendant's actions had made a significant contribution to the victim's death (answer C). Answer A is incorrect as the lack of medical treatment was caused by McCLEOD's assault. Answer B is incorrect as although the ulcer is the *actual* cause of death, it ruptured because of a lack of medical treatment, which could not be given because of the brain damage caused by the assault. Answer D is incorrect as the ruptured ulcer is not an intervening act.

Investigators' Manual, paras 1.2.5, 1.2.6

Answer 1.7

Answer **D** — Whether an accessory will be liable for the actions of the principal offender will depend on the nature and extent of the offence that was initially agreed to and contemplated by the accessory. The offence agreed to in this scenario was the theft of a car; this is entirely different to the wounding that BASRAN commits. In these circumstances, PYE will not be liable because BASRAN has gone 'beyond what has been tacitly agreed as part of the common enterprise' (*R* v *Anderson* [1966] 2 QB 110). In addition, there need be no physical assistance by the accessory to attract liability.

Investigators' Manual, paras 1.2.7 to 1.2.7.2

Answer 1.8

Answer **B** — Answer A is incorrect as the offence of conspiracy to defraud can take two forms—one is as per answer A, and the other is an agreement by two or more persons, by dishonesty, to deprive a person of something which is his or to which he is or would or might be entitled [or] an agreement by two or more by dishonesty to injure some proprietary right [of the victim] (Viscount Dilhorne in *Scott* v *Metropolitan Police Commissioner* [1975] AC 819). This definition means that answers C and D are incorrect.

Investigators' Manual, para. 1.3.3.2

Answer 1.9

Answer **B** — Although there has been an agreement that if carried out in accordance with the conspirators' intentions will involve the commission of an offence, the offence of statutory conspiracy is not made out. This is because a defendant cannot be convicted of statutory conspiracy if the *only* other party to the agreement is his/ her spouse, a child/children under 10 years of age or the intended victim.

Investigators' Manual, para. 1.3.3.1

Answer 1.10

Answer **D** — The defendant's actions must be shown to have gone beyond mere preparation towards the commission of the substantive offence. The courts have accepted an approach of questioning whether the defendant had 'embarked on the crime proper' (*R* v *Gullefer* [1990] 1 WLR 1063), although there is no requirement for the defendant to have passed a point of no return if the intention of the defendant can be ascertained. Up to point C, WISEDALE has not 'embarked on the crime proper'. In *R* v *Geddes* [1996] Crim LR 894, G was found in a boys' toilet of a school in possession of articles that suggested his reason for being there was to kidnap a child. His conviction for attempted false imprisonment was quashed. Even clear evidence of what he had in mind 'did not throw light on whether he had begun to carry out the commission of the offence'.

Investigators' Manual, para. 1.3.4

Answer 1.11

Answer **B** — You may consider that the offence cannot be committed because the goods from the container have been recovered by the police and returned to their rightful owner. Under s. 24(3) of the Theft Act 1968 this would mean that the goods shall no longer be regarded as stolen goods. However, s. 1(2) of the Criminal Attempts Act 1981 states: 'A person may be guilty of attempting to commit an offence to which this section applies even though the facts are such that the commission of the offence is impossible.' This makes answer A incorrect and also answer C as the offence is not a legal impossibility. Answer D is incorrect as KRAY has already 'embarked on the crime proper' by moving the boxes from one vehicle to another.

Investigators' Manual, paras 1.3.4, 1.3.5

Answer 1.12

Answer **B** — If a drug dealer supplies drugs to another person who then kills him-/herself by overdose, the dealer cannot, without more, be said to have caused the death. Death would have been brought about by the deliberate exercise of free will by the user, making answers A and C incorrect. Answer D is incorrect as the Court of Appeal has accepted that, under certain circumstances, where a person buys a controlled drug from another and immediately injects it, resulting in his/her death, the supplier can attract liability for the person's death.

Investigators' Manual, para. 1.2.6

Answer 1.13

Answer **C** — Answer A is incorrect as if an accessory 'aids, abets, counsels or procures' an offence then he/she will be treated by a court in the same way as a principal offender for an indictable offence (Accessories and Abettors Act 1861, s. 8). Answer B is incorrect as the expression 'aid, abet, counsel or procure' is generally used in its entirety when charging a defendant, without separating out the particular element that applies. Answer D is incorrect as if you are trying to show that a defendant 'procured' an offence, you *must* show a causal link between his/her conduct and the offence.

Investigators' Manual, para. 1.2.7

Answer 1.14

Answer **A** — Although actions by the victim will sometimes be significant in the chain of causation, the victim's behaviour will not necessarily be regarded as a new intervening act. If the victim's actions are those which might reasonably be anticipated from any victim in such a situation, there will be no new and intervening act and the defendant will be responsible for the consequences flowing from them, i.e. being hit by a car in escaping. If you threaten someone with a knife telling them they will be stabbed if they do not hand over their wallet it is a thoroughly understandable reaction from the victim to try to escape from such a threat. Therefore, LATIF is responsible for the injury to ENLY, making answers B and D incorrect. Answer C is incorrect as if ENLY did die from the injury received then LATIF would be liable for his death—a simple example of the chain of causation in action.

Investigators' Manual, paras 1.2.5, 1.2.6

Answer 1.15

Answer **B** — Intention can be inferred in two ways (i) by virtue of s. 8 of the Criminal Justice Act 1967 or (ii) by the body of case law that has developed around the subject. There is no requirement for a confession to exist (otherwise very few intention-based offences would be proved), making answer C incorrect. Answer A is incorrect as the word 'intent' is not defined by any statute and intent means different things for different offences. Answer D is incorrect as whether a defendant intends a particular consequence will be a question of fact left to the jury or magistrate(s) as appropriate.

Investigators' Manual, para. 1.1.3

Answer 1.16

Answer **A** — Negligence is concerned with the defendant's compliance with the standards of reasonableness of ordinary people (answer A) and not the standards of the defendant, making answer C incorrect. Like strict liability, the concept focuses on the consequences (not the conduct) of the defendant rather than demanding proof of a particular state of mind at the time, making answer D incorrect. However, negligence does not have such a close relationship with strict liability so as to mean that only the act needs to be proved—there is still the requirement to illustrate 'fault' or 'blame' of the defendant who must be shown to have acted in a way that runs contrary to the expectations of the reasonable person (making answer B incorrect).

Investigators' Manual, para. 1.1.10

Answer 1.17

Answer **C** — Companies have been prosecuted for offences of strict liability (*Alphacell Ltd* v *Woodward* [1972] AC 824) but they have also been prosecuted for offences involving *mens rea* (*Tesco Supermarkets Ltd* v *Nattrass* [1972] AC 153) and also as accessories (*R* v *Robert Millar (Contractors) Ltd* [1970] 2 QB 54), making answers A, B and D incorrect. There are occasions where the courts will accept that the knowledge of certain employees will be extended to the company (see, e.g. *Tesco Stores Ltd* v *Brent Borough Council* [1993] 1 WLR 1037).

Investigators' Manual, para. 1.2.8

Answer 1.18

Answer **D** — The offence under s. 46 of the Act is committed when a person does an act (the request by PINTER to SANDY) capable of encouraging or assisting the commission of one or more of a number of offences (kidnap and sexual assault) and he *believes* that one or more of those offences will be committed and that his act will encourage or assist in the commission of one or more of them. One conversation is ample, making answer B incorrect. Only a *belief* is required (not intention—that is under s. 44 of the Act and makes answer C incorrect). Answer A is incorrect as the offence can be committed regardless of whether the encouragement or assistance has the effect the defendant intended or believed it would have.

Investigators' Manual, para. 1.3.2

Answer 1.19

Answer **D** — The first thing to consider here is what kind of offence is ARUN trying to encourage FLATLEY to commit? The answer to that would be an offence under s. 9 of the Sexual Offences Act 2003—sexual activity with a child. That offence exists to protect children under 16 from this kind of sexual activity. So ARUN is encouraging FLATLEY to commit an offence that exists for her own protection. Section 51 of the Act limits the liability of the offence by setting out in statute the common law exception established in *R* v *Tyrell* [1894] 1 QB 710. A person cannot be guilty of an offence under s. 44, 45 or 46 if, in relation to the offence, it is a 'protective' offence and the person who does the act capable of encouraging or assisting that offence (ARUN in this question) falls within the category of persons that the offence was designed to protect and would be considered a victim.

Investigators' Manual, para. 1.3.2

Answer 1.20

Answer **C** — When proving *actus reus* you must show that the defendant's conduct was voluntary and that it occurred while the defendant still had the required *mens rea*.

Investigators' Manual, para. 1.2.1

Answer 1.21

Answer **C** — The doctrine of transferred *mens rea* will only apply if the nature of the offence remains the same. When SPARROW throws a chair at HARDWARE he intends to cause *someone* harm and that is the end result when the chair hits GROUCOTT. So SPARROW is liable for the attempted injury to HARDWARE (the attempted s. 18) and the actual injury caused to GROUCOTT (a s. 18 offence), making answers A and B incorrect. SPARROW is not liable for the damage to the vase as the nature of the offence (assault to criminal damage) has changed, making answer D incorrect.

Investigators' Manual, para. 1.1.12

Answer 1.22

Answer **B** — MINACK and LORIMER have embarked on the commission of an offence and have a common goal (to break into a house)—that is a joint enterprise. As the parties to a joint enterprise share a combined purpose, each will be liable for the consequences of the actions of the other in the pursuit of the joint enterprise. This is the case even if the consequences of the joint enterprise are a result of a mistake (as in the question). Here, MINACK and LORIMER have agreed to carry out a burglary—the fact that MINACK goes to the wrong house will not prevent LORIMER being liable for burglary. This makes answers C and D incorrect. However, where the nature of the offence changes liability will not exist. LORIMER did not know that MINACK had a knife and the stabbing of the occupier of the house is a clear departure from the nature and type of crime that was envisaged by LORIMER. It is so fundamentally different that LORIMER would not be liable for the injury, making answer A incorrect.

Investigators' Manual, paras 1.2.7 to 1.2.7.2

Answer 1.23

Answer **C** — This question checks whether you know the exceptions regarding the Criminal Attempts Act 1981. You cannot attempt to conspire, making answer A incorrect. You cannot attempt to counsel, making answer B incorrect and you cannot attempt to procure the commission of an offence, making answer D incorrect.

Investigators' Manual, para. 1.3.4

Answer 1.24

Answer **C** — The offence under s. 45 of the Serious Crime Act 2007 will be committed if a person does an act capable of encouraging or assisting in the commission of an offence and he believes that the offence will be committed and that his act will encourage or assist its commission. CRADDOCK does not believe that PATAVAN will commit the offence and therefore the offence under s. 45 is not committed, making answers B and D incorrect. The fact that PATAVAN does not go on to commit an offence (if all the other elements were present) would not prevent CRADDOCK committing the offence, making answer A incorrect.

Investigators' Manual, para. 1.3.2

2 Regulation of Investigatory Powers Act 2000

QUESTIONS

Question 2.1

TI GRIFFIN has spoken to a number of people on the telephone in respect of crime taking place in and around her police station. She is concerned that her contacts may well fall into the definition of a CHIS (Covert Human Intelligence Source) and approaches you for some advice on the matter. She describes the conversations and activities that have taken place on the telephone.

Which of the following statements is correct?

A KELLY is a member of the public who has contacted TI GRIFFIN to supply some general information regarding crime in the locality. TI GRIFFIN should treat KELLY as a CHIS.

B MOSELEY is a member of staff at a bank who has come across information in the ordinary course of her job and suspects criminal activity. TI GRIFFIN should treat MOSELEY as a CHIS.

C PARSAD heard about a drug deal taking place in a pub. TI GRIFFIN asked PARSAD to return to the pub and find out who was involved and what future deals were planned. TI GRIFFIN should treat PARSAD as a CHIS.

D TI GRIFFIN would not need to treat any person as a CHIS if the information being passed to the officer is being communicated by telephone.

Question 2.2

DC EVAN is approached by TREDMAN (who is 13 years old). TREDMAN tells DC EVAN that he can supply a large amount of quality information about the activities of a gang of burglars operating in DC EVAN's area. DC EVAN is keen to utilise TREDMAN as a CHIS (Covert Human Intelligence Source).

Which of the following statements is correct in respect of TREDMAN?

A A juvenile cannot be utilised as a CHIS in any circumstances.

B A superintendent could authorise the use of TREDMAN as a CHIS for a maximum period of three months.

C An assistant chief constable can authorise the use of TREDMAN as a CHIS for a maximum period of one month.

D A juvenile CHIS can only be authorised by an officer of the rank of chief constable or his/her nominated deputy for a maximum period of one week.

Question 2.3

DC HUNT is tasked with dealing with a number of robberies that have occurred near a cash-point in a shopping centre. Victims are being attacked near the cash-point just after they have withdrawn cash and the offender runs off and out of the shopping centre. The shopping centre has an overt high-quality CCTV system with several cameras that can cover the cash-point and nearby area. It is DC HUNT's intention to use the CCTV system to specifically focus on the area of the cash-point while other officers are stationed nearby. Should an incident take place, DC HUNT will notify his colleagues, who will move into the shopping centre and make an arrest.

With regard to directed surveillance, which of the following statements is correct?

A DC HUNT is covertly and specifically using the CCTV system in connection with a planned operation and this may amount to directed surveillance.

B The monitoring of a CCTV system could never be covered by the Regulation of Investigatory Powers Act 2000 (RIPA 2000).

C As DC HUNT is not using the CCTV system to search for an individual specifically identified for the purposes of the operation, this would not qualify as directed surveillance.

D This is not directed surveillance as the CCTV cameras in the centre are not 'covert'.

Question 2.4

DS DONNELLY wishes to carry out intrusive surveillance as part of a large ongoing drugs operation against KIRK.

Who will authorise this surveillance?

A An officer of the rank of inspector or above.

B An officer of the rank of superintendent or above.

C An officer of the rank of chief constable.

D The Home Secretary.

Question 2.5

DC FAIRWEATHER wishes to place a surveillance device inside a private vehicle owned by RODAN who is the suspected leader of a gang carrying out high-value armed robberies. The officer hopes to obtain intelligence and evidence in respect of RODAN's criminal activities by recording RODAN's conversations with other members of the gang inside the private vehicle.

With regard to the Regulation of Investigatory Powers Act 2000, which of the following statements is correct?

A This is intrusive surveillance and if authorised would last for a period of one month.

B This is directed surveillance and if authorised would last for a period of one month.

C This is intrusive surveillance and if authorised would last for a period of three months.

D This is directed surveillance and if authorised would last for a period of three months.

Question 2.6

TIs DAILY and EAVES are discussing the use of covert human intelligences sources (CHIS) and in doing so make a number of comments about them.

Which of the following statements made by the officers is correct?

A TI DAILY states that the power to authorise the use of a CHIS is limited to the police, the National Crime Agency (NCA), the military and the intelligence services.

B TI EAVES states that if a CHIS may obtain confidential information as a result of their activities, the relevant authority for CHIS authorisation is increased to that of an assistant chief constable.

C TI DAILY states that use of a CHIS may only be authorised if the authorising officer believes it is necessary to do so for the purpose of preventing or detecting crime or in the interests of national security.

D TI EAVES states that a single authorisation can cover more than one regulated activity (e.g. the use of surveillance and the use of a CHIS).

Question 2.7

DC KENT is approached by JAMAL who tells the officer that he can provide him with information about a paedophile ring operating in the officer's policing area. JAMAL tells the officer the ring has been discussing killing any child they abuse to avoid leaving witnesses and other evidence. JAMAL tells DC KENT the ring is meeting in 2 hours' time. DC KENT requires urgent authorisation to make JAMAL a CHIS.

Which of the following comments is correct in respect of such urgent authorisation?

A In an urgent case, a superintendent can give authorisation for JAMAL's CHIS activities. This authorisation must be written and will last for 48 hours.

B In an urgent case, an inspector can give authorisation for JAMAL's CHIS activity. The authorisation can be oral or written and will last for 48 hours.

C In an urgent case, a superintendent can give authorisation for JAMAL's CHIS activities. The authorisation must be written and will last for 72 hours.

D In an urgent case, an inspector can give authorisation for JAMAL's CHIS activities. The authorisation must be written and will last for 72 hours.

Question 2.8

The Regulation of Investigatory Powers Act 2000 governs the use of surveillance when it is directed or intrusive and it provides definitions of such activities that all police officers should be aware of so that they do not carry out unlawful activities.

In respect of those definitions, which of the following comments is correct?

A PC ILKS is in a shop situated 20 metres away from a house he is watching. The officer is using long-range audio equipment to monitor the conversations of the occupants of the house. The equipment is of such quality that it provides the same kind of results that a device actually placed in the house would. This is directed surveillance.

B A police officer who is on plain clothes patrol sees a suspicious male hanging around near a jewellers shop. The officer hides behind a bush to watch the male and see what he does. This is directed surveillance.

C DC KULLA wishes to place a recording device in a hotel room occupied by GODSEN to record conversations that take place in the room. This is intrusive surveillance.

D DC QUEEN wants to attach a 'tracker' device to a car driven by HENNIMORE to provide information about the location of the vehicle. This is intrusive surveillance.

Question 2.9

DC VEMEER wishes to obtain evidence about the people-smuggling activities of DUNN and to do so he needs to obtain an authorisation for directed surveillance to watch/record DUNN in his workplace and an intrusive surveillance authorisation to watch/record DUNN'S activities in his home. DC VEMEER considers the surveillance could last a considerable period of time.

Which of the following comments is correct in respect of those authorisations?

A An authorisation for directed surveillance will ordinarily cease to have effect after one month, beginning on the day it was granted.

B An intrusive surveillance authorisation will not take effect until a Surveillance Commissioner has approved it and given written notification to that effect to the authorising officer.

C Authorisation for both types of surveillance would last for three months and can be renewed but only after they cease to have effect.

D If the situation became urgent, an inspector could authorise intrusive surveillance for a maximum period of 72 hours.

ANSWERS

Answer 2.1

Answer **C** — A CHIS is someone who establishes or maintains a relationship with another person for the covert purpose of obtaining information or providing access to information. Clearly this can be accomplished on the telephone, making answer D incorrect. However, the definition would not cover activities of a member of the public passing general information to the police (answer A) or a person who passes information to the police that they have come across in the ordinary course of their job (answer B). If a person supplying information is asked by the police to do something further to develop or enhance it this could well make the individual a CHIS.

Investigators' Manual, para. 1.4.3

Answer 2.2

Answer **C** — A juvenile CHIS can be used for certain activities (making answer A incorrect). The use of a juvenile CHIS is authorised by an officer of the rank of assistant chief constable or above for a maximum period of one month, making answers B and D incorrect.

Investigators' Manual, para. 1.4.3.2

Answer 2.3

Answer **A** — CCTV will not normally be covered by RIPA 2000 as in most cases it is not covert. However, the use of the cameras in the way the officer is considering could well make such activities 'directed surveillance'. This is because the surveillance is (i) covert, (ii) for the purposes of a specific operation, (iii) likely to result in the obtaining of private information about a person (whether or not that person has been specifically identified for the purposes of the operation) and (iv) not in immediate response to events.

Investigators' Manual, paras 1.4.4, 1.4.4.1

Answer 2.4

Answer **C** — The authorising officer for intrusive surveillance by the police is the chief constable.

Investigators' Manual, para. 1.4.4.2

Answer 2.5

Answer **C** — Answers B and D are incorrect as this is intrusive surveillance. Intrusive surveillance is surveillance that is covert, carried out in relation to anything taking place on any residential premises or in any private vehicle and involves the presence of an individual on the premises or in the vehicle, or is carried out by means of a surveillance device. Intrusive surveillance, if authorised, will be authorised for a period of three months, making answer A incorrect.

Investigators' Manual, para. 1.4.4.2

Answer 2.6

Answer **D** — The power to authorise a CHIS extends to public authorities and is not limited to the police, NCA, the military and intelligence services, making answer A incorrect. Answer B is incorrect as if CHIS activity may lead to the obtaining of confidential information, the authorisation level is that of a chief constable. CHIS activity can be authorised:

- for the purpose of preventing or detecting crime or of preventing disorder;
- in the interests of national security, public safety or the economic well-being of the United Kingdom;
- for the purposes of protecting health or collecting or assessing any tax, duty, etc.;
- for any purpose specified by an order made by the Secretary of State.

This makes answer C incorrect. Single authorisations can cover more than one type of activity.

Investigators' Manual, para. 1.4.3.2

Answer 2.7

Answer **D** — Urgent authorisation for CHIS activity can be given by a superintendent or an inspector. That authorisation will last for 72 hours, making answers A and B incorrect. However, an inspector cannot give an oral authorisation (a superintendent can)—any authorisation by an inspector must be written.

Investigators' Manual, para. 1.4.3.2

Answer 2.8

Answer **C** — If a police officer is acting in immediate response to events/circumstances where it would not be reasonably practicable to seek prior authorisation for surveillance and that surveillance is not intrusive, then no authorisation for the officer's activities will be required, making answer B incorrect. Answer A is incorrect as although the officer might not be in the residential premises he is monitoring, if the device he uses produces such images/sound as to give the same result as if the device were on the premises, then this is intrusive surveillance. Placing a 'tracker' device on or even in a vehicle to provide information about its geographical location is directed surveillance, making answer D incorrect. Hotel rooms are considered to be residential premises and placing a recording device in a hotel room would be intrusive surveillance.

Investigators' Manual, paras 1.4.4 to 1.4.4.2

Answer 2.9

Answer **B** — An officer of the rank of inspector cannot authorise intrusive surveillance in any circumstances, making answer D incorrect. Surveillance can be renewed and this can take place before the operating authorisations cease to have effect as long as the criteria for authorisation are still satisfied, making answer C incorrect. Directed surveillance will last for three months from the date it is granted (72 hours if urgent), making answer A incorrect. Intrusive surveillance has to wait until the Surveillance Commissioner gives written approval (unless it is an urgent situation when the surveillance can commence when authorised by a chief constable or his/her deputy).

Investigators' Manual, paras 1.4.4 to 1.4.4.2

3 Entry, Search and Seizure/ Code B

QUESTIONS

Question 3.1

DS GRETTEN carries out a search of a house along with DC WALKER (who has 10 years' police service) and PC LOWE (a probationary constable with 11 months' police service). The search is being carried out as a result of a long investigation and subsequent arrest carried out by DC WALKER, who is extremely familiar with the facts of the case.

Considering Code B of the Codes of Practice, which of the following comments is correct in respect of who should be in charge of the search?

A The officer in charge of the search must be the most senior officer present (DS GRETTEN).

B DS GRETTEN should normally be in charge of the search but as DC WALKER is more conversant with the facts of the case, DS GRETTEN may appoint him as the officer in charge.

C DS GRETTEN or DC WALKER could be in charge of the search. PC LOWE could not be in charge of the search in any circumstances as she is a probationary constable.

D In normal circumstances any one of the three officers could be in charge of the search.

Question 3.2

DC BENTLEY wishes to make an application for a search warrant to search two sets of premises in respect of drug-related offences.

Which of the following statements is correct with regard to the officer's application?

A The application for a search warrant must be made with the written authority of an officer of the rank of superintendent or above.

B The application for a search warrant must be made with the written authority of an officer of the rank of inspector or above.

C The application for a search warrant must be made with the authority of an officer of the rank of inspector or above. The authority can be oral or written.

D An application for a search warrant must be made with the written authority of a magistrate.

Question 3.3

DC EMERY receives intelligence which indicates that HALL has committed an offence of handling stolen goods (contrary to s. 22 of the Theft Act 1968). DC EMERY's intelligence indicates that there are stolen goods located at HALL's home address and also in a lock-up garage belonging to HALL, the location of which is unknown. DC EMERY makes an application for an all-premises search warrant under s. 8 of the Police and Criminal Evidence Act 1984 (PACE).

Which of the following comments is correct?

A The application will be refused because handling stolen goods is not an indictable only offence.

B If the application is granted then the warrant must be executed within one month from the date of its issue.

C If an all-premises warrant is granted then premises which are not specified in it may only be entered and searched if an officer of the rank of inspector or above authorises the search in writing.

D An all-premises warrant can only authorise entry to premises on one occasion.

Question 3.4

HANSON is in a café when it is raided by the police and he is arrested by DC KHAN for an offence of possessing a controlled drug. HANSON breaks down on arrest and tells the officer that there are several dozen stolen Sony PlayStation 3 game consoles at his home address that were stolen from an electrical store by his flatmate three weeks ago. He tells the officer he is unlikely to find them as they are well hidden and his flatmate may well dispose of them if he hears of HANSON's arrest.

Which of the following statements is correct?

A DC KHAN could take HANSON to his home address and search the address before HANSON is taken to a police station under the powers of s. 18 of the Police and Criminal Evidence Act 1984 (PACE).

B DC KHAN could take HANSON to his home address and search it by virtue of s. 32 of PACE.

C DC KHAN could search HANSON's home address under s. 17 of PACE.

D DC KHAN could not utilise his powers under s. 17, 18 or 32 to search HANSON's home address in these circumstances.

Question 3.5

In certain circumstances it is permissible to search premises with the consent of a person entitled to grant entry to the premises. Code B of the Codes of Practice details the practice and procedure for such searches.

In respect of such a search, which of the following statements is correct?

A In a lodging house, a search of a lodger's room can be made solely on the basis of the landlord's consent.

B A search based on the consent of a person entitled to grant entry cannot be made unless an officer of the rank of inspector or above authorises it.

C If it is proposed to search premises with the consent of a person entitled to grant entry then that consent should, if practicable, be given in writing on the Notice of Powers and Rights before the search.

D If an occupier has given his consent to a search but then withdraws that consent before the search is complete, the search may continue until it is completed.

Question 3.6

DC EASTWOOD is the officer in charge of a search carried out under a warrant granted by virtue of s. 8 of the Police and Criminal Evidence Act 1984. The search is being carried out at the home address of GRAINGER. GRAINGER demands that his friend, ORTON, be allowed to witness the search. ORTON lives three hours away from the scene of the search.

Which of the following comments is correct?

A ORTON may be allowed to witness the search but this will not stop the search beginning immediately.

B GRAINGER does not have the right to have a friend, neighbour or other person witness the search of his house.

C DC EASTWOOD can refuse to allow ORTON to witness the search but only if he believes ORTON's presence will endanger officers or other people.

D The search must be delayed until ORTON arrives at GRAINGER's address to witness the search.

Question 3.7

DS CHILDS is the officer in charge of a search where seize and sift powers were utilised (under s. 50 of the Criminal Justice and Police Act 2001) due to the fact that it was going to take a lengthy period of time and a large number of officers to separate material relevant to the offence and other material. The material seized was a large amount of papers contained in over 50 crates.

Which of the following statements is correct in relation to those seize and sift powers?

A Section 50 allows for the seizure of material that is reasonably believed to be legally privileged where it is not reasonably practicable to separate it.

B Section 50 provides for extended seizure of materials found on people who are being lawfully searched.

C Section 50 provides a freestanding power to seize property.

D Section 50 should not have been used by DS CHILDS as the power is only relevant to material stored on computers.

Question 3.8

DC KIRK has arrested OPLINGTON for numerous offences of handling stolen goods and has brought him to a designated police station. OPLINGTON gives the custody officer his home address and after being processed is placed in a cell. DC KIRK has reasonable grounds for suspecting there is evidence at OPLINGTON's home address regarding handling offences. The officer makes further enquiries regarding OPLINGTON and discovers that he owns a lock-up garage near to his home address. He carries out intelligence checks on OPLINGTON and finds out that the lock-up garage has been linked with a separate criminal enterprise of OPLINGTON's, namely the supply of drugs. Intelligence also suggests that OPLINGTON has been linked with a shop (as he is supposed to own it) where the stolen goods are sold. All of the intelligence is of a good quality and causes the officer to suspect OPLINGTON controls the shop premises and that there are drugs in the lock-up garage. DC KIRK wishes to search all three premises (house, lock-up and shop) using s. 18 of the Police and Criminal Evidence Act 1984 to do so.

Which of the following statements is correct in respect of the use of the power?

A Only OPLINGTON's home address can be searched under s. 18.

B Only OPLINGTON's home address and the lock-up garage can be searched under s. 18.

C All three premises can be searched under s. 18.

D Only OPLINGTON's home address and the shop can be searched under s. 18.

Question 3.9

PC DRAPER is called to the scene of a robbery. The property stolen in the offence consists of a gold ring and a gold watch. The victim identifies BROWN as the offender and provides a description of BROWN to PC DRAPER. BROWN's details are circulated along with a warning that BROWN is known to be a violent drug dealer who has attempted to stab officers with hypodermic needles in the past. Shortly after the circulation, DCs HEMMINGWAY and LE FORT see BROWN standing outside a busy shopping centre. The officers stop BROWN and arrest him for the robbery offence. The officers propose to search BROWN at the location of the arrest under s. 32 of the Police and Criminal Evidence Act 1984.

Which of the following statements is correct in respect of this power?

A The officers could search BROWN but only for the stolen property.

B This power would not authorise the search of BROWN's mouth.

C Such a search could involve BROWN being required to take off his shoes.

D The officers could search the location where BROWN was arrested.

Question 3.10

PC ROSE (a uniformed officer) has arrested MARKOU for an offence of theft and is transporting him to a police station. While being transported to the police station, he manages to escape from custody. A search for MARKOU takes place but he is not found. Two days later, DC GOWER (who is working in plain clothes) hears about the incident and remembers that he dealt with MARKOU six months ago for a theft and at that time he was living with a girlfriend at an address nearby. DC GOWER believes that MARKOU is at the address and contacts PC ROSE and together the two officers visit the address. The officers knock on the front door which is answered by DELPH (MARKOU's girlfriend). DELPH tells the officers that she no longer has anything to do with MARKOU and has not seen him for three months.

Can the officers enter the address under s. 17 of the Police and Criminal Evidence Act 1984?

A No, as MARKOU is not an escaped HMP prisoner.

B Yes, but the power is only available to an officer in uniform.

C No, because they are not in 'fresh' pursuit of MARKOU.

D Yes, the power is available to either police officer, in uniform or not.

Question 3.11

DC JACKS is making enquiries regarding an armed robbery at an electrical store where a large amount of TV/audio equipment was stolen. He is in the process of visiting houses near to the store to try and locate witnesses and sees that a house opposite the store, belonging to LOMAS, has a security camera system which might possibly have captured the robbery. DC JACKS visits LOMAS who invites the officer into her house. Whilst chatting to LOMAS in the lounge of the house, DC JACKS notices some documentation on a coffee table that appears to be useful intelligence regarding crime in the area and decides to seize it. When LOMAS asks what is going on, DC JACKS tells her, to which she responds, '*Well you can fuck off then!*' DC JACKS is ushered towards the front door by LOMAS but before he leaves he sees the recording device for the security cameras and ejects and seizes the CD in the device as he suspects it may contain evidence of the armed robbery.

Taking into account the powers under s. 19 of the Police and Criminal Evidence Act 1984 only, which of the following comments is true?

A DC JACKS has legitimately seized the intelligence material and the CD.

B DC JACKS has legitimately seized the intelligence but not the CD as he was a trespasser at this point.

C DC JACKS has legitimately seized the CD but not the intelligence.

D DC JACKS has no power to seize either item.

Question 3.12

TI ROBERT wishes to apply for a warrant under s. 8 of PACE 1984 to search a house belonging to GRISHAM who is suspected of involvement in a burglary (contrary to s. 9(1)(a) of the Theft Act 1968).

Which of the following comments is correct?

A If the application is successful, the warrant can only authorise entry on one occasion.

B A s. 8 warrant can authorise an unlimited number of entries to GRISHAM's house.

C A s. 8 warrant will only permit a search of one specific premises, which must be clearly identified in the warrant.

D A s. 8 warrant permits the large-scale seizure of all material found on premises to be 'sifted' at another location.

Question 3.13

DC KIDBY receives information that WESTGATE is in possession of a significant quantity of stolen property from a burglary that occurred two days ago. The information states that WESTGATE is a traveller and moves around the country in a car and is at present camped in a tent in a field in DC KIDBY's police area. The stolen property is being kept inside the tent and also in WESTGATE's car.

Considering s. 15 of PACE 1984 (in respect of an application for a warrant), which of the following comments is correct?

A A warrant could not be granted to search a car or a tent.

B A warrant could be granted to search both the car and the tent.

C A warrant could be granted to search the car but not the tent.

D A warrant could be granted to search the tent but not the car.

ANSWERS

Answer 3.1

Answer **B** — Code B states that the officer in charge of a search should *normally* be the most senior officer present (DS GRETTEN), making answers A and D incorrect. However, an exception to this is when the supervising officer who attends or assists at the scene of the premises appoints an officer of lower rank as officer in charge (OIC) of the search because that officer is more conversant with the facts (answer B). The senior officer could appoint any officer to be in charge of the search if that officer is a more appropriate officer to be in charge of the search, making answer C incorrect.

Investigators' Manual, para. 1.5.3.5

Answer 3.2

Answer **B** — Applications for all search warrants must be made with the written authority of an officer of at least the rank of inspector (Code B, para. 3.4). However, in cases of urgency where no such officer is 'readily available', the senior officer on duty may authorise the application.

Investigators' Manual, para. 1.5.4

Answer 3.3

Answer **C** — A s. 8 warrant must relate to the fact that an indictable offence has been committed. Handling stolen goods is an either-way offence, which means that it is indictable and would qualify (it does not have to be indictable only), making answer A incorrect. Entry and search under a warrant must be within three months from the date of issue, making answer B incorrect. An all-premises warrant may authorise entry and search on more than one occasion if, on the application, the justice of the peace is satisfied that it is necessary to authorise multiple entries in order to achieve the purpose for which he issues the warrant, therefore answer D is incorrect.

Investigators' Manual, para. 1.5.3.7

Answer 3.4

Answer **D** — Section 18 cannot be utilised unless DC KHAN is searching for evidence that relates to the offence which HANSON is under arrest for or to some other indictable offence which is connected with or similar to that offence, making answer A incorrect. Section 32 searches can only take place to find evidence relating to the offence for which the person was arrested, making answer B incorrect. Section 17 of PACE is a power of entry rather than a power of search, making answer C incorrect.

Investigators' Manual, para. 1.5.5.3

Answer 3.5

Answer **C** — A lodger's room should not be searched based solely on the permission of the landlord unless the situation is urgent and the lodger is unavailable, making answer A incorrect. Answer B is incorrect as the authority of an inspector is not required when carrying out a search by consent. If an occupier gives his/her consent but then withdraws it the search must stop at that point, making answer D incorrect.

Investigators' Manual, paras 1.5.5.3 to 1.5.6.1

Answer 3.6

Answer **A** — Code B allows a friend, neighbour or other person to witness a search, making answer B incorrect. That can be refused if the OIC of the search has reasonable grounds for believing that this would seriously hinder the investigation or endanger officers or others, making answer C incorrect. A search need not be unreasonably delayed for this purpose, making answer D incorrect.

Investigators' Manual, para. 1.5.7

Answer 3.7

Answer **A** — Section 50 of the Act relates to material at the scene of the search and not on individuals (this is s. 51 of the Act), making answer B incorrect. Answer C is incorrect as these powers can only be used to extend the scope of an existing power and do not allow for seizure as a freestanding power. Answer D is incorrect as these powers can be utilised in a variety of situations and considerations relating to the use of the power would include the length of time and the number of people that would be required to separate the material on the premises (s. 50(3)).

Investigators' Manual, paras 1.5.8.6, 1.5.8.7

Answer 3.8

Answer **A** — Section 18 searches can only take place at premises occupied or controlled by the arrested person; suspicion that the person occupies or controls the premises is not sufficient and therefore the lock-up garage and shop are eliminated, making answers B, C and D incorrect. Further, the premises searched must be searched because the officer has reasonable grounds to suspect that there is evidence on the premises of that offence (the offence the person has been arrested for) or to some other indictable offence which is connected with or similar to that offence. The suspected drug dealing is entirely separate from the handling so the lock-up garage is further eliminated.

Investigators' Manual, para. 1.5.5.3

Answer 3.9

Answer **D** — A search under s. 32 allows a constable to search for anything that may present a danger to himself or others, that the person might use to assist him to escape from lawful custody, or that might be evidence relating to an offence. The officers can therefore search for the stolen property and the needles, making answer A incorrect. Such a search will not authorise the removal, in public, of more than the jacket, outer coat and gloves of the person, so answer C is incorrect. Such a search does authorise the search of a person's mouth, making answer B incorrect. The power under s. 32 authorises a search to take place where the person was arrested (other than at a police station).

Investigators' Manual, para. 1.5.5.2

Answer 3.10

Answer **C** — Section 17 provides a power of entry in a large variety of situations. One of those is to recapture a person who is 'unlawfully at large'. This term is not defined and could include someone who has escaped from custody, making answer A incorrect. Wearing a uniform is irrelevant to the power of entry for such a purpose, making answer B incorrect. However, the pursuit of the person unlawfully at large must be 'fresh'—calling at an address two days after the event is not and makes answer D incorrect.

Investigators' Manual, para. 1.5.5.1

Answer 3.11

Answer **D** — The power under s. 19 allows an officer who is legitimately, i.e. lawfully, on premises to seize anything which the officer reasonably *believes* is evidence of an offence or has been obtained in consequence of an offence to prevent it being lost, altered, damaged or destroyed. This is not a power to seize property purely for the purposes of intelligence so answers A and B are incorrect. Telling the officer to 'fuck off' does not turn him into a trespasser (you need to be more explicit and clearly communicate that fact) but the officer only suspects the CD is evidence, making answer C incorrect.

Investigators' Manual, para. 1.5.8.1

Answer 3.12

Answer **B** — Answer A is incorrect as a s. 8 warrant can permit entry on a number of occasions. Answer C is incorrect as the warrant may be a 'specific premises' warrant or an 'all premises' warrant. Answer D is incorrect as possession of a warrant under s. 8 does not authorise police officers to seize all material found on relevant premises to be taken away and 'sifted' somewhere else (*R* v *Chesterfield Justices, ex parte Bramley* [2000] 2 WLR 409).

Investigators' Manual, para. 1.5.3.7

Answer 3.13

Answer **B** — The 'premises' that are referred to in the legislation include any place, and in particular (a) any vehicle, vessel, aircraft or hovercraft; (b) any offshore installation; (c) any renewable energy installation; (d) any tent or moveable structure (s. 23 of the Act). The car and the tent can be searched under the terms of a warrant, making answers A, C and D incorrect.

Investigators' Manual, para. 1.5.3.3

4 Detention and Treatment of Persons by Police Officers/ Code C

QUESTIONS

Question 4.1

DC MANLER arrests DAWSON for an offence of theft. Due to the circumstances surrounding the arrest, DC MANLER takes DAWSON to a non-designated police station where DC ROBERTS (who is not involved in the investigation) performs the role of custody officer.

As the acting custody officer, whom, if anyone, should DC ROBERTS inform of these circumstances?

A There is no requirement for DC ROBERTS to inform anyone of the circumstances.
B The custody officer at a designated police station.
C An officer of the rank of inspector or above at a designated police station.
D An officer of the rank of superintendent or above at a designated police station.

Question 4.2

DC JOPLIN has arrested FARROW for an offence of aggravated burglary. In the custody block, FARROW requests that he be allowed to telephone his girlfriend, ROWE. ROWE lives with FARROW and DC JOPLIN is concerned that if ROWE speaks to FARROW, she will dispose of any property relating to the aggravated burglary before he searches the home address of FARROW.

In these circumstances, can FARROW be prevented from making the telephone call to ROWE?

A Yes, with the authorisation of an officer of the rank of superintendent or above.

B No, this right cannot be withheld in any circumstances.

C Yes, if an officer of the rank of inspector or above authorises it.

D No, because FARROW has not been arrested for a drug trafficking offence.

Question 4.3

MULLAN is in custody for an offence of kidnapping and requests that TURNER (a solicitor friend of MULLAN) represents him whilst he is in police custody. DC SAUL is in charge of the investigation and is genuinely concerned that if MULLAN is allowed to use TURNER as a solicitor, TURNER will, inadvertently or otherwise, act in a way that will interfere with evidence connected to the kidnapping.

Which of the following statements is correct?

A DC SAUL should seek a superintendent's authority to deny MULLAN access to legal advice from TURNER.

B MULLAN should be allowed to speak with TURNER, but to ensure that TURNER acts ethically, his consultations with MULLAN can be monitored by a police officer.

C Once the decision to deny MULLAN his legal advice has been taken, the authorisation applies to all solicitors or legal advisers and lasts up to a maximum of 36 hours.

D MULLAN cannot be denied access to legal advice from TURNER in these circumstances.

Question 4.4

WHORWOOD has been arrested for burglary and has requested the services of a solicitor, a fact that has been recorded on the custody record. Before the custody officer has had a chance to contact WHORWOOD's nominated solicitor, she changes her mind and states that she does not want or need a solicitor.

What course of action should be taken to deal with this situation?

A The custody officer should enquire as to WHORWOOD's change of mind and record the fact that WHORWOOD wishes to proceed without a solicitor on the custody record.

B An officer of inspector rank or above should enquire as to WHORWOOD's reasons for her change of mind and give authority for the interview to proceed and

WHORWOOD should agree to be interviewed without a solicitor in writing or in interview.

C When WHORWOOD is interviewed she should be asked to explain her reasons for her change of mind on tape and state the fact that she is willing to be interviewed without the presence of her solicitor.

D The solicitor should be contacted regardless of her change of mind. If WHORWOOD informs the solicitor that she wishes to continue without his/her presence, this should be recorded on the custody record.

Question 4.5

PARRISH voluntarily attends at a police station in your force area to be dealt with for an offence of theft; he arrives at the police station at 10.00 hrs and is arrested at 10.15 hrs. You have circulated PARRISH as wanted for an offence of rape and you are informed of his detention. You travel to the police station where PARRISH is detained and arrest him for the offence at 13.00 hrs. At no stage has PARRISH been questioned in relation to the offence of rape. You escort PARRISH back to your police station and arrive at 14.00 hrs.

From what time will PARRISH's 'relevant time' be calculated?

A 10.00 hrs.

B 10.15 hrs.

C 13.00 hrs.

D 14.00 hrs.

Question 4.6

DYTHAM is arrested for murder and has been in custody for 20 hours. DS KNIBBS, the officer in charge of the case, considers that the investigating and interviewing officers need more time to carry out their enquiries and realises that this will take more than the 24-hour basic period of detention. DS KNIBBS believes that it is unlikely that more than 36 hours will be needed to conclude matters.

Who will approve the 12-hour extension required by DS KNIBBS?

A The custody officer.

B An officer of the rank of inspector or above.

C An officer of the rank of superintendent or above.

D A magistrates' court.

Question 4.7

MURPHY (aged 15 years) is arrested for burglary. Due to problems with MURPHY's family, SERCOMBE (a responsible adult aged over 18 years) is called out to act as the appropriate adult during MURPHY's interview. MURPHY requests that he be allowed to consult a solicitor and HEMSTOCK (a solicitor) attends the police station. MURPHY asks for a consultation with HEMSTOCK but demands that SERCOMBE be excluded from the consultation.

Which of the following statements is correct?

A SERCOMBE will not be excluded as otherwise she cannot advise and assist MURPHY in her role as an appropriate adult.

B If SERCOMBE were related to MURPHY she could not be excluded but as she has no relationship with MURPHY, she can be excluded.

C The solicitor, HEMSTOCK, will make the decision as to whether SERCOMBE will be allowed into the consultation.

D If MURPHY wishes to have a private consultation with HEMSTOCK without SERCOMBE being present, he must be permitted to do so.

Question 4.8

At 10.00 hrs DC HEATHCOCK arrests DEBNEY (aged 15 years) for an offence of supplying a controlled drug (contrary to s. 4(3) of the Misuse of Drugs Act 1971). DEBNEY arrives at a police station at 11.00 hrs and as well as his father he requests that his friend, GRUNDY, be informed of his arrest. DC HEATHCOCK is concerned that if GRUNDY is contacted it will lead to interference with evidence relating to the offence.

With regard to DEBNEY's right to have someone informed (s. 56 of the Police and Criminal Evidence Act 1984), which of the following comments is correct?

A This right cannot be delayed in any circumstances.

B In these circumstances, DEBNEY's right can be delayed and this delay can continue until 23.00 hrs the following day.

C An officer of the rank of superintendent or above may authorise the delay in DEBNEY having someone informed of his arrest.

D DEBNEY's rights can be delayed with the authority of an inspector but cannot be delayed after 10.00 hrs the following day.

Question 4.9

Section 118 of the Police and Criminal Evidence Act 1984 defines the meaning of 'police detention'.

In which of the following circumstances would the named person not be classed as being in 'police detention'?

A OGDEN is arrested at a police station after attending voluntarily at the station.

B DUNKLEY is arrested by PC WEST and is sitting with the officer in a police livery vehicle waiting to go into a custody block.

C PELHAM is being escorted from the scene of her arrest to a police station by HALSETT (a designated escort officer).

D KHAN is in court after being charged with burglary and is in the charge of PC WYATT.

Question 4.10

DC BAKER arrests ZAFAR for an offence of theft and takes him to a designated police station. On arrival it becomes apparent that there is no custody officer readily available to deal with ZAFAR. PC CHARLES is allocated to perform the role of custody officer and begins to deal with ZAFAR in the custody block. Several minutes later Sergeant EDEN telephones PC CHARLES to see how he is doing. Sergeant EDEN is supervising a road check one mile away from the designated police station.

Considering the law with regard to the provision of custody officers, which of the following statements is correct?

A A constable can only perform the role of custody officer at a non-designated police station.

B PC CHARLES cannot perform the role of custody officer as an officer of at least the rank of sergeant must perform it.

C As a sergeant is not readily available, then PC CHARLES can perform the role of custody officer.

D Sergeant EDEN would be considered available to carry out the role of custody officer and allowing PC CHARLES to continue in the role would be unlawful.

Question 4.11

DC MOHAMMED arrests WALSH in connection with an offence of aggravated burglary. When WALSH arrives at a police station he indicates that he wishes to have a solicitor to represent him. Due to the circumstances surrounding the offence, DC

MOHAMMED wants to take non-intimate samples for evidential purposes from WALSH and also carry out an urgent interview without a solicitor being present (under the provisions of Code C, para. 6.6). WALSH tells DC MOHAMMED that he will not consent to the taking of the non-intimate samples or answer questions in any interview.

Which of the following statements is correct in these circumstances?

A As WALSH has requested a solicitor, any evidence gained from an interview carried out in such circumstances will be inadmissible because no solicitor was present.

B If WALSH refuses to answer any questions during the course of the urgent interview it may lead to a court drawing an inference from that failure.

C DC MOHAMMED can take non-intimate samples without consent even if WALSH has not consulted his solicitor.

D If an officer of the rank of inspector or above authorises it, an urgent interview can take place.

Question 4.12

BAXTER has been detained under the Terrorism Act 2000.

When should BAXTER's first review of detention take place?

A As soon as reasonably practicable after his arrest.

B 6 hours after his arrest.

C 12 hours after his arrest.

D 24 hours after his arrest.

Question 4.13

FERRY is arrested for an offence of burglary and is charged with the offence. Seven months after being charged the CPS decide to take no further action against FERRY and the case is dropped. After hearing that it has been decided to take no further action against him, FERRY attends the police station where he was detained for the offence and asks for a copy of his custody record.

Is FERRY entitled to a copy of his custody record?

A No, as the entitlement does not exist when it is decided that no further action will be taken against an individual.

B Yes, as the entitlement lasts for 12 months after his release from custody.

C No, as the entitlement only lasts for 6 months after his release from custody.

D Yes, but this request must be made by FERRY's legal representative.

Question 4.14

COURTNEY is a juvenile and has been arrested for an offence of robbery. COURTNEY is taken to a designated police station and booked into custody by PS BARNES. The custody block is extremely busy and there is a shortage of space for persons in custody meaning there is no secure accommodation available for COURTNEY; PS BARNES is considering what to do with COURTNEY.

With regard to the Codes of Practice and in particular issues surrounding conditions of detention, which of the following comments is correct?

A PS BARNES could place COURTNEY in a cell with HUCK, an adult who has been detained in respect of an offence of theft.

B COURTNEY cannot be placed in a cell under any circumstances.

C COURTNEY can be placed in a cell if PS BARNES considers it is not practicable to supervise him otherwise.

D COURTNEY can be placed in a cell if an officer of the rank of inspector or above authorises it.

Question 4.15

DC WHITTAKER has arrested HENDERSON for supplying a controlled drug (contrary to s. 4(3) of the Misuse of Drugs Act 1971). As HENDERSON was being arrested he swallowed a small amount of what DC WHITTAKER suspected was a controlled drug. This information was passed to the custody officer, PS SADRETTIN, when HENDERSON was brought into custody.

Considering Code C of the Codes of Practice, which of the following comments is correct?

A HENDERSON should be visited and roused every 15 minutes.

B HENDERSON should be visited and roused every 30 minutes.

C HENDERSON should be visited and roused every 60 minutes.

D HENDERSON should be visited and roused every 90 minutes.

Question 4.16

ATWAL has been arrested for an offence of assault (contrary to s. 20 of the Offences Against the Person Act 1861) and has been brought to a designated police station where the facts of the arrest are related to the custody officer, PS WEBSTER. ATWAL complains that he is suffering pain in his stomach as a consequence of the fight that led to his arrest. PS WEBSTER tells ATWAL that a health care professional will be called out to examine him regarding the pain but ATWAL is not happy with this and insists that his local doctor, Dr SCOTT, also examine him.

Which of the following statements is correct in respect of the action to be taken?

A PS WEBSTER should call out a health care professional; ATWAL's wishes to be examined by Dr SCOTT should be ignored.

B PS WEBSTER should have ATWAL examined by a health care professional and also by Dr SCOTT. Dr SCOTT's examination will be funded by the police.

C PS WEBSTER can choose between having ATWAL examined by a health care professional or Dr SCOTT.

D ATWAL should be examined by a health care professional and Dr SCOTT. However, ATWAL will fund the examination by Dr SCOTT.

Question 4.17

HUMBER (a juvenile aged 15 years) has been arrested in connection with an offence of murder. HUMBER has been in custody for a number of hours and her second review is due.

In respect of this review, which of the following comments is correct?

A The review must take place in person.

B The review can take place either in person or by telephone.

C The review can take place either in person or by video conferencing.

D The review can take place in person, by telephone or by video conferencing.

Question 4.18

WARDALE has been arrested for an offence of s. 20 wounding by DC HERRIOT. During the course of the audio-recorded interview, WARDALE replied '*No comment*' to all the questions put to him apart from the question '*Who was responsible for the assault?*', to which WARDALE replied, '*It wasn't me.*' WARDALE is charged with the offence and, after the custody officer charges and cautions him, WARDALE replies, '*I can tell you who committed the assault if you want me to.*'

Could WARDALE be interviewed about his comments?

A No, a detainee may not be interviewed about an offence after they have been charged with it, or informed they will be prosecuted for it.

B Yes, to clear up any ambiguity in a previous answer or statement.

C No, this can only be done to prevent or minimise harm or loss to some other person, or the public.

D Yes, as long as WARDALE agrees in writing to be re-interviewed regarding his comments.

Question 4.19

Sections 38 and 39 of the Police Reform Act 2002 allow persons employed by the Local Policing Body or persons employed by a contractor of the Local Policing Body (in relation to detention officers and escort officers) to be designated as investigating officers, detention officers and escort officers. Schedule 4 to the Police Reform Act 2002 outlines the powers of these individuals.

In relation to the powers of detention officers and escort officers, which of the following statements is correct?

A A detention officer can carry out an examination of a person detained at a police station in order to identify the person concerned via marks on their body (such as a tattoo).

B An escort officer cannot conduct an non-intimate search of a detainee.

C A detention officer cannot carry out an intimate search of a detained person.

D An escort officer can photograph detained persons in the same way as constables.

Question 4.20

Section 30 of the Police and Criminal Evidence Act 1984 requires that persons who have been arrested must be taken to a police station as soon as practicable after arrest. A prisoner who will be detained (or is likely to be detained) for a certain period of time must go to a 'designated' police station.

What is that time period?

A A prisoner who will be detained (or is likely to be detained) for more than six hours must go to a 'designated' police station.

B A prisoner who will be detained (or is likely to be detained) for more than 12 hours must go to a 'designated' police station.

C A prisoner who will be detained (or is likely to be detained) for more than 18 hours must go to a 'designated' police station.

D A prisoner who will be detained (or is likely to be detained) for more than 24 hours must go to a 'designated' police station.

Question 4.21

STUBBS (who is 15 years old) is brought to a police station by HAWTHORNE (the 30-year-old uncle of STUBBS) and ADEY (who is 25 years old and a friend of the family). HAWTHORNE has discovered that STUBBS had stolen £2,000 from him and he wants HAWTHORNE dealt with by the police. When they arrive at the police station, they speak to PC BUTCHER about the matter. PC BUTCHER asks ADEY why he has come along and ADEY responds, '*I know he's stolen the money as he told me he has, but I want to help out.*' After hearing the facts, PC BUTCHER arrests STUBBS for the offence of theft.

Who, if anyone, could act as an appropriate adult for STUBBS?

A HAWTHORNE only.

B ADEY only.

C HAWTHORNE or ADEY.

D HAWTHORNE and ADEY could not be appropriate adults for STUBBS.

Question 4.22

WIDMER is 17 years old and has been arrested for an offence of burglary and taken to a designated police station. The custody officer, PS DETMER, is dealing with WIDMER.

Considering Code C of the Codes of Practice in relation to detained persons, which of the following comments is correct?

A PS DETMER would not require an appropriate adult to look after WIDMER's welfare as he is 17 years old.

B PS DETMER must ascertain the identity of a person responsible for WIDMER's welfare and as soon as practicable inform that person of the place and time that WIDMER was arrested.

C WIDMER should be informed that an appropriate adult will look after his welfare and that he can consult privately with such an appropriate adult at any time.

D Contact should be made with an appropriate adult; however, whether the custody officer informs the appropriate adult of the grounds for WIDMER's detention is a matter of choice for the custody officer.

Question 4.23

RASBAND has been arrested on suspicion of committing an offence of burglary and is transported to a designated police station. At the station he is presented to PS BOX (the custody officer), and the arresting officer, TI GRAVLIN, informs PS BOX of the circumstances of the arrest. PS BOX then considers the issues in relation to RASBAND's property.

Considering s. 54 of the Police and Criminal Evidence Act 1984 and Code C of the Codes of Practice, which of the following comments is correct?

A Section 54 imposes an absolute requirement that RASBAND must be searched on his arrival at the designated police station.

B If PS BOX authorises a search of RASBAND it must be carried out by a constable who is the same sex as RASBAND.

C An intimate search can be authorised by PS BOX under s. 54 of PACE.

D As soon as RASBAND arrives at the designated police station, TI GRAVLIN can search him under s. 54 of PACE as the use of this power does not require the approval of the custody officer.

Question 4.24

STRIKER, a citizen of Australia (an independent Commonwealth country), is out drinking with COWEE (who is a citizen of the Republic of Ireland). The two men become involved in a brawl resulting in both men being arrested for assault and public order offences. The custody officer, PS WEATHER, is dealing with the two men and is considering what Code C states about citizens of independent Commonwealth countries and foreign nationals.

Which of the following comments is correct?

A STRIKER and COWEE can, on request, consult with the appropriate High Commission, Embassy or Consulate at any time.

B STRIKER could consult with his High Commission, Embassy or Consulate at any time; COWEE (as a citizen of the Republic of Ireland) does not have this facility available.

C STRIKER and COWEE have the right to contact their High Commission, Embassy or Consulate on one occasion only and that is after their detention has been authorised by PS WEATHER.

D If either STRIKER or COWEE asks to communicate with their High Commission, Embassy or Consulate this should be acted upon immediately.

Question 4.25

AUBUCHON (who is a citizen of France) has been arrested for an offence of robbery and has been brought to a designated police station. AUBUCHON can speak some

English but his command of the English language is not particularly good and so the custody officer, PS BAGGERLEY, calls an interpreter to assist in communication whilst AUBUCHON is at the police station. PIERRON is called to the station as an interpreter to facilitate communication. AUBUCHON is interviewed regarding the offence but the interview does not last long as AUBUCHON claims that PIERRON is a poor quality interpreter. AUBUCHON tells PS BAGGERLEY that he wants a different interpreter.

Which of the following statements is correct in respect of this situation?

A PS BAGGERLEY must arrange for a different interpreter to attend the police station.

B PS BAGGERLEY is responsible for deciding whether a different interpreter should be called to the police station.

C If PS BAGGERLEY decides that a different interpreter should not be called, and AUBUCHON challenges the decision, the matter should be reported to an officer of the rank of superintendent or above.

D A police officer or a member of police staff could be used to assist in communication in the interview.

Question 4.26

SMITH is wanted by West Midlands Police for an offence of attempted murder. He is arrested in Glasgow by Scottish police officers for an unrelated burglary offence that took place in Glasgow. West Midlands Police are notified of the arrest of SMITH and DCs TRAINER and LOWBRIDGE travel to Scotland to pick up SMITH and transport him back to the West Midlands. The officers arrive in Glasgow at 11.00 hrs and pick SMITH up. They leave Glasgow immediately and cross the border between Scotland and England at 12.45 hrs the same day. Later in the day, they arrive in the West Midlands force area at 16.45 hrs and arrive at the first police station in the West Midlands at 17.15 hrs (all on the same day).

What time will SMITH's 'relevant time' begin in relation to the attempted murder offence?

A 11.00 hrs.

B 12.45 hrs.

C 16.45 hrs.

D 17.15 hrs.

Question 4.27

HANE has been arrested on suspicion of murder. Due to the complex nature of the offence and the large-scale enquiries connected with it, HANE has spent 27 hours in police custody (a superintendent lawfully authorised an extension of HANE's detention). The Senior Investigating Officer is considering her options regarding obtaining a further extension of HANE's detention by way of a warrant of further detention.

In respect of such a warrant of further detention, which of the following comments is correct?

A A warrant of further detention can only be made with the written authorisation of an officer of the rank of superintendent or above.

B An application for a warrant of further detention must be made by an officer of the rank of inspector or above.

C An application for a warrant of further detention is made in the Crown Court.

D An application for a warrant of further detention can be made at any time, even before a superintendent's review has been carried out.

Question 4.28

NOREM has been arrested on suspicion of being a terrorist (under s. 41 of the Terrorism Act 2000) and a large-scale investigation is under way regarding his activities.

In relation to warrants of further detention and terrorism cases, which of the following statements is correct?

A A court could extend NOREM's period of detention up to a total of 14 days (starting at the time NOREM was arrested).

B NOREM could be held for a period of 96 hours without charge before an application must be made to issue or extend a warrant of further detention.

C An extension of detention in such a matter will normally be for a five-day period.

D An application for a warrant of further detention in a terrorism case can only be made by a Crown Prosecutor.

Question 4.29

At 06.00 hrs today, PALER is arrested for an offence of rape. He is escorted to a designated police station by the arresting officer, DC FULLWOOD, and they arrive at the station at 06.30 hrs. PALER's detention is authorised by PS MOSES at 06.50 hrs. PALER remains in police custody while the investigation progresses—he has not yet been charged with any offence.

Considering any review of PALER's detention, which of the following statements is correct?

A As PALER has not been charged with an offence, the 'review officer' will be the custody officer.

B The first review of PALER's detention shall be no more than six hours after his arrival at a designated police station.

C The first review of PALER's detention shall be no more than six hours after his detention was first authorised.

D The first review of PALER's detention shall be no more than nine hours after his detention was first authorised.

Question 4.30

CHARNOCK is an extremely violent 14-year-old child who has been arrested for an offence of s. 18 wounding which was committed using a razor blade of some description. He is brought into custody by DC ALMACK and, when the circumstances of the arrest are provided, CHARNOCK states, '*The blade is right up my arse where you can't get it!*' Inspector KEYS is in the custody block when this exchange takes place and consequently has reasonable grounds for believing that CHARNOCK may have concealed upon himself something which he could and might use to cause physical injury to himself or others at the station.

Could an intimate search of CHARNOCK be authorised?

A Yes, but it would have to be carried out by a registered medical practitioner or a registered nurse.

B No, as CHARNOCK has not been arrested for supplying a Class A drug.

C Yes, as long as an officer of the rank of inspector or above authorised it to take place.

D No, not unless an appropriate adult has given their consent to the search taking place.

ANSWERS

Answer 4.1

Answer **C** — Where an officer performs the duties of a custody officer in the circumstances described in the question, that officer shall inform an officer, who (a) is attached to a designated police station and (b) is of at least the rank of inspector, that he has done so.

Investigators' Manual, para. 1.6.2

Answer 4.2

Answer **C** — Code C, para. 5.6 states that the detained person shall, on request, be given writing materials and/or be allowed to telephone one person for a reasonable time. This privilege may be denied or delayed if an officer of the rank of inspector or above considers sending the letter or making the telephone call may result in any of the consequences set out in Annex B, paras 1 and 2 of Code C (making answer B incorrect). One of those consequences is that the inspector believes the exercise of the right will hinder the recovery of property obtained in consequence of the commission of such an offence.

Investigators' Manual, paras 1.6.9, 1.6.9.1

Answer 4.3

Answer **A** — If an authorising officer, of superintendent rank or above, considers that access to a solicitor will interfere with evidence relating to an indictable offence, then access to that solicitor may be delayed, making answer D incorrect. This authorisation to delay access is not a 'blanket' authorisation to deny access to *all* legal advisers and in the example given in the question, the authorising officer should consider offering the detained person access to another solicitor on the Duty Solicitor scheme, making answer C incorrect. The consultation with a solicitor must be in private (Code C, para. 6.1). In *Brennan* v *United Kingdom* (2001) 34 EHRR 507, the court held that a suspect's right to communicate confidentially with a solicitor 'is part of the basic requirements of a fair trial'. The court found that there had been a breach of Article 6(3)(c) because a police officer had been present during a suspect's first interview with his solicitor, making answer B incorrect.

Investigators' Manual, paras 1.6.10, 1.6.10.1

Answer 4.4

Answer **B** — Paragraph 6.6(d) of Code C deals with the situation where the detainee changes their mind about wanting legal advice. In these circumstances, the interview may be started or continued without delay provided:

(a) an officer of the rank of inspector or above speaks to the interview to the detainee to enquire about the reason for their change of mind;
(b) the detainee's reason is recorded in the custody record;
(c) the detainee confirms in writing that they do not want a solicitor;
(d) an inspector gives authority for the interview to proceed; and
(e) confirmation of the previous factors is recorded in the interview.

Investigators' Manual, paras 1.6.10, 1.6.10.1

Answer 4.5

Answer **B** — Section 41(2)(c) of the Police and Criminal Evidence Act 1984 states that in the case of a person who attends voluntarily at a police station or accompanies a constable to a police station without having been arrested, and is arrested, the 'relevant time' will begin at the time of his/her arrest. In situations where a person is arrested at one police station and has been circulated as wanted by another police station in the same force area, the detention clock for the second offence (in this case for the offence of rape) starts at the same time as for the original offence for which they were arrested.

Investigators' Manual, para. 1.6.16.1

Answer 4.6

Answer **C** — Section 42(1) of the Police and Criminal Evidence Act 1984 permits an officer of superintendent rank or above who is responsible for the station at which the person is detained to authorise detention beyond 24 hours and up to a maximum of 36 hours (Code C, para. 15.2). The offence investigated must be an indictable offence and the senior officer must be satisfied that there is not sufficient evidence to charge, that the investigation is being conducted diligently and expeditiously and that the person's detention is necessary to secure or preserve evidence relating to the offence or to obtain such evidence by questioning that person.

Investigators' Manual, para. 1.6.16

Answer 4.7

Answer **D** — The right to have a private consultation with a solicitor also applies to juveniles (Code C). If a juvenile wishes to have a private consultation without the presence of an appropriate adult, they must be permitted to do so.

Investigators' Manual, paras 1.6.10, 1.6.10.1

Answer 4.8

Answer **B** — The right under s. 56 of the Act can be delayed (making answer A incorrect). The delay can be authorised by an officer of the rank of inspector or above, making answer C incorrect. Answer D is incorrect as although the authorisation level is correct, the right can only be delayed up to a maximum of 36 hours (48 in cases involving terrorism) and this 36-hour period is calculated from the 'relevant time'. The 'relevant time' is the time that DEBNEY arrives at the police station, i.e. 11.00 hrs, and so the right could be delayed up to 23.00 hrs on the following day, making answer B correct.

Investigators' Manual, paras 1.6.9, 1.6.9.1

Answer 4.9

Answer **D** — Section 118 states that a person will be in police detention for the purposes of the Act if (i) he has been taken to a police station after being arrested for an offence or after being arrested under s. 41 of the Terrorism Act 2000, or (ii) he is arrested at a police station after attending voluntarily at the station (answer A) or accompanying a constable to it, or is detained there or is detained elsewhere in the charge of a constable (answer B), except that a person who is at court after being charged *is not* in police detention for those purposes (answer D). In addition, where a person is in another's lawful custody by virtue of para. 22, 34(1) (a designated escort officer and answer C) or 35(3) of sch. 4 to the Police Reform Act 2002, he shall be treated as being in police detention.

Investigators' Manual, para. 1.6.5.2

Answer 4.10

Answer **C** — Section 36(3) states that a custody officer must be an officer of at least the rank of sergeant (answer B); however, s. 36(4) allows an officer of any rank to perform the functions of a custody officer if a sergeant is not readily available to perform them (answer C). An officer of any rank can perform the role at a designated or non-designated police station, making answer A incorrect. The effect of these sections is that the practice of allowing an officer of any rank to perform the role of custody officer where a sergeant (*who has no other role to perform*) is in the police station must therefore be unlawful. Answer D has Sergeant EDEN (i) performing another role and (ii) *out* of the police station.

Investigators' Manual, para. 1.6.2

Answer 4.11

Answer **C** — As long as the interview under Code C, para. 6.6 can be justified at court, the interview will be admissible, making answer A incorrect. Where a suspect is in an authorised place of detention and fails to answer questions, no inference will be drawn from that failure if he/she has not been allowed the opportunity to consult a solicitor prior to being questioned, making answer B incorrect. Answer D is incorrect as an interview under Code C, para. 6.6 can only take place if an officer of the rank of superintendent or above authorises it. It is not necessary to await the arrival of a solicitor to take a non-intimate sample without consent for evidential purposes.

Investigators' Manual, paras 1.6.10, 1.6.10.1

Answer 4.12

Answer **A** — In cases where the person has been detained under the Terrorism Act 2000, the first review should be conducted as soon as reasonably practicable after his/her arrest. It must be conducted by a superintendent after the 24-hour period.

Investigators' Manual, para. 1.6.16.13

Answer 4.13

Answer **B** — When a detainee leaves police detention or is taken before a court they, their legal representative or appropriate adult shall be given, on request, a copy of the custody record as soon as practicable. This entitlement lasts for 12 months after release.

Investigators' Manual, para. 1.6.6

Answer 4.14

Answer **C** — A juvenile may not be placed in a cell with a detained adult, making answer A incorrect. COURTNEY can be placed in a cell (making answer B incorrect) if there is no other secure accommodation available and the custody officer considers it is not practicable to supervise him if he is not placed in a cell or that the cell provides more comfortable accommodation than other secure accommodation in the station (Code C, para. 8.8). This does not require the authority of an inspector, making answer D incorrect.

Investigators' Manual, para. 1.6.12

Answer 4.15

Answer **B** — Detainees should be visited every hour but if it is suspected that they are intoxicated through drink or drugs or having swallowed a drug or there are concerns about a detainee's level of consciousness, they should be visited and roused at least every half hour (Code C, para. 9.3).

Investigators' Manual, para. 1.6.13

Answer 4.16

Answer **D** — The custody officer must make sure a detainee receives appropriate clinical attention as soon as reasonably practicable if the person is injured. The detainee may also be examined by a medical practitioner of their choice at their expense (Code C, para. 9.8).

Investigators' Manual, para. 1.6.13

Answer 4.17

Answer **D** — The decision on whether the review takes place in person or by telephone or by video conferencing (video conferencing is subject to the introduction of regulations by the Secretary of State) is a matter for the review officer.

Investigators' Manual, para. 1.6.16.12

Answer 4.18

Answer **B** — Answer A is incorrect as Code C, para. 16.5 details the occasions when it is permissible to re-interview a suspect after they have been charged or informed that they will be prosecuted for an offence. There is no requirement for the suspect to agree in writing to this taking place, making answer D incorrect. The re-interviewing of a suspect can take place if it is necessary to (i) prevent or minimise harm or loss to some other person or the public, or (ii) clear up any ambiguity in a previous answer or statement, or (iii) in the interests of justice for the detainee to have put to them, and have an opportunity to comment on, information concerning the offence which has come to light since they were charged or informed that they might be prosecuted. The reasons for re-interviewing could be any one of these, making answer C incorrect.

Investigators' Manual, para. 1.6.17

Answer 4.19

Answer **A** — A detention officer can carry out an examination of a person detained at a police station in order to identify the person concerned via marks on their body (such as a tattoo). Answers B and C are incorrect as these are all powers available to detention officers and escort officers. The power to photograph a detained person is not available to an escort officer, making answer D incorrect.

Investigators' Manual, paras 1.6.3.2, 1.6.3.3

Answer 4.20

Answer **A** — A prisoner who will be detained (or is likely to be detained) for more than six hours must go to a 'designated' police station.

Investigators' Manual, para. 1.6.4

Answer 4.21

Answer **D** — HAWTHORNE and ADEY could both potentially act as an appropriate adult for STUBBS; however, a person should not be an appropriate adult if he/she is the victim of an offence (HAWTHORNE) or has received admissions prior to attending to act as an appropriate adult (ADEY).

Investigators' Manual, para. 1.6.5.4

Answer 4.22

Answer **C** — Code C, para. 3.13 states that if a person is a juvenile, the custody officer must, if it is practicable, ascertain the identity of a person responsible for their welfare. Paragraph 1.5A extends the obligations in para. 3.13 to 17-year-old detainees, making answer A incorrect. Paragraph 3.15 states that the custody officer must, as soon as practicable, inform the appropriate adult of the grounds for the juvenile's detention (making answer D incorrect) and their whereabouts. It does not require the custody officer to inform the appropriate adult of the time and place of the juvenile's arrest (making answer B incorrect). Paragraph 3.18 points out that the juvenile should be informed that they can consult privately with the appropriate adult at any time.

Investigators' Manual, para. 1.6.7

Answer 4.23

Answer **B** — Not all detained persons need to be searched; s. 54(1) and para. 4.1 of Code C require a detainee to be searched when it is clear that the custody officer will have continuing duties in relation to the detainee or when that detainee's behaviour or offence makes an inventory appropriate. They do not require every detainee to be searched, making answer A incorrect. Answer C is incorrect as although a custody officer can authorise a strip search, an intimate search can only be authorised by an officer of the rank of inspector or above. Answer D is incorrect as the custody officer must first authorise any search and the extent of the search—officers should not search a person until the authority has been given. Section 54(9) states that such a search is a same-sex process (answer B).

Investigators' Manual, para. 1.6.8.1

Answer 4.24

Answer **A** — You may consider this a strange question for a Trainee Investigator to consider, but the reason it is asked is that s. 7 of Code C, which deals with citizens of independent Commonwealth countries and foreign nationals, has been questioned in a number of examinations. Code C, para. 7.1 states that a detainee who is a citizen of an independent Commonwealth country or a national of a foreign country, including the Republic of Ireland (so answer B is incorrect), has the right, upon request, to communicate at any time (making answer C incorrect) with the appropriate High Commission, Embassy or Consulate. Such a request should be acted upon as soon as practicable (making answer D incorrect).

Investigators' Manual, para. 1.6.11

Answer 4.25

Answer **B** — Code C, para. 13.9 states that a police officer or any other police staff cannot be used for the purpose described in the question, making answer D incorrect. Paragraph 13.10A states that if a detainee complains that they are not satisfied with the quality of the interpretation, the custody officer or (as the case may be) the interviewer is responsible for deciding whether a different interpreter should be called (this makes answer A incorrect). Paragraph 13.10D states that if a suspect challenges the decision of the custody officer (or interviewer) not to provide a different interpreter, that matter should be reported to an inspector to deal with as a complaint (making answer C incorrect).

Investigators' Manual, para. 1.6.14

Answer 4.26

Answer **D** — This scenario has long been an exam favourite. Section 41(2)(b) states that where a person is arrested outside England and Wales, the 'relevant time' shall be the time at which that person arrives at the first police station to which he/she is taken in the police area in England and Wales in which the offence for which he/she was arrested is being investigated or the time 24 hours after the time of that person's entry into England and Wales, whichever is the sooner. Therefore, the time of arrival at the first police station in the West Midlands is the 'relevant time', i.e. 17.15 hrs. This makes answers A, B and C incorrect.

Investigators' Manual, para. 1.6.16.1

Answer 4.27

Answer **D** — There is no requirement for the written authorisation of a superintendent in order to apply for a warrant of further detention, nor is there a need for the application to be made by an officer of the rank of inspector or above, making answers A and B incorrect. The application for the warrant is made in the magistrates' court, making answer C incorrect.

Investigators' Manual, paras 1.6.16.7 to 1.6.16.8

Answer 4.28

Answer **A** — The court can extend the period of detention of a person up to a total of 14 days—this will start at the time of arrest when a person is arrested under s. 41 of the Terrorism Act 2000 (correct answer A). A person detained in these circumstances may only be held for a maximum of 48 hours without charge before an application must be made (making answer B incorrect). Answer C is incorrect as extensions by the court will normally be for a seven-day period. Answer D is incorrect as applications to the court can be made by a superintendent or a Crown Prosecutor.

Investigators' Manual, para. 1.6.16.11

Answer 4.29

Answer **C** — In the case of a person arrested but not charged, the 'review officer' will be an officer of at least inspector rank not directly involved in the investigation, making answer A incorrect. Answers B and D are incorrect as the first review shall not be later than six hours after detention was first authorised (not nine hours and not calculated from the time of arrival at the designated police station).

Investigators' Manual, para. 1.6.16.12

Answer 4.30

Answer **C** — Answer A is incorrect as an intimate search may only be carried out by a registered medical practitioner or a registered nurse, unless an officer of the rank of at least inspector considers that this is not practicable, in which case a police officer could carry out the search (very much a last resort—see Code C, paras 3 and 3A of Annex A). Answer B is incorrect as whilst an intimate search could be authorised in connection with Class A drugs, it can also be authorised if an officer of the rank of inspector or above has reasonable grounds for believing that the person may have concealed upon themselves anything which they could and might use to cause physical injury to themselves or others at the station. Answer D is incorrect as consent is not required for an intimate search to take place in the circumstances described.

Investigators' Manual, para. 1.6.19

5 Interviews/Code C/Code E/ Code F

QUESTIONS

Question 5.1

JENKINS (aged 15 years) has stolen several bottles of concentrated acid from his school chemistry laboratory and has hidden them in an unknown location on the school premises. The principal of the school has detained JENKINS and contacted the police to deal with the matter. PC McATEER attends the school and is concerned that if the acid is not located immediately it will lead to physical harm to other people. PC McATEER wishes to interview JENKINS regarding the location of the stolen acid and believes that contacting JENKINS's parents would cause an unreasonable delay in the circumstances.

Which of the following statements is correct?

A The principal cannot act as an appropriate adult because JENKINS is suspected of an offence against his educational establishment.

B Under no circumstances can PC McATEER interview JENKINS at his place of education.

C Regardless of the circumstances, JENKINS's parents must be notified of the interview and be present when the interview is carried out.

D If waiting for JENKINS's parents to attend would cause an unreasonable delay, the principal can act as an appropriate adult.

Question 5.2

DC BUTLIN is interviewing FLATMAN in relation to the kidnapping of his ex-wife. Before the kidnapping took place, FLATMAN told HARLOWE (a civilian witness) that he had considered kidnapping his ex-wife to teach her a lesson after she retained possession of their marital home in the divorce settlement between them. HARLOWE has provided DC BUTLIN with a witness statement to this effect.

Considering the Codes of Practice in relation to significant statements, what action should DC BUTLIN take with regard to FLATMAN's comment to HARLOWE?

A DC BUTLIN should introduce the comment made to HARLOWE at the start of the interview after caution, as it is a significant statement.

B DC BUTLIN may introduce the comment made to HARLOWE at any time during the interview, as unless the comment is a direct admission of guilt it is not a significant statement.

C DC BUTLIN may introduce the comment made to HARLOWE at any time during the course of the interview, even though the comment is a significant statement.

D DC BUTLIN may introduce the comment made to HARLOWE at any time during the course of the interview, as it would not be classed as a significant statement.

Question 5.3

DCs CHURCHLEY and RAY are conducting an audio-recorded interview with HOLLAND for an offence of robbery. Also present in the interview is HOLLAND's solicitor, MASPERO. Thirty minutes after the interview has started, HOLLAND asks for a short two-minute break in the interview while he gathers his thoughts. During the short break, DCs CHURCHLEY and RAY will remain in the interview room with HOLLAND and MASPERO.

Considering Code E of the Codes of Practice, what action should the interviewing officers take?

A The Codes of Practice do not allow for short breaks to be taken. The officers should stop the recording media and vacate the interview room.

B The officers should remove the recording media from the audio recorder and follow the procedures as if the interview had been concluded.

C As this is only a short break, the officers may turn off the audio recorder and when the interview recommences, continue the interview on the same tapes.

D The officers should leave the audio machine running for the duration of the short break and then continue the interview on the same recording media.

Question 5.4

CROXTON is arrested for an offence of supplying a Class A controlled drug and on arrival in the custody block he requests the presence of his solicitor, Mr JONES. Mr JONES is contacted but tells the custody officer it will be ten hours before he can get to the police station. The arresting officer, DC ROACH, speaks to her duty superintendent who authorises an interview without the presence of Mr JONES on the grounds that to await his arrival would cause an unreasonable delay to the process of the investigation. During the course of this interview, CROXTON's reply to all the questions put to him is, '*No comment*'.

Considering only s. 34 of the Criminal Justice and Public Order Act 1994, what effect will CROXTON's '*No comment*' response have on the case?

A A court could draw an inference from CROXTON's failure to provide an answer to DC ROACH's questions.

B A court will draw no inference unless there is additional evidence produced by the prosecution to prove the case.

C Should a court draw an inference from CROXTON's failure to answer questions, CROXTON can be convicted on that inference alone.

D A court will draw no inference, as CROXTON was not allowed to consult a solicitor prior to being questioned.

Question 5.5

VOWLES makes a statement to the police complaining that THOMAS assaulted him with a knuckle-duster. VOWLES states that during the assault he managed to punch THOMAS on his left cheek. The next day, DCs STOKOE and McCROW visit THOMAS's home address and arrest him for a s. 20 grievous bodily harm (contrary to the Offences Against the Person Act 1861) on VOWLES. On his arrest, DC STOKOE notices that THOMAS has a large bruise on his left cheekbone. During the arrest, DC McCROW seizes a knuckle-duster from THOMAS's living room. In interview, THOMAS tells DC STOKOE that he got the bruised cheekbone playing football the previous day but refuses to answer any questions relating to the knuckle-duster. DC STOKOE believes that THOMAS's bruised cheekbone and the knuckle-duster are attributable to THOMAS taking part in the offence.

Considering only s. 36 of the Criminal Justice and Public Order Act 1994, which, if any, of the following would DC STOKOE be able to give THOMAS a special warning for?

A THOMAS's bruised cheekbone.

B The knuckle-duster recovered at THOMAS's home address.

C THOMAS's bruised cheekbone and the knuckle-duster recovered at THOMAS's home address.

D Special warnings are not applicable for either the bruised cheekbone or the knuckle-duster.

Question 5.6

DCs KENT and TORBIN are interviewing SPONDEN in respect of an arson offence and associated offences of witness intimidation. The interview is being audio-recorded. SPONDEN is a particularly violent suspect and has a history of violent behaviour towards witnesses and also towards police officers. DC KENT believes that if she discloses her name during the course of interviewing SPONDEN it will put her in danger; DC TORBIN believes that if he discloses his name during the course of interviewing SPONDEN it will put his family in danger.

Considering Code E of the Codes of Practice, which of the following statements is correct?

A Both officers must provide their names in the interview as the case does not involve enquiries into the investigation of terrorism.

B DC KENT may use her warrant number and police station as a means of identification in interview; DC TORBIN must use his name.

C DC TORBIN may use his warrant number as a means of identification; DC KENT must use her name.

D Both officers may withhold their names and use their warrant numbers and police stations as a means of identification.

Question 5.7

DC ENGLISH and TI JONES are in the process of interviewing HAY on audio recording media regarding an offence of burglary. Thirty minutes into the interview, the audio recording machine malfunctions and stops. Despite the interviewing officers' best efforts, the machine cannot be fixed. No other interviewing room or recording facility is available.

According to Code E of the Codes of Practice, what should occur?

A The interview must be suspended until an appropriate interviewing room or device becomes available.

B The interview may be continued without being audio-recorded but the officers will need to seek the authority of an officer of the rank of inspector or above to do so.

C The interview may be continued without being audio-recorded but the officers will need to seek the authority of the custody officer to do so.

D The interview may be continued without being audio-recorded. No particular authority is required in such a situation.

Question 5.8

DC MORRIN (who has 10 years' police service) and TI EDMOND (who has 12 years' police service) are interviewing YOUNG about an allegation of fraud. At the conclusion of the interview DC MORRIN seals the master recording of the interview, signs the master recording label and asks YOUNG to sign the label. YOUNG refuses to do so.

Which of the following comments is correct in such a situation?

A The senior police officer in the interview (TI EDMOND) should sign the label to the effect that YOUNG would not sign the seal.

B Either DC MORRIN or TI EDMOND can sign the label to the effect that YOUNG would not sign the seal.

C The custody officer should be called into the interview room and he/she should sign the label.

D An officer of the rank of inspector or above should be called into the interview room and sign the label.

Question 5.9

TI DIOLA is the officer in charge of an investigation into a series of burglaries. The suspect, BOURNE, was interviewed on audio recording media and released on bail. A record of the interview with BOURNE is required for the court file but the working copy of the audio recording media is accidentally destroyed. The only remaining audio recording media is the master recording which has been sealed according to the rules governing such matters. TI DIOLA needs to access the master recording to create a record of the interview.

Can TI DIOLA break the seal on the master recording?

A Yes, but this can only be done with the authority of an officer of the rank of superintendent or above.

B No, unless TI DIOLA arranges for the seal to be broken in the presence of a representative of the Crown Prosecution Service.

C Yes, but the seal must be broken in a magistrates' court.

D No, unless TI DIOLA obtains an authorisation from the Crown Court.

Question 5.10

DUCLIN has been arrested for an offence of rape and is in his cell awaiting interview. DCs HUTTON and PAGE tell the custody officer they are ready to interview DUCLIN but when the custody officer assistant attempts to get DUCLIN out of his cell, he refuses to attend and shouts that he will not leave his cell. DUCLIN is spoken to by the custody officer but continues to refuse to leave his cell.

Could DUCLIN be interviewed in his cell?

A Yes, as long as the custody office considers, on reasonable grounds, that the interview should not be delayed the interview can be conducted in DUCLIN's cell using portable recording equipment.

B No, interviews must not take place in cells.

C Yes, if an officer of the rank of inspector or above believes that it will cause an unreasonable delay to act otherwise, the interview can be recorded using portable recording equipment.

D No, because of the seriousness of the allegation (an offence of rape) the interview must be conducted in an interview room.

Question 5.11

DC NUMAN is working on an enquiry into the activities of PROSSER who is suspected of working for an organised crime syndicate as an 'enforcer'. PROSSER is arrested for several offences of s. 18 grievous bodily harm/wounding and DC NUMAN is asked to take part in the visually recorded interview of PROSSER. Due to certain elements of DC NUMAN's personal life, the officer reasonably believes that to provide his name during the course of the interview would put him in danger.

Considering the guidance provided by Code F of the Codes of Practice on such matters, which of the following comments is correct?

A The interview should take place as normal but DC NUMAN should only provide his warrant number (instead of his name).

B As DC NUMAN would be recognised in a visually recorded interview, he cannot take part in it.

C If an officer of the rank of at least inspector certifies that it is necessary for the officer's safety, DC NUMAN should give his warrant number (instead of his name) and also state the police station to which he is attached.

D DC NUMAN can take part in the interview but should have his back to the camera and give his warrant number (not his name) and the name of the police station to which he is attached.

Question 5.12

DC BOLTON has arrested PIKE (who is 19 years old and profoundly deaf) and DAPSON (who is 15 years old) for an offence of robbery. PIKE and DAPSON are taken to a custody block where an interpreter is called out for PIKE and an appropriate adult called for DAPSON. Several interview rooms in the custody block have the ability to visually record interviews with suspects; there are also interview rooms in the custody block that only record sound.

Considering Code F of the Codes of Practice, which of the following statements is correct?

A DC BOLTON must interview PIKE using a visual recording interview room; it does not matter what type of interview recording is used for DAPSON.

B DAPSON must be interviewed in a visual recording interview room; it does not matter what type of interview recording is used for PIKE.

C As PIKE is deaf and DAPSON is a juvenile, Code F states that both suspects must be interviewed in a visual recording interview room if one is available.

D There is no requirement for either suspect to be interviewed in a visual recording interview room.

Question 5.13

PRIEST has been arrested in connection with an offence of rape and is being interviewed by DCs ROWLEY and SKILLEN. The officers decide to give PRIEST a special warning under s. 36 of the Criminal Justice and Public Order Act 1994.

Which of the following is correct with regard to the delivery of the special warning?

A PRIEST does not need to be told what offence is being investigated.

B PRIEST does not need to be told what fact he is being asked to account for.

C PRIEST does not need to be told that a record is being made of the interview and that it may be given in evidence at any subsequent trial.

D PRIEST does not need to be cautioned at the conclusion of the special warning.

ANSWERS

Answer 5.1

Answer **A** — Code C, para. 11.16 states that a juvenile can be interviewed at his/her place of education in exceptional circumstances and with the agreement of the principal or the principal's nominee, making answer B incorrect. The parents of the juvenile should be notified and allowed a reasonable time to attend unless waiting for the appropriate adult would cause an unreasonable delay in which case the principal or his/her nominee can act as an appropriate adult, making answer C incorrect. However, if the juvenile is suspected of an offence against the educational establishment then the principal or his/her nominee cannot act as an appropriate adult, making answer D incorrect.

Investigators' Manual, para. 1.7.3.2

Answer 5.2

Answer **D** — Code C, para. 11.4A states that a significant statement is one that appears capable of being used in evidence against the suspect, in particular a direct admission of guilt, making answer B incorrect. FLATMAN's comment to HARLOWE would appear to be a significant statement on that basis. However, para. 11.4 states that a significant statement is a statement that occurred in the presence and hearing of a police officer or a civilian interviewer before the start of the interview and this is not the case with the comment made to a civilian witness. Therefore, the comment is not a significant statement, making answers A and C incorrect. Answer C is further incorrect as a significant statement should be put to the suspect at the beginning of the interview after caution.

Investigators' Manual, para. 1.7.3

Answer 5.3

Answer **C** — Code E, para. 4.13 allows for short breaks to be taken during an audio-recorded interview, making answer A incorrect. This paragraph states that if the break is to be a short one and both the suspect and the interviewer are to remain in the room, then the audio-recorder may be turned off. There is no need to remove the tapes and when the interview recommences the tape recording should continue on the same tapes, making answers B and D incorrect.

Investigators' Manual, para. 1.7.10.6

Answer 5.4

Answer **D** — Section 34(2A) states that if the defendant has not been allowed an opportunity to consult a solicitor prior to being questioned then no inference will be drawn by the court on the defendant's silence, refusal or failure to give an account. This section was introduced because of the judgment of the European Court of Human Rights in the case of *Murray* v *United Kingdom* (1996) 22 EHRR 29. The court held that inferences being drawn from the silence of the accused when denied access to legal advice constituted a breach of Article 6(1) in conjunction with Article 6(3) of the European Convention on Human Rights (right to a fair trial).

Investigators' Manual, para. 1.7.2.3

Answer 5.5

Answer **B** — Special warnings under s. 36 of the Act are applicable if a person is arrested by a constable and there is (i) on his person, or (ii) in or on his clothing or footwear, or (iii) otherwise in his possession or (iv) in any place in which he is at the time of his arrest, any object, substance or mark, or there is any mark on any such object which the officer reasonably believes may be attributable to the participation of the arrested person in the commission of an offence. This would mean that both the bruised cheekbone (a mark on the person) and the knuckle-duster (an object in any place in which the person is at the time of the arrest) could form part of a special warning. However, the special warning should only be given if the defendant fails or refuses to account for the fact. THOMAS has answered the question relating to the bruised cheekbone, making answers A and C incorrect. He refuses to answer questions relating to the knuckle-duster and so a special warning may be given regarding this item, making answer D incorrect.

Investigators' Manual, paras 1.7.2.4 to 1.7.2.5

Answer 5.6

Answer **B** — Nothing in Code E requires the identity of officers or police staff conducting interviews to be recorded or disclosed:

(a) in the case of enquiries linked to the investigation of terrorism; or
(b) if the interviewer reasonably believes recording or disclosing their name might put them in danger.

In these cases interviewers should use warrant or other identification numbers and the name of their police station.

Therefore, answer A is incorrect as it is not only in terrorism cases where this facility exists. Answers C and D are incorrect as DC TORBIN believes disclosing his name will put his family *and not him* in danger. Answer C is additionally incorrect as identification must be a warrant number *and* the individual's police station.

Investigators' Manual, para. 1.7.8

Answer 5.7

Answer **C** — Where there is a failure of the recording media and it is not possible to continue recording on that recorder and no replacement recorder is readily available, the interview may continue without being audio-recorded (making answer A incorrect). Should this occur, authority to continue the interview without it being audio-recorded is required from the custody officer (making answers B and D incorrect).

Investigators' Manual, para. 1.7.10.8

Answer 5.8

Answer **D** — Answers A, B and C are incorrect as if a suspect or a third party present during the interview refuses to sign the master recording label an officer of at least inspector rank, or if not available the custody officer, shall be called into the interview room and asked (subject to para. 2.3 of Code E) to sign it.

Investigators' Manual, para 1.7.10.10

Answer 5.9

Answer **B** — No actual 'authorisation' is required to break the seal on a master recording, making answers A and D incorrect. There are also no rules as to where the seal should be broken, making answer C incorrect. However, if the seal is to be broken it must be broken in the presence of a representative of the Crown Prosecution Service.

Investigators' Manual, para. 1.7.12

Answer 5.10

Answer **A** — Interviews can take place in cells, making answer B incorrect. This is the case regardless of the seriousness of the offence the suspect is to be interviewed for, making answer D incorrect. The decision as to whether this takes place is at the discretion of the custody officer, making answer C incorrect. Such an interview can take place if the custody officer considers, on reasonable grounds, that the interview should not be delayed. It can be conducted using portable recording equipment or, if none is available, recorded in writing (Code E, para. 3.4).

Investigators' Manual, para. 1.7.9

Answer 5.11

Answer **D** — Code F, para. 2.5 states that nothing in the Code requires the identity of the officer to be recorded or disclosed if the interview or record relates to a person detained under the Terrorism Act 2000 or otherwise where the officer reasonably believes that recording or disclosing their name might put them in danger. In these cases, the officer will have their back to the camera and shall use their warrant number or other identification number and the name of the police station to which they are attached.

Investigators' Manual, para. 1.7.15

Answer 5.12

Answer **D** — Code F does not enforce the use of visually recorded interviews but offers advice on when such use '*might be appropriate*'. Two examples are where the interview is with a deaf person or with anyone who requires the presence of an 'appropriate adult'.

Investigators' Manual, para. 1.7.16

Answer 5.13

Answer **D** — Answers A, B and C are all incorrect as all of these are requirements when delivering a special warning to a suspect. Answer D is correct, as the suspect *does not have* to be cautioned at the conclusion of the special warning.

Investigators' Manual, para. 1.7.2.4

6 Identification/Code D

QUESTIONS

Question 6.1

SALISBURY is looking out of her bedroom window when she sees COX attempting to break into her neighbour's house. SALISBURY watches COX for a continuous period of five minutes and then telephones the police to tell them what she has seen. SALISBURY describes the approximate age of COX and the clothes he is wearing. The police arrive and COX is arrested. In interview, COX disputes being the person responsible for the offence but does not request an identification parade.

Considering the law with regard to identification, which of the following statements is correct?

A A suspect's failure to request an identification parade means that the police may proceed without one.

B This would not be classed as an identification within the terms of the Codes of Practice as SALISBURY has only described the clothing and approximate age of COX.

C The Codes of Practice are clear; where a witness is available and the suspect disputes being the person responsible for the offence, an identification procedure shall be held.

D Following the decision in *R* v *Forbes*, if the police are in possession of sufficient evidence to justify an arrest of a suspect and any identification is disputed then an identification procedure should be held.

Question 6.2

PITCHER commits a robbery and is filmed on a town centre CCTV system carrying out the offence. DC THORPE wishes to trace witnesses to the offence and obtains a still image from the CCTV and places this in the local newspaper. MAYBURY recognises PITCHER from the still image and contacts DC THORPE, who subsequently arrests PITCHER.

Considering Code D of the Codes of Practice, which of the following statements is correct?

A There is no requirement for PITCHER or his solicitor to view the material released to the media before any identification procedure is carried out.

B As MAYBURY has recognised PITCHER from a still image placed in a newspaper, she would not be allowed to take part in any further identification procedures.

C DC THORPE may keep a copy of the material released to the media for the purposes of recognising or tracing the suspect.

D The fact that MAYBURY identified PITCHER from a still image in a newspaper would not stop her taking part in any further identification procedures.

Question 6.3

You have arrested TRAVIS on suspicion of committing 30 bogus-official type burglaries. Descriptions of the offender have been obtained for every incident and there is a reasonable chance that each victim would be able to identify the offender. During her interview, TRAVIS denies any involvement in the offences. TRAVIS states that she will stand on an identification parade to prove her innocence.

What action will you take?

A As TRAVIS disputes her involvement, there is an identification issue. In these circumstances you must arrange an identification in the first instance.

B As there is an identification issue, you must initially offer TRAVIS the choice between taking part in a video identification or standing on an identification parade.

C You should initially offer a video identification to TRAVIS.

D As the officer in the case you may choose freely between a video identification and an identification parade.

Question 6.4

CHURCH is involved in large-scale crowd violence at a football match during which he takes part in a violent disorder. The incident is caught on CCTV film. As well as the CCTV film of the incident, an E-fit is released to the public to identify CHURCH, who is recognised from the E-fit by DRAPER. As a result, CHURCH is later arrested, charged and bailed for the offence. On his release, CHURCH makes a series of threatening telephone calls to DRAPER, who tape-records the threats.

Considering the law relating to photographs, images and sound, which of the following statements is correct?

A The interpretation of images on film is a matter for the jury; expert evidence would not be admitted to interpret such images.
B The Codes of Practice preclude the use of aural identification procedures.
C A police officer familiar with the CCTV of the crowd violence may be allowed to assist the court in interpreting and explaining events shown within the film.
D DRAPER would not be allowed to give evidence identifying CHURCH's voice.

Question 6.5

GROUCOTT admits to an offence of theft (a recordable offence) and is cautioned. At the time of her caution she had an injury to her left hand that meant no fingerprints relating to that hand could be taken.

Considering the powers to take fingerprints under s. 61 of the Police and Criminal Evidence Act 1984, which of the following statements is correct?

A GROUCOTT cannot be required to provide any further fingerprints in connection with a case for which she was cautioned.
B Section 61 of the Act is only applicable if the person has been convicted of a recordable offence.
C The authority of an inspector would be required to take further fingerprints from GROUCOTT.
D The custody officer must authorise the taking of such prints from GROUCOTT.

Question 6.6

You are investigating a s. 20 wounding where the blood of the offender has been found on the clothing of the victim. You strongly suspect that HARPER is responsible for the offence but you have no direct evidence to implicate him. A colleague suggests obtaining an intimate sample (of blood) for DNA analysis from HARPER for elimination purposes.

Is this possible?

A Yes, with an inspector's authorisation and the consent of HARPER.
B No, an intimate sample could only be obtained from HARPER if he was in police detention.
C Yes, with a superintendent's authorisation and the consent of HARPER.
D No, because this is not an indictable offence.

Question 6.7

Section 62 of the Police and Criminal Evidence Act 1984 sets out police powers to take intimate samples.

Which of the following comments is correct with regard to those powers?

A An intimate sample cannot be taken by a police officer in any circumstances.

B Intimate samples can only be obtained from a suspect who is in police detention.

C Where an intimate sample is taken from a child under 14 years of age consent must be obtained from the child and also from his/her parents or guardian.

D An intimate sample can only be obtained with the consent of the suspect and this consent must be in writing.

Question 6.8

SMALLWOOD has been arrested on suspicion of burglary. A scenes of crime examination of the scene of the offence led to the recovery of several samples of head hair. DC FELLOWS, the officer in the case, wants to obtain samples of head hair from SMALLWOOD. No samples have been obtained from SMALLWOOD at this stage of the enquiry.

Which of the following statements is correct in respect of obtaining those head hair samples?

A Head hair samples cannot be obtained from SMALLWOOD unless he provides his consent, which must be in writing.

B Head hair samples can be obtained from SMALLWOOD by force if necessary as long as an inspector authorises the taking of the sample.

C The authority of an inspector is not required as SMALLWOOD is in police detention for a recordable offence and has not had a non-intimate sample of the same type and from the same part of the body taken in the course of the investigation.

D Head hair samples should only be obtained from SMALLWOOD if an inspector believes that the sample will tend to prove or disprove his involvement in the commission of the offence.

Question 6.9

HILL has been arrested for an offence of rape. His alleged victim has provided a witness statement detailing HILL's description. The victim states that HILL had a tattoo of a snake on his stomach. The officer in the case, DS BARRY, wishes to examine HILL's stomach to establish if he has such a tattoo.

With regard to any examination of HILL under s. 54A(1) of the Police and Criminal Evidence Act 1984, which of the following statements is correct?

A An inspector must give an authorisation for HILL's stomach to be examined regardless of whether HILL provides his consent to the examination.

B If HILL refuses, then an officer of the rank of inspector or above can orally authorise that HILL be examined.

C HILL cannot be examined for the tattoo under this section as it can only be used to establish the identity of the person examined.

D HILL can be examined for the tattoo but not with the use of force.

Question 6.10

OAKMOOR (aged 12 years) has been arrested for an offence of burglary. DC COPELAND wishes to obtain impressions of OAKMOOR's footwear to compare against marks found at the scene. OAKMOOR has not had an impression of his footwear taken in connection with the investigation of the offence.

Which of the following comments is correct?

A As OAKMOOR is under 14 years of age, his footwear impressions cannot be obtained unless an appropriate adult has given their permission for them to be taken.

B OAKMOOR must consent to the taking of a footwear impression.

C If OAKMOOR does not consent, then an inspector must authorise the obtaining of footwear impressions.

D PACE allows footwear impressions to be taken without consent in such circumstances.

Question 6.11

TI ORPINGDON is discussing a case of robbery with her supervisor, DS FRIEND. The issue of identification is raised and TI ORPINGDON asks DS FRIEND what the term 'available' means in respect of Code D of the Codes of Practice.

In respect of that term, which of the following comments is correct?

A 'Available' means that a suspect will be immediately available or will be within a reasonably short time and willing to take an effective part in a video identification, an identification parade or a group identification.

B 'Available' means that the location of the suspect is known to the police.

C 'Available' means that a suspect has been arrested by the police in connection with the offence and has indicated that they are willing to take an effective part in a video identification or identification parade.

D 'Available' means that the suspect has informed the police that they will take part in an identification parade, a video identification or a group identification.

Question 6.12

Annex A of Code D governs the rules relating to a video identification.

With regard to the number of images in a video identification parade, which of the following statements is true?

A The set of images must include the suspect and at least seven other people who, so far as possible, resemble the suspect in age, general appearance and position in life.

B The set of images must include the suspect and at least eight other people who, so far as possible, resemble the suspect in age, general appearance and position in life.

C The set of images must include the suspect and at least nine other people who, so far as possible, resemble the suspect in age, general appearance and position in life.

D The set of images must include the suspect and at least twelve other people who, so far as possible, resemble the suspect in age, general appearance and position in life.

Question 6.13

DC GUDDEN and TI INCE are working alongside uniform colleagues whilst policing a large-scale demonstration against the building of an airport in a rural area. Intelligence suggests that the protesters plan to cause damage and use violence and it is anticipated that a significant number of arrests will be made in respect of public order and other offences. In a briefing it is suggested that persons who are arrested should have their photograph taken with the arresting officer. TI INCE asks DC GUDDEN about this idea and whether it complies with the Police and Criminal Evidence Act 1984 and the Codes of Practice.

Which of the following responses is correct?

A Photographs cannot be taken of an arrested person unless that person is at a police station.

B Photographs of an arrested person can be taken elsewhere than a police station if that person has been arrested by a constable for an offence.

C An arrested person can be photographed elsewhere than at a police station but the photograph must be obtained with that person's consent.

D Photographs of arrested persons can be obtained if an officer of the rank of inspector or above authorises them to be taken.

Question 6.14

CLEVE and O'SULLIVAN both live in a small village where a murder takes place. The Senior Investigating Officer in charge of the murder investigation decides to ask all village residents for a set of their fingerprints for elimination purposes as part of intelligence-led screening to assist in the investigation of the offence. When an officer calls at CLEVE's house, he refuses to participate. When an officer calls at O'SULLIVAN's house, O'SULLIVAN agrees to provide his fingerprints but only on the strict understanding that they will be destroyed after the investigation has been concluded. O'SULLIVAN has a set of prints taken and signs a consent form which specifically states his prints will be destroyed at the end of the case and that they will only be compared to fingerprints from the murder enquiry. Unfortunately, nobody is ever convicted or even arrested in connection with the murder.

Considering Code D of the Codes of Practice, which of the following comments is correct?

A A set of prints for elimination purposes may be obtained from CLEVE (at the time of their request) by force if necessary.

B Regardless of the form that O'SULLIVAN signed, his fingerprints could be retained to be used in the investigation of other offences.

C Fingerprints obtained in such a mass screening exercise must always be destroyed at the end of the investigation.

D O'SULLIVAN may witness the destruction of the set of fingerprints he supplied if he asks to do so within five days of being informed that their destruction is required.

Question 6.15

DC SERSAN and TI MITCHUM are discussing the taking of intimate and non-intimate samples from persons in custody.

Which of the following statements is correct?

A DC SERSAN states that a dental impression is a non-intimate sample.

B TI MITCHUM states that a sample of saliva is an intimate sample.

C DC SERSAN states that a sample of urine is an intimate sample.

D TI MITCHUM states that a sample of tissue fluid is a non-intimate sample.

ANSWERS

Answer 6.1

Answer **B** — Answer A is incorrect as a suspect's failure to request an identification parade does not mean the police may proceed without one (*R* v *Graham* [1994] Crim LR 212). Answer C is incorrect as (under Code D, para. 3.12) an identification procedure does not need to be held if it is not practicable or would serve no useful purpose in proving or disproving whether the suspect committed the offence. Answer D is incorrect as the exceptions that apply for answer C also apply to decisions when considering *R* v *Forbes*. This question is based on the case of *D* v *DPP* (1998) The Times, 7 August, where it was held that an identification had not been made (as per answer B). An identification parade would have served no useful purpose since the clothing would have changed and those persons used for the parade would have been the same approximate age.

Investigators' Manual, para. 1.8.4.4

Answer 6.2

Answer **D** — Code D, paras 3.28 and 3.29 govern identification when the media has been used. When a broadcast or publication is made, a copy of the relevant material released to the media for the purposes of recognising or tracing the suspect must be kept, making answer C incorrect. The suspect or their solicitor must be allowed to view the material released to the media prior to any identification procedure, provided it is practicable and would not unreasonably delay the investigation, making answer A incorrect. The fact that MAYBURY has recognised PITCHER would not preclude her participation in any future identification procedure, therefore answer B is incorrect. However, each witness will be asked, after they have taken part, whether they have seen any broadcast or published films or photographs relating to the offence and any description of the suspect and their replies shall be recorded.

Investigators' Manual, para. 1.8.4.10

Answer 6.3

Answer **C** — The circumstances of this question would mean that an identification would be held (Code D, para. 3.21). Under Code D, para. 3.14, where an identification is to be held, the suspect shall initially be offered a video identification.

Investigators' Manual, paras 1.8.4.6, 1.8.4.8

Answer 6.4

Answer **C** — Expert evidence may be admitted to interpret images on film (*R* v *Stockwell* (1993) 97 Cr App R 260), making answer A incorrect. The Codes of Practice do not preclude the police making use of aural identification procedures, making answer B incorrect. Answer C is correct as police officers who are familiar with a particular film clip (e.g. crowd violence at a football match) may be allowed to assist the court in interpreting and explaining events shown within it (*R* v *Clare and Peach* (1995) 2 Cr App Rep 333). Generally, a witness (DRAPER) may give evidence identifying the defendant's voice (*R* v *Robb* (1991) 93 Cr App R 161), making answer D incorrect.

Investigators' Manual, paras 1.8.4.11, 1.8.4.13

Answer 6.5

Answer **C** — Section 61(6) of the Police and Criminal Evidence Act 1984 provides that a person who has been given a caution (making answers A and B incorrect) in respect of a recordable offence which, at the time of the caution, the person admitted may be required to provide fingerprints if, since their caution, their fingerprints have not been taken or their fingerprints which have been taken do not constitute a complete set or some, or all, of the fingerprints are not of sufficient quality to allow satisfactory analysis, comparison or matching. In either case, an officer of the rank of inspector (making D incorrect) or above must be satisfied that taking the fingerprints is necessary to assist in the prevention or detection of crime and authorise the taking.

Investigators' Manual, para. 1.8.5

Answer 6.6

Answer **A** — The Criminal Justice and Police Act 2001, s. 80(1) provides that the authorisation level required to obtain an intimate sample is that of an inspector or above, making answer C incorrect. Section 62(2)(a) of the Police and Criminal Evidence Act 1984 states that the type of offence for which an intimate sample may be taken need only be a recordable offence and not an indictable offence, making answer D incorrect. Code D recognises that an intimate sample may be taken from a person not in police detention, for the purposes of elimination, providing his/her consent is given, making answer B incorrect.

Investigators' Manual, paras 1.8.7 to 1.8.7.3

Answer 6.7

Answer **D** — Urine (an intimate sample) can be obtained by a police officer, making answer A incorrect. An intimate sample may be taken from a person not in police detention, making answer B incorrect. An intimate sample taken from a child under the age of 14 years requires the consent of his/her parents alone, making answer C incorrect. Answer D is correct as the consent of a suspect must be given in writing (Code D, para. 6.2).

Investigators' Manual, para. 1.8.7.2

Answer 6.8

Answer **C** — The authority of an inspector to take a non-intimate sample from SMALLWOOD is not required in these circumstances, making answers B and D incorrect. SMALLWOOD's consent will be sought (answer A) and it should be in writing; however, if he will not provide it then the sample can be taken by force as per answer C.

Investigators' Manual, paras 1.8.7 and 1.8.7.4

Answer 6.9

Answer **B** — If HILL refuses then an inspector can provide oral authorisation that he be examined, although this will have to be confirmed in writing as soon as practicable (Code D, para. 5.8). HILL's consent is not required but if it is given then an inspector's authority is not required, making answer A incorrect. The power can be used to establish the identity of an individual or to identify them as a person involved in the commission of an offence, making answer C incorrect. Force can be used if necessary, making answer D incorrect.

Investigators' Manual, para. 1.8.6

Answer 6.10

Answer **D** — Section 61A of the Police and Criminal Evidence Act 1984 provides a power for police officers to take footwear impressions without consent from any person over the age of ten who is detained at a police station in consequence of being arrested for a recordable offence and they have not had an impression of their footwear taken in the course of the investigation of the offence.

Investigators' Manual, para. 1.8.5.4

Answer 6.11

Answer **A** — A suspect being 'available' means that they are immediately available or will be within a reasonably short time and willing to take an effective part in at least one of the following which it is practicable to arrange:

- video identification;
- identification parade; or
- group identification.

This makes answers B, C and D incorrect.

Investigators' Manual, para. 1.8.4.4

Answer 6.12

Answer **B** — The set of images for a video identification must include the suspect and at least *eight* other people who, so far as possible, resemble the suspect in age, general appearance and position in life. Only one suspect shall appear in any set unless there are two suspects of roughly similar appearance, in which case they may be shown together with at least twelve other people.

Investigators' Manual, para. 1.8.8

Answer 6.13

Answer **B** — Section 64A of the Police and Criminal Evidence Act 1984 governs the taking of photographs of persons. Such photographs will be taken of a person whilst they are detained at a police station but can also be taken elsewhere, making answer A incorrect. Neither the consent of the person being photographed nor the authority of an officer of the rank of inspector or above is required to do so, making answers C and D incorrect.

Investigators' Manual, para. 1.8.6

Answer 6.14

Answer **D** — Force cannot be used to obtain elimination prints, making answer A incorrect. Fingerprints obtained in mass screening exercises do not always have to be destroyed if they were taken for the purposes of an investigation for which a person has been convicted and fingerprints were also taken from the convicted person for the purposes of the investigation, making answer C incorrect. This is further the case as the person from whom the prints were obtained may sign a form allowing the prints to be used in the prevention or detection of crime. Answer B is incorrect as fingerprints may not be used in the investigation of any offence or in evidence against a person who is, or would be, entitled to its destruction.

Investigators' Manual, para. 1.8.13

Answer 6.15

Answer **C** — A dental impression is an intimate sample, making answer A incorrect. A sample of saliva is a non-intimate sample, making answer B incorrect. A sample of tissue fluid is an intimate sample, making answer D incorrect.

Investigators' Manual, para. 1.8.7.2

7 Bail

QUESTIONS

Question 7.1

LOVETT has a previous conviction for attempted rape for which he served three years' imprisonment. LOVETT is arrested and charged in connection with a s. 18 wounding.

Considering the bail restrictions under s. 25 of the Criminal Justice and Public Order Act 1994, which of the following statements is correct?

A This section only applies to defendants who have a previous conviction for murder, attempted murder or manslaughter and would not affect the granting of bail for LOVETT.

B A previous conviction for attempted rape is covered by this section, as is the charge of s. 18 wounding; bail should only be granted to LOVETT if there are exceptional circumstances which justify it.

C This section only applies to defendants if they have previously been convicted by or before a court in the United Kingdom of culpable homicide and so LOVETT's previous conviction will not affect the granting of bail.

D Although LOVETT's previous conviction for attempted rape is relevant, a s. 18 wounding is not and so will not alter the decision to grant bail.

Question 7.2

DC WRAGG arrests SYMONS for three robberies and tells the custody officer that SYMONS has carried out the offences with PARTINGTON who has yet to be arrested. The custody officer asks for SYMONS's name and address to which SYMONS replies, '*I'll never say.*' DC WRAGG tells the custody officer that SYMONS has failed to answer bail on two previous occasions. Several hours later SYMONS is charged with the offences of robbery although DC WRAGG still has some further enquiries to make regarding the offences. The issue of bail is now being considered.

For which one of the following reasons could the custody officer refuse to bail SYMONS?

A SYMONS has failed to comply with s. 38(1) of the Police and Criminal Evidence Act 1984 as he has refused to provide his name and address.

B If released, SYMONS will interfere with the administration of justice, as the police have still to arrest PARTINGTON.

C There is a risk that SYMONS will abscond and this is evidenced by his previous failure to answer bail.

D SYMONS will interfere with the administration of justice because there are still further enquiries to make regarding the offences.

Question 7.3

You are the officer in charge of a case involving MOUNTFORD. You arrested MOUNTFORD for a fraud-related offence and charged him at your police station. MOUNTFORD was bailed to appear at your local magistrates' court and the custody officer at the time of his charging, PS GLEDHILL, granted bail on the condition that MOUNTFORD would report to your police station on a daily basis at 18.00 hrs. MOUNTFORD contacts you and asks if it is possible for his bail conditions to be modified as he has injured his leg and will have difficulty getting to the police station every day at the appointed time.

What will you tell MOUNTFORD?

A MOUNTFORD should make the request to any custody officer at your police station.

B Once bail conditions have been imposed, only a magistrates' court can alter them.

C Only PS GLEDHILL can alter the bail conditions.

D MOUNTFORD can make his request to any custody officer serving at any police station in your force.

Question 7.4

BOON is arrested for burglary. The custody officer decides to give him bail on the condition that he obtains a surety to secure his surrender to custody. BOON suggests that his cousin, MAGEE, will stand as a surety. MAGEE is contacted by the police for this purpose.

Which of the following statements is true?

A MAGEE would have a liability if BOON committed any further offences or interfered with witnesses whilst on bail.

B MAGEE cannot be a surety for BOON because they are related to each other.

C MAGEE would be required to forfeit the entire sum in which he stood surety.

D In order for MAGEE to forfeit the sum in which he stood surety, it would be necessary to prove that he had some involvement in BOON's non-appearance.

Question 7.5

You have arrested MILBURN (aged 13 years) on suspicion of burglary. During interview, MILBURN tells you that he has committed at least 30 other burglaries and wants to confess to them. You are considering charging MILBURN with the burglary that he has been arrested for and requesting a remand in police custody under s. 128 of the Magistrates' Courts Act 1980 with a view to interviewing MILBURN for the other 30 offences.

Will such a request be successful?

A Yes, the court can remand MILBURN into local authority accommodation for a period not exceeding three days.

B No, such a remand can only be given if MILBURN has attained the age of 15 and the offences are of a violent or sexual nature.

C Yes, MILBURN may be remanded to police custody for a period not exceeding 24 hours.

D No, such a remand may only be sought if its purpose is to make enquiries into the offence for which MILBURN has been charged.

Question 7.6

Sergeant ANDERSON is acting as a custody officer and is considering granting bail to FRAZER. It appears necessary to impose bail conditions on FRAZER in order to prevent him from failing to surrender to custody and to prevent him committing an offence whilst on bail.

Which of the following conditions would Sergeant ANDERSON be unable to impose on FRAZER?

A A requirement that FRAZER resides in a bail hostel or probation hostel.

B A requirement that FRAZER surrenders his passport.

C A requirement restricting FRAZER from entering a certain area or building or to go within a specified distance of a specified address.

D A requirement that FRAZER provides a surety or security.

Question 7.7

FRAZER has been arrested for a complex offence of fraud. DC AZAR informs the custody officer, PS HARRY, of the detailed nature of the offence and the large number of enquiries that need to be carried out in relation to it. As a consequence, PS HARRY has granted bail to FRAZER whilst investigations continue into the offence. As he is released on bail, FRAZER asks DC AZAR what the time limit is for which his bail may be granted.

Considering the issues of pre-charge bail and the Police and Criminal Evidence Act 1984, how should DC AZAR respond?

A There is no time limit for which bail may be granted.

B Bail may be granted and is subject to a time limit of six months.

C Bail may be granted and is subject to a time limit of one year.

D Bail may be granted and is subject to a time limit of two years.

Question 7.8

KELLY (aged 11 years) has been arrested in relation to an offence of s. 18 wounding and for a variety of reasons, including the fact that it is necessary to protect the public from serious harm, PS NYMAN has authorised that KELLY be detained.

Which of the following comments is correct in relation to KELLY?

A KELLY must be moved to local authority accommodation unless this is impracticable or there is no secure accommodation available and the custody officer considers that the local authority accommodation would be inadequate to protect the public from serious harm.

B KELLY must be moved to local authority accommodation unless this is impracticable. The type of accommodation in which the local authority proposes to place KELLY is not a factor which PS NYMAN may take into account when considering whether the transfer is acceptable.

C KELLY must be moved to local authority accommodation; there are no exceptions to this requirement.

D KELLY must be moved to local authority accommodation unless PS NYMAN considers the accommodation the local authority are considering placing KELLY in is unsuitable and consequently poses a risk of serious harm to the public.

Question 7.9

PC CROWTHER arrests JONES in relation to a minor offence of theft and decides to grant JONES 'street bail' (as per s. 30A of the Police and Criminal Evidence Act 1984).

In relation to the granting of bail in these circumstances, which of the following statements is correct?

A Whilst there is no time limit for which 'street bail' may be granted, Home Office guidance suggests a normal maximum time of six weeks.

B PC CROWTHER may require JONES to provide a surety in order to ensure that he surrenders himself at a police station.

C PC CROWTHER may grant JONES 'street bail' but only after she has obtained permission to do so from a custody officer serving within the relevant area in which JONES was arrested.

D PC CROWTHER may grant JONES 'street bail' but cannot attach any conditions to such bail.

Question 7.10

EBBY was arrested and charged with an offence of theft and bailed (without conditions) to appear back at the same police station to enable further enquiries to be made in respect of the offence. Due to an administrative error, the custody officer forgot to provide EBBY with a copy of the record of the decision to bail him. Several weeks later, EBBY is at home thinking that he has to attend the police station the following morning then suddenly remembers that he was supposed to attend the police station that morning—when he looks at his watch, he sees he is three hours late. He drives to the police station but on the way decides to have a couple of drinks at his local pub as he thinks it does not matter now that he is already late. EBBY stays in the pub for two hours and then attends the police station.

Considering the offence of absconding (contrary to s. 6 of the Bail Act 1976), which of the following statements is correct?

A No offence has been committed by EBBY as the custody officer failed to provide him with a record of the decision to bail him.

B EBBY has committed the offence which, in this form, is a summary-only offence.

C No offence has been committed by EBBY as the offence does not apply to bail granted to a suspect to appear at a police station.

D EBBY would have a reasonable excuse for committing the offence as he was mistaken about the day on which he should have appeared.

ANSWERS

Answer 7.1

Answer **D** — Section 25 of the Criminal Justice and Public Order Act 1994 states that bail will only be granted to a defendant who is affected by it in the most exceptional circumstances. A defendant will be subject to this section if he/she has a previous conviction for murder, attempted murder, manslaughter, rape or attempted rape; this makes answers A and C incorrect. LOVETT's previous conviction for attempted rape is, therefore, relevant. However, the defendant must not only have a previous conviction for one of the stated offences but also be charged with one of those offences. LOVETT is charged with a s. 18 wounding which is not covered by the legislation; this makes answer B incorrect.

Investigators' Manual, para. 1.9.5

Answer 7.2

Answer **C** — The fact that SYMONS refuses to give his name and address does not satisfy the grounds on which bail can be refused under s. 38 of the Police and Criminal Evidence Act 1984; this is only so if the name and address *cannot be ascertained*, making answer A incorrect. Although refusing bail on the grounds that the defendant will interfere with the administration of justice is a reason for refusing bail, this ground would not apply for the purposes of the police making further enquiries or where other suspects are still to be arrested, making answers B and D incorrect.

Investigators' Manual, para. 1.9.6

Answer 7.3

Answer **A** — Section 3A of the Bail Act 1976 applies to bail granted by a custody officer and amends s. 3 of the Act. Section 3A(4) states that where a custody officer has granted bail in criminal proceedings *he or another* custody officer serving *at the same police station* may, at the request of the person to whom it was granted, vary the conditions of bail and in doing so he may impose conditions or more onerous conditions.

Investigators' Manual, para. 1.9.7.3

Answer 7.4

Answer **C** — A surety has no responsibility or liability should the defendant commit further offences or interfere with witnesses whilst on bail, making answer A incorrect. The decision as to whether a surety is suitable rests with the custody officer. The fact that there is a relationship between the two is a consideration but not a bar, making answer B incorrect. It is not necessary to prove that the surety has any involvement in the defendant's non-appearance (*R* v *Warwick Crown Court, ex parte Smalley* [1987] 1 WLR 237), making answer D incorrect.

Investigators' Manual, para. 1.9.7.4

Answer 7.5

Answer **C** — Section 128 of the Magistrates' Courts Act 1980 provides that a magistrates' court may remand a person to *police custody* for a period not exceeding three days (*24 hours for a person under 18*) for the purposes of enquiries into other offences (*other than the offence for which he/she appears before a court*).

Investigators' Manual, para. 1.9.12

Answer 7.6

Answer **A** — Section 3A of the Bail Act 1976 applies to bail granted specifically by a custody officer. Section 3A(5) provides for the occasions when a custody officer can consider imposing bail conditions. Answers B, C and D are all conditions that can be imposed. However, there is no authority under s. 3A to bail a defendant to a bail hostel or a probation hostel as this has been omitted from this part of the Act.

Investigators' Manual, paras 1.9.7.1, 1.9.7.2

Answer 7.7

Answer **A** — There is NO time limit for which bail may be granted under the 1984 Act and the courts will only intervene if there are exceptional circumstances. In *Fitzpatrick* v *Commissioner of the Police of the Metropolis* [2012] EWHC 12 (QB) police bail was granted on 12 September 2007 and the suspects remained on police bail and subject to investigation until it was confirmed that no action would be taken against them in June 2009. The court held that there had been no breach of Article 8 of the

European Convention on Human Rights (the right to respect for private and family life) due to the complex nature of the case.

Investigators' Manual, para. 1.9.3

Answer 7.8

Answer **B** — The Children (Secure Accommodation) Regulations 1991 (SI 1991/1505 as amended by SI 2012/3134) provide that a child who is detained by the police under s. 38(6) of the Police and Criminal Evidence Act 1984, and who is aged 12 or over but under the age of 17, must be moved to local authority accommodation unless this is impracticable or there is no secure accommodation available and local authority accommodation would be inadequate to protect the child or public from serious harm. Where no secure accommodation is available and the serious harm criterion is met, the child can be kept in police detention.

Where the detained child is aged 10 or 11 (KELLY), the police *must* move the child to local authority accommodation (making answer A incorrect) unless this is impracticable, e.g. in extreme weather conditions (making answer C incorrect). The type of accommodation in which the local authority proposes to place the youth is not a factor which the custody officer may take into account in considering whether the transfer is acceptable (making answer D incorrect).

Investigators' Manual, para. 1.9.8

Answer 7.9

Answer **A** — Section 30A(3A)(c) states that where a constable releases a person on 'street bail', the person shall not be required to provide a surety or sureties for his/her surrender to custody, making answer B incorrect. Answer C is incorrect as no authority is required to grant 'street bail'. Answer D is incorrect as s. 30A(3B) states that a constable may impose conditions when granting 'street bail'. Guidance on street bail is contained in Home Office Circular 61/2003, *Bail Elsewhere than at a Police Station*. Although there is no limit on the time for which 'street bail' may be granted, the Circular suggests a normal maximum time of six weeks (answer A).

Investigators' Manual, para. 1.9.2

Answer 7.10

Answer **B** — Section 6 applies where:

- the police grant bail to a suspect to appear at the police station (making answer C incorrect);
- the police grant bail to a defendant to appear at court on the first appearance;
- the court grants bail to the defendant to return to court at a later date.

The burden of proof in relation to showing 'reasonable cause' (s. 6(1)) is a matter for the accused (s. 6(3)). A person who has 'reasonable cause' still commits the offence if he/she fails to surrender 'as soon after the appointed time as is reasonably practicable'. Where an accused was half an hour late in appearing at court it was held that he/she had absconded (*R* v *Scott* [2007] EWCA Crim 2757). In *Laidlaw* v *Atkinson* (1986) The Times, 2 August, it was held that being mistaken about the day on which one should have appeared was not a reasonable excuse (making answer D incorrect). Failure to give to a person granted bail in criminal proceedings a copy of the record of the decision does not constitute reasonable cause for that person's failure to surrender to custody (s. 6(4)), making answer A incorrect. The offence in this form is a summary offence and the decision to initiate proceedings is for the police/prosecutor using the written charge and requisition procedure (answer B).

Investigators' Manual, para. 1.9.11

8 Disclosure of Evidence

QUESTIONS

Question 8.1

DC SMART is the OIC in a case involving ELDIN who has been charged with an offence of s. 18 assault. ELDIN's solicitor makes a request for advanced information to help decide whether ELDIN will plead guilty or not guilty. ELDIN's solicitor requests a summary of the prosecution case together with copies of the statements of the proposed prosecution witnesses. DC SMART considers that providing copies of the witness statements might lead to a witness being intimidated.

What course of action should DC SMART take?

A The officer should consult with the CPS as the rules allow the prosecutor to limit disclosure of some or all of the prosecution case.

B The officer must disclose all the material requested by the defence solicitor in order to comply with Article 6 of the European Convention on Human Rights and the Human Rights Act 1998.

C DC SMART need not disclose any statements to the defence at this stage, as they have no entitlement to any material.

D Unless the material undermines the prosecution case, there is no requirement for the statements of witnesses to be disclosed.

Question 8.2

LUNN is arrested and charged with an offence of rape and the case goes to trial. The OIC of the case, DC ATTWOOD, accidentally fails to comply with disclosure rules under the Criminal Procedure and Investigations Act 1996, although there is sufficient credible evidence available which would justify a safe conviction.

Which of the following statements is true with regard to the effect this non-compliance will have on the trial?

A An accidental failure to disclose will not affect the trial and the accused will still have to make defence disclosure to the prosecution.

B A failure to comply with disclosure rules in these circumstances will not automatically mean the trial will be stayed for an abuse of process.

C The prosecution will offer no evidence as otherwise the trial will be stayed on the grounds that there has been an abuse of process.

D The courts are obliged to adjourn the trial in order for the prosecution to make adequate disclosure to the defence.

Question 8.3

BARBER is charged with an offence of murder and is committed to Crown Court for trial.

When should the prosecution make primary disclosure?

A 7 days after BARBER is committed to Crown Court.

B 14 days after BARBER is committed to Crown Court.

C 21 days after BARBER is committed to Crown Court.

D As soon as practicable after the duty arises.

Question 8.4

DS CHRISTIE is overseeing the prosecution of a series of aggravated burglaries committed by KEYWOOD. The operation to arrest KEYWOOD was intelligence-led and KEYWOOD was the subject of numerous intelligence reports eventually leading to his arrest. On arrest, KEYWOOD assaulted DC POULOS, resulting in KEYWOOD being charged with a s. 47 assault against the officer. Due to the amount of material generated in the investigation, DS CHRISTIE decides to appoint a disclosure officer for the case.

Which of the following statements is true with regard to the appointment of a disclosure officer by DS CHRISTIE?

A An unsworn member of support staff would not be allowed to perform this function.

B DS CHRISTIE could appoint DC POULOS as the disclosure officer.

C Generally speaking, there is no restriction on who can perform the role of disclosure officer.

D There can only be one disclosure officer for each case.

Question 8.5

WATTIS has been arrested and charged with an offence of rape. You are the officer in charge of the case and have the assistance of PC SMEDLEY who is acting as the disclosure officer. PC SMEDLEY approaches you and asks your advice regarding the disclosure of material that may be relevant to the investigation.

Which of the comments is correct in respect of relevant material?

A A draft version of a witness statement where the content of the draft version differs from the final version of the statement would not be classed as relevant material.

B A written record of an interview with a potential witness would not be classed as relevant material.

C The identity of a potential witness to the arrest of WATTIS would not be classed as relevant material.

D The fact that house-to-house enquiries were made and that no one witnessed anything would not be classed as relevant material.

Question 8.6

DCs MIDDLEMORE and KHOJA receive information that HENLEY is dealing in drugs outside a school. The officers drive to the school in an unmarked police vehicle and park near the front gates where they can observe HENLEY. The officers witness HENLEY dealing drugs and arrest him for supplying a controlled drug. HENLEY is charged and the case goes to trial. During the trial the defence apply to cross-examine the officers on the location of their observations in order to test what they could see. This includes the colour, make and model of the vehicle the officers used.

Considering the ruling in *R* v *Johnson*, will the prosecution be able to withhold this information?

A Yes, the court will follow the ruling in *R* v *Johnson* which states that the exact location of the observations need not be revealed.

B No, the ruling in *R* v *Johnson* is based on the protection of the owner or occupier of premises and would not apply in this case.

C Yes, although the prosecution will have to supply details of the location of the vehicle.

D No, under no circumstances can the location of observation posts be withheld from the defence.

Question 8.7

HOOD is being prosecuted for an offence of s. 18 wounding (contrary to the Offences Against the Person Act 1861) (an indictable only offence). The prosecution make primary disclosure to HOOD's defence team who, in line with s. 5 of the Criminal Procedure and Investigations Act 1996, must now provide a defence statement to the court and the prosecutor.

Although the courts can extend the period, within what time period must HOOD's defence team normally provide the defence statement?

A Within 7 days of the prosecution making primary disclosure.

B Within 14 days of the prosecution making primary disclosure.

C Within 21 days of the prosecution making primary disclosure.

D Within 28 days of the prosecution making primary disclosure.

Question 8.8

LEXINGTON is convicted of an offence of theft and is sentenced to three months' imprisonment for the offence; he is released after having served one month of the sentence.

For how long should material relating to this case be retained?

A Until LEXINGTON is released from his custodial sentence.

B Three months from the date of LEXINGTON's conviction for theft.

C Six months from the date of LEXINGTON's conviction for theft.

D Twelve months from the date of LEXINGTON's conviction for theft.

Question 8.9

DC REWSON is the disclosure officer in a case of s. 20 wounding (contrary to the Offences Against the Person Act 1861) where the offender is alleged to have passed the HIV virus to a sexual partner. DC REWSON is aware that a nearby hospital and a local GP both have records regarding the medical condition of the defendant that are relevant to the prosecution case. DC REWSON reasonably considers that this material might be capable of undermining the prosecution case.

Which of the following comments is correct in respect of this material?

A DC REWSON should seek access to the material at the hospital and from the GP but if access is refused there is nothing further that can be done.

B DC REWSON will be able to access the material held by the hospital but would not be able to access material held by the GP in any circumstances.

C Should the hospital or GP refuse access to the material and DC REWSON believes it is still reasonable to seek its production then the prosecutor should apply for a witness summons causing a representative of the hospital and GP to produce the material at court.

D If information regarding the medical condition of the offender comes into the possession of the prosecution from the hospital or from the GP then whether it is disclosed is entirely a matter for the prosecutor.

ANSWERS

Answer 8.1

Answer **A** — The prosecution is required, on request, to supply the defence with a summary of the prosecution case and/or copies of the statements of the proposed witnesses, making answer C incorrect. The defence are entitled to this disclosure to consider whether the defendant will plead guilty or not guilty and this has no relevance to whether the material undermines the prosecution case, making answer D incorrect. However, if the OIC considers that such disclosure may lead to witnesses being intimidated or some other interference with justice, the prosecutor may limit some or all of the prosecution case, making answer B incorrect.

Investigators' Manual, paras 1.10.3, 1.10.3.1

Answer 8.2

Answer **B** — Any failure to comply with the rules of disclosure, by the prosecution or the defence, may affect the trial. A failure by the prosecution to comply with their obligations means the accused does not have to make defence disclosure, making answer A incorrect. The court is under no obligation to adjourn the trial, making answer D incorrect. Although a failure to comply may mean the trial is stayed for abuse of process, this is not necessarily always the case (*R* v *Feltham Magistrates' Court, ex parte Ebrahim*; *Mouat* v *DPP*; *R* v *Feltham Magistrates' Court, ex parte DPP* [2001] 1 WLR 1293). In this case it was stated that in such circumstances the trial should proceed, leaving the defendant to seek to persuade the jury or magistrates not to convict because evidence that might otherwise have been available was not before the court through no fault of the defendant, making answer C incorrect.

Investigators' Manual, para. 1.10.2

Answer 8.3

Answer **D** — The Criminal Procedure and Investigations Act 1996 in effect only applies once a defendant has been committed/transferred to the Crown Court or is proceeding to trial in the magistrates' or youth court. While there are provisions to set specific time periods by which primary disclosure must be met, none currently exists. Until such times, primary disclosure must be made as soon as practicable after the duty arises, making answers A, B and C incorrect.

Investigators' Manual, para. 1.10.10.2

Answer 8.4

Answer **C** — For investigations carried out by the police, generally speaking there is no restriction on who performs the role of the 'Disclosure Officer'. The role could be performed by unsworn support staff (Criminal Procedure and Investigations Act 1996, Codes of Practice, paras 2.1 and 3.3), making answer A incorrect. However, para. 7 of the Attorney General's Guidelines on disclosure states that an individual must not be appointed as disclosure officer if that role is likely to result in a conflict of interest, for example, if the disclosure officer is a victim of the alleged crime which is the subject of criminal proceedings. Therefore, DC POULOS should not be appointed, making answer B incorrect. There may be occasions where the police investigation has been intelligence-led and there may be an additional disclosure officer appointed to deal with the intelligence material, making answer D incorrect.

Investigators' Manual, paras 1.10.5, 1.10.6

Answer 8.5

Answer **C** — Paragraph 5.4 of the Code of Practice for the Criminal Procedure and Investigations Act 1996 gives details of material that might be considered to be relevant material. This *includes* the items listed at answers A, B and D, making those answers incorrect. In *DPP* v *Metten*, 22 January 1999, the defence claimed that officers knew the identity of potential witnesses to the arrest of the offender and that these had not been disclosed. The court stated that this was not relevant to the case as it concerned the time of the arrest and not what happened at the time the offence was committed.

Investigators' Manual, paras 1.10.5.4, 1.10.8

Answer 8.6

Answer **B** — In *R* v *Johnson* [1988] 1 WLR 1377, the judge ruled that the exact location of premises used to carry out observations need not be revealed, making answer D incorrect. The rule is based on the protection of the owner or occupier of premises and not on the identity of the observation post. So, in *R* v *Brown* (1987) 87 Cr App R 52, where a surveillance operation was conducted from an unmarked police car, information relating to the surveillance and the colour, make and model of the vehicle should not be withheld, making answers A and C incorrect.

Investigators' Manual, para. 1.10.9.5

Answer 8.7

Answer **D** — Once the prosecution provides the initial disclosure, the defence have 14 days in respect of summary proceedings, or 28 days in respect of Crown Court proceedings within which the accused in criminal proceedings must give: a compulsory defence statement under s. 5 of the Act; a voluntary defence statement under s. 6 of the Act; or a notice of his/her intention to call any person, other than him-/herself, as a witness under s. 6C of the Act (alibi witness).

Investigators' Manual, para. 1.10.11.4

Answer 8.8

Answer **C** — All material which may be relevant must be retained at least until:

- the person is released from custody or discharged from hospital in cases where the court imposes a custodial sentence or hospital order;
- in all other cases, for six months from the date of conviction.

If the person is released from the custodial sentence or discharged from hospital earlier than six months from the date of conviction (LEXINGTON), the material must be retained for at least six months from the date of conviction.

Investigators' Manual, para. 1.10.8

Answer 8.9

Answer **C** — If the investigator, disclosure officer or prosecutor seeks access to material or information held by a third party (e.g. a local authority, a social services department, a hospital, a doctor, etc.) but the third party declines or refuses to allow access to it, the matter should not be left, making answer A incorrect. If, despite any reasons offered by the third party it is still believed reasonable to seek production of the material or information, and the requirements of s. 2 of the Criminal Procedure (Attendance of Witnesses) Act 1965 or as appropriate s. 97 of the Magistrates' Courts Act 1980 are satisfied, then the prosecutor or investigator should apply for a witness summons causing a representative of the third party to produce that material at court, making answer B incorrect. Answer D is incorrect as when such information comes into the possession of the prosecution, consultation with the other agency should take place before disclosure is made.

Investigators' Manual, para. 1.10.6.5

9 Issues in Evidence and Offences against the Administration of Justice and Public Interest

QUESTIONS

Question 9.1

Even though evidence may be admissible in criminal cases, at common law the trial judge has a general discretion to exclude legally admissible evidence tendered by the prosecution. In addition, evidence may be excluded for a variety of reasons.

Which of the following statements is correct in respect of a reason for excluding admissible evidence?

A In deciding whether the evidence should be admitted, the question the judge has to ask is whether the evidence was obtained fairly or by unfair means.
B Evidence could not be excluded because of the incompetence of a witness.
C The judge generally has the discretion to exclude relevant admissible evidence on the ground that it was obtained improperly.
D Evidence may be excluded if it is non-expert opinion evidence.

Question 9.2

The 'facts in issue' of a case are those which must be proved by the prosecution in order to establish the defendant's guilt, or in exceptional circumstances those facts which are the essential elements of a defence, where the burden of proof is on the defendant to prove a defence.

Which of the following comments is correct is respect of these 'facts in issue'?

A 'Facts in issue' would not include the identity of the defendant.

B The relevant criminal conduct (*actus reus*) and state of mind (*mens rea*) will always be facts in issue.

C The standard of proof for the defence is the same as the prosecution, i.e. 'beyond all reasonable doubt'.

D It is only when attempting to utilise a statutory defence that the burden of proof will shift to the defence.

Question 9.3

DC BROWN receives an anonymous telephone call stating that stolen goods are being stored at a house owned by GIBBS who has several convictions for theft and handling stolen goods. DC BROWN believes the information to be true. DC BROWN swears out a search warrant for GIBBS's home address and during this process the magistrate asks DC BROWN what corroboration she has sought for the information provided. DC BROWN has not sought corroboration but rather than lose the chance to arrest GIBBS she tells the magistrate that the information has come from a tried and tested source who has always been accurate in the past.

Is DC BROWN guilty of an offence of perjury in judicial proceedings (contrary to s. 1 of the Perjury Act 1911)?

A Yes, DC BROWN has committed the offence, although corroboration will be required in relation to the falsity of her statement.

B No, as swearing out a search warrant is not classed as 'judicial proceedings' for the purposes of this Act.

C Yes, the officer is guilty but to prove the offence, corroboration will be required to prove the fact that she actually made the alleged statement.

D No, as DC BROWN believes the information to be true she is not guilty of the offence.

Question 9.4

ROWLEY is an independent candidate for forthcoming council elections and campaigns that asylum seekers should not be allowed to live locally. To gain public sympathy and thereby votes, he causes several bruises to his face and reports the matter as an assault to DC TROMANS. ROWLEY tells the officer that he was attacked by two Iraqi men who objected to his views. ROWLEY intends his report to be taken seriously by the police but tells DC TROMANS that he cannot identify his attackers as they were disguised. As a result, the investigation only amounts to one day's work for the officer before being filed.

With regard to the offence of perverting the course of justice, which of the following statements is true?

A These circumstances do not amount to an offence, as the allegations made by ROWLEY are incapable of identifying specific individuals.

B For a charge to succeed, the prosecution must show that a lot of police time and resources were involved in the investigation; this is not the case with ROWLEY.

C Making a false allegation of an offence would mean that ROWLEY commits the offence.

D ROWLEY commits the offence but the consent of the Director of Public Prosecutions is required before a charge can be brought against him.

Question 9.5

Eighteen months ago, PROSSER gave evidence against HILL regarding an assault. HILL was sentenced to three years' imprisonment but is released early. HILL wants revenge against PROSSER and is walking the streets searching for him. HILL sees PROSSER's sister, AUCOTE, out shopping and approaches her saying, '*Don't think I've forgotten your brother and the little story in court, his house will be burnt down tonight.*' HILL intends to cause PROSSER to fear that harm will be caused to his property.

Why is no offence of harming witnesses (contrary to s. 40 of the Criminal Justice and Police Act 2001) committed?

A HILL commits no offence as it is over a year since the proceedings were concluded.

B HILL commits no offence as he does not intend to pervert or interfere with the course of justice.

C HILL commits no offence as the harm done or threatened must be physical and not to the person's property.

D HILL commits no offence as the threat has not been made in the presence of the person who would be harmed.

Question 9.6

CLINTON and GREEN share a flat. One afternoon, GREEN tells CLINTON about a robbery that she has just committed that netted her £1,000. The next day, GREEN goes to Spain for a week's holiday. Two days later, DC LAGRAM comes to the flat and asks CLINTON if she knows where GREEN is. When CLINTON asks why, the officer tells her that he needs to speak with GREEN about a theft committed that day. CLINTON knows that GREEN has not committed the offence because she was out of the country but is worried that she will lose her flat-mate and so tells the officer that GREEN moved out a month ago and no longer lives at the address.

Has CLINTON committed an offence of assisting an offender (contrary to s. 4 of the Criminal Law Act 1967)?

A No, because CLINTON knows that GREEN has not committed the offence of theft.

B Yes, but GREEN will have to be convicted of the offence of robbery before CLINTON can be prosecuted for the offence.

C No, because the 'positive act' of providing misleading information to DC LAGRAM must relate to the robbery.

D Yes, CLINTON knows GREEN has committed a relevant offence and has provided misleading information with intent to impede her apprehension.

Question 9.7

BARKER commits an offence of assisting an offender (contrary to s. 4 of the Criminal Law Act 1967). The original offence was a burglary of a dwelling (punishable with 14 years' imprisonment).

As a consequence, what is the maximum sentence that could be imposed on BARKER?

A 5 years' imprisonment.

B 7 years' imprisonment.

C 9 years' imprisonment.

D 14 years' imprisonment.

Question 9.8

DC NEWMAN has arrested GRIFFIN for an offence of burglary. She believes that BISHOP may have assisted GRIFFIN and has consequently committed an offence of assisting an offender (s. 4 of the Criminal Law Act 1967). DC NEWMAN asks DS ENVER for some advice regarding this offence.

Which of the following statements is correct?

A The relevant offence committed by GRIFFIN must be one that carries more than five years' imprisonment for this offence to be committed.

B BISHOP can commit the offence before GRIFFIN is convicted of committing the burglary.

C BISHOP could attempt to commit this offence.

D The offence requires the consent of the Attorney General before a prosecution is brought.

Question 9.9

PALTRY has her purse stolen. The purse was worth £10 and contained £50 in cash and several personal items with a combined value of £30. PALTRY is annoyed by the theft and makes enquiries into who was responsible for the offence. She finds out that JAMES took her purse. PALTRY confronts JAMES who confesses to the theft. JAMES states that he is truly sorry for what he did and that to make up for the loss PALTRY suffered he would like to compensate her loss by giving her £90 in cash. PALTRY agrees and accepts the money offered by JAMES.

Considering the offence of concealing relevant offences (contrary to s. 5 of the Criminal Law Act 1967), which of the following statements is correct?

A PALTRY has committed the offence but the permission of the Attorney General is required before a prosecution could take place.

B PALTRY has not committed the offence in this situation because concealing relevant offences is only applicable to offences with a maximum sentence of 10 years' imprisonment.

C PALTRY has committed the offence but the consent of the DPP would be required before a prosecution can be brought.

D PALTRY has not committed the offence as she has only accepted reasonable compensation for the loss caused by the theft.

Question 9.10

WHEELER is a witness to a civil proceedings matter. The defendant is CLAYDON and the proceedings are being heard in a county court. While WHEELER is waiting outside the court to give evidence, she is approached by TURNBULL, a friend of CLAYDON's. TURNBULL is aware that WHEELER is a witness in the case and, intending to intimidate WHEELER into not providing her evidence, tells WHEELER that all the windows in her house will be broken that evening if she provides evidence against CLAYDON. WHEELER does not believe TURNBULL and carries on to give her evidence.

Considering the offence of intimidation of witnesses (contrary to s. 39 of the Criminal Justice and Police Act 2001), which of the following comments is correct?

A The offence has not been committed as the case was being heard in a county court and not a High Court.

B The offence has not been committed as the act of intimidation takes place after the commencement of the proceedings.

C The offence has not been committed as the threat is to damage property and not to injure WHEELER.

D TURNBULL has committed the offence in this situation.

Question 9.11

CARTER comes home and speaks to her nephew, CYRIL, and tells him that while she was out shopping she stole an iPod from a shop on a nearby high street and not to tell anybody. CARTER leaves the stolen iPod on a table in the front lounge of the house. Later that day the police visit CARTER's house on an unconnected matter. CYRIL sees the police at the front door and when they knock at the door he does not answer as he fears that they are making enquiries about the theft of the iPod. When the police leave, CYRIL removes the iPod from the house and takes it down to the local tip and disposes of it.

Considering the offence of assisting an offender contrary to s. 4 of the Criminal Law Act 1967, does CYRIL commit the offence?

A No, as he was not present at the time of the original theft.

B Yes, he commits the offence when he does not answer the door.

C No, as CYRIL was only aware of the offence after the crime had been committed.

D Yes, he commits the offence when he disposes of the iPod.

Question 9.12

The offence of escaping is one dealt with by the common law; it is triable on indictment only and has an unlimited punishment in terms of sentencing.

Which of the following statements is correct in respect of this offence?

A This offence could not be committed by a person escaping from police detention as it only applies to a person escaping custody following their conviction for a criminal offence.

B The offence can only be committed by a person who escapes from the lawful custody of a sworn police officer.

C A person who is detained under s. 136 of the Mental Health Act 1983 can commit this offence.

D A person would commit this offence even if the custody they escaped from was later proved to be 'unlawful'.

Question 9.13

HEATH is serving 10 years' imprisonment for committing an offence of robbery. He is visited in prison by KELLY who offers to help HEATH escape from the prison. HEATH agrees to escape as a consequence of KELLY's offer. KELLY hides some clothes and cash in a bush just outside the prison one evening with the idea that HEATH can change into the clothes and use the cash as soon as he gets out of the prison. The following day KELLY visits HEATH in the prison. When KELLY enters the prison he is carrying a skeleton key which he intends to pass to HEATH during his visit. KELLY is subject to a search before he enters the visiting area and the key is discovered.

At what stage, if at all, is the offence of assisting escape (contrary to s. 39 of the Prison Act 1952) first committed?

A When KELLY makes the offer to help HEATH escape from the prison.

B When KELLY hides the clothes and cash outside the prison.

C When KELLY takes the skeleton key into the prison.

D The offence is not committed in these circumstances.

ANSWERS

Answer 9.1

Answer **D** — In deciding whether the evidence should be admitted, the question the judge asks him/herself is whether it is fair to allow the evidence, *not* whether it is obtained fairly or by unfair means, making answer A incorrect. The judge generally *has no discretion* whether to exclude relevant admissible evidence on the ground that it was obtained improperly, making answer C incorrect. Evidence may be excluded for a number of reasons amongst which is the incompetence of a witness, making answer B incorrect.

Investigators' Manual, para. 1.11.2.2

Answer 9.2

Answer **B** — 'Facts in issue' will include the *identity of the defendant*, the *actus reus* and the *mens rea* of an offence (making answer A incorrect). The standard of proof for the defence is 'on the balance of probabilities', making answer C incorrect. The evidential burden may shift to the defence in a variety of situations; statute (e.g. diminished responsibility) or common law (e.g. the defence of insanity), making answer D incorrect.

Investigators' Manual, paras 1.11.3 to 1.11.4.2

Answer 9.3

Answer **A** — Section 1(2) of the Act describes the term 'judicial proceedings' as including proceedings before any court, tribunal, *or person having by law power to hear, receive, and examine evidence on oath*, making answer B incorrect. Corroboration is required in cases of perjury (see Perjury Act 1911, s. 13) but not of the fact that the defendant actually made the alleged statement, making answer C incorrect. The fact that the officer believes the original anonymous information to be true does not stop her committing the offence. First, an application for a search warrant may not be made on the basis of information from an anonymous source if corroboration has not been sought (Code B, para. 3.1). Secondly, the offence is committed when a lawfully sworn witness makes a statement in proceedings, which he/she knows to be false, or does not believe to be true. DC BROWN's statement on the quality and source of the information would fall into this category, making answer D incorrect.

Investigators' Manual, para. 1.12.1

Answer 9.4

Answer **C** — The consent of the DPP is not required to charge with this offence, making answer D incorrect. The fact that the allegations made by ROWLEY are incapable of identifying specific individuals is immaterial if the defendant intends that the allegation be taken seriously as in *R* v *Cotter and Others* [2002] EWCA Crim 1033, making answer A incorrect. The requirement to show that a great deal of police time and resources have been expended on the investigation was raised in *R* v *Sookoo* [2002] EWCA Crim 800 but is associated with giving false details to the police on arrest, making answer B incorrect. Making a false allegation of an offence means ROWLEY commits the offence (*R* v *Goodwin* (1989) 11 Cr App R (S) 194 (rape)).

Investigators' Manual, para. 1.12.2

Answer 9.5

Answer **A** — This offence is aimed to protect those who have been involved in relevant proceedings and so there is no requirement for an intention to pervert or interfere with justice, making answer B incorrect. The harm threatened can be physical or financial and can be made to a person or to property, making answer C incorrect. It is immaterial whether the threat is made in the presence of the person who would be harmed, making answer D incorrect. The offence must take place between the start of the proceedings and one year after they are concluded.

Investigators' Manual, para. 1.12.4

Answer 9.6

Answer **D** — Section 4 of the Act states 'where a person has committed a relevant offence, any other person who, knowing or believing him to be guilty of the offence *or some other relevant offence*, does without lawful authority or reasonable excuse any act with intent to impede his apprehension or prosecution shall be guilty of an offence'. The fact that CLINTON knows GREEN has not committed the theft is immaterial as she knows she has committed a robbery, i.e. she knows GREEN is guilty of *some other arrestable offence*, making answer A incorrect. The 'positive act' carried out by the defendant is about the behaviour of the defendant, not the offence to which it relates, making answer C incorrect. CLINTON can commit the offence before GREEN is convicted of the robbery, making answer B incorrect.

Investigators' Manual, para. 1.12.5

Answer 9.7

Answer **B** — Where the sentence for the original offence is 14 years, this offence would be punishable with a sentence of seven years' imprisonment, making answers A, C and D incorrect.

Investigators' Manual, para. 1.12.5

Answer 9.8

Answer **B** — There is no limitation placed on the sentence for the offence the defendant has assisted, making answer A incorrect. This offence cannot be attempted, making answer C incorrect. The consent of the DPP and not the Attorney General is required before a prosecution is brought, making answer D incorrect.

Investigators' Manual, para. 1.12.5

Answer 9.9

Answer **D** — Permission to prosecute for the offence is required from the DPP, making answer A incorrect. This does not make C correct as although the prosecuting permission is correctly identified in the answer (from the DPP), PALTRY *has not* committed the offence. Answer B is incorrect as the offence applies to all 'relevant' offences and does not exclude offences on the grounds of length of sentence. As PALTRY has only received reasonable compensation for her loss she does not commit the offence.

Investigators' Manual, para. 1.12.6

Answer 9.10

Answer **D** — The offence is committed when an intimidatory act is carried out by an individual who knows or believes that the victim is or may be a witness in any relevant proceedings, intending by their act to cause the course of justice to be obstructed, perverted or interfered with, and when the act is done after the commencement of those proceedings. The last point makes answer B incorrect. The fact that the threat is against property is immaterial, making answer C incorrect. Proceedings in any court are covered under s. 41(1) of the Act, making answer A incorrect.

Investigators' Manual, para. 1.12.3

Answer 9.11

Answer **D** — Section 4(1) of the Criminal Law Act 1967 states that where a person has committed a *relevant offence* (one that is fixed by law or an offence for which a person aged 18+ who has not previously been convicted, could be sent to prison for five years, i.e. theft (seven years)), any other person who knowing or believing him/her to be guilty of the offence or of some other relevant offence, does without lawful authority or reasonable excuse any act with intent to impede his/her apprehension or prosecution shall be guilty of an offence. The fact that CYRIL was not present at the scene of the original crime and only became aware of it at a later stage will not alter the fact that he is liable (making answers A and C incorrect). This offence must be an act so when he does not answer the door, this inaction cannot create liability, making answer B incorrect. He commits the offence when he disposes of the iPod as at that time he knew or believed CARTER to be guilty of a relevant offence. Please note that this offence cannot be attempted.

Investigators' Manual, para. 1.12.5

Answer 9.12

Answer **C** — The custody from which a person escapes must be shown to be lawful, making answer D incorrect. The offence applies to both police custody (or police detention as per s. 118 of the Police and Criminal Evidence Act 1984) or custody following conviction, making answer A incorrect. Answer B is incorrect as a person might be in lawful custody even if not directly in the custody of a sworn police officer, for example those people being dealt with by an investigating officer or escort officers under sch. 4 to the Police Reform Act 2002. People detained under the Mental Health Act 1983, s. 136, are in lawful custody.

Investigators' Manual, para. 1.12.7

Answer 9.13

Answer **B** — The offence under s. 39 can be committed in a variety of ways. Under s. 39(1)(b) any person who, intending to facilitate the escape of a prisoner (i) brings, throws or otherwise conveys anything into prison, (ii) causes another person to bring, throw or otherwise convey anything into prison, or (iii) gives anything to a prisoner or leaves anything in any place (whether inside or outside a prison) will commit the offence. Merely offering to assist an escape would not suffice (making answer A incorrect). The offence is first committed at point B, satisfying the conditions of s. 39(1)(b)(iii), therefore answers C and D are incorrect.

Investigators' Manual, para. 1.12.7

PART TWO

Property Offences

10 Theft

QUESTIONS

Question 10.1

BOYLAN and HAMILL are employed in a small shop and regularly chat to each other. During one such conversation, BOYLAN asks if HAMILL will help her with a problem. She tells HAMILL that over 12 months ago she lent £2,000 to IRONS, another shop employee, and that since then IRONS has flatly refused to pay any part of the money back. BOYLAN offers HAMILL £200 to act on her behalf and recover the loan from IRONS. HAMILL tells BOYLAN not to worry and that he will somehow resolve the situation. After work, HAMILL goes to IRONS's home and breaks into and takes IRONS's car, worth £2,000, from the drive. He takes the car to BOYLAN's house and presents it to BOYLAN as payment of the loan.

With regard to s. 2 of the Theft Act 1968, which of the following statements is correct?

A HAMILL's actions will not be dishonest if he honestly believes that he has a right in law to deprive IRONS of the car on behalf of BOYLAN.

B HAMILL must have a reasonable belief that he has a right in law to act as he did. If this is not the case then he has acted dishonestly.

C Section 2 of the Theft Act 1968 only allows an individual to appropriate property on behalf of himself and not, as in this case, on behalf of a third person.

D HAMILL's behaviour is dishonest as it falls below the standards of reasonable and honest people.

Question 10.2

CANHAM is a committed anti-vivisectionist and is a long-standing member of the Animal Liberation Front. He breaks into a laboratory and releases a variety of animals used for testing medicines. CANHAM personally believes that freeing the animals from captivity is not dishonest but an ethically and morally correct and proper decision. He does realise that, according to the ordinary standards of reasonable and honest people, what he has done would be considered dishonest. As he leaves the laboratory he is caught and arrested. At his trial, CANHAM maintains that his behaviour was not 'dishonest'.

Considering the ruling in *R* v *Ghosh*, which of the following statements is correct?

A A jury must take into account the fact that CANHAM's behaviour has not been dishonest according to his own moral values and in such a situation he should be acquitted of the charge.

B The only test the jury will apply is whether CANHAM's actions were dishonest according to the standards of reasonable and honest people.

C In such a situation, if s. 2 of the Theft Act 1968 is not applicable or helpful, the decision regarding whether CANHAM was dishonest is a matter for the judge to decide.

D CANHAM's actions can still be dishonest as what he did will be tested against the ordinary standards of reasonable and honest people along with the fact that he knew his actions were dishonest by those standards.

Question 10.3

MILSOM is shopping in his local supermarket when he notices that a member of staff has left a price-labelling machine on a display stand. He thinks it will be funny to create new price labels for goods in the store and cause chaos as a result. MILSOM walks around the store placing new and cheaper price labels on a wide variety of goods. MILSOM's only intention is to create confusion, not to benefit himself or any other customers in the supermarket.

Considering s. 3 of the Theft Act 1968 (appropriation) only, which of the following statements is correct?

A Although MILSOM swaps price labels, he is not appropriating the property. To do this effectively, he must pay for the goods.

B MILSOM's actions fall short of a full appropriation. This can only be accomplished by a combination of label swapping and the removal of an item from the shelf.

C It does not matter that MILSOM's further intention is to cause chaos and confusion; his conduct would constitute an appropriation.

D In order for MILSOM to appropriate property, he must have a dishonest intention. As this is not present, he does not appropriate.

Question 10.4

PC TROTMAN starts an attachment to the CID. He is told to take over the workload of a colleague who has retired. A few days later, PC TROTMAN approaches you with numerous reports that have been recorded as thefts. He believes that several of these reports do not represent offences of theft as there are some elements of the offence missing.

In which one of the following reports will you tell the officer that there has been an offence of theft?

A JOBLING was stopped in a stolen Mercedes. He had bought the car in good faith, paying a reasonable price for it but refused to hand it back to the original owner when he found out it was stolen.

B YU speaks little English. He shows ADEY, a taxi driver, a written address and gives him £10. The fare should be £9.50. ADEY indicates that this is not enough and takes a £50 note from YU's wallet. YU permits him to do so.

C PIT was arrested for stealing a caravan. The caravan was never recovered by the police and was left in a lay-by while PIT was interviewed. When he was released and before the true owner recovered the caravan, PIT took the caravan again.

D RODWELL was stop searched and found in possession of a £1,000 gold ring stolen in a theft. RODWELL states that when he innocently found the ring he believed he would never find the true owner.

Question 10.5

EALES rents a house under a tenancy agreement from his local council. EALES is short of money and decides to sell off several items from the house to help him through his cash crisis.

At what stage, if at all, does EALES first commit an offence of theft?

A When he picks flowers from the front garden of the house to sell commercially at a car-boot sale.

B When he severs a large amount of topsoil to sell to his neighbour.

C When he removes a fireplace to sell at a nearby second-hand shop.

D As EALES is in possession of the land under a tenancy agreement, he cannot steal land, things forming part of the land or severed from it or fixtures or structures let which are to be used with the land.

Question 10.6

LONGWORTH is a medical student with a keen interest in human anatomy. To satisfy her desire for experimentation she enters a university laboratory and takes a whole human body and several amputated and preserved body parts.

Which of the following statements is correct?

A LONGWORTH would be guilty of the theft of the human body and of the preserved body parts.

B LONGWORTH would only be guilty of the theft of the human body.

C LONGWORTH would be guilty of the theft of the preserved body parts.

D LONGWORTH would not be guilty of theft as human bodies and preserved body parts are not property for the purposes of s. 4 of the Theft Act 1968.

Question 10.7

GRATTON is a registered charity collector and is collecting in a shopping precinct. WHITBREAD approaches GRATTON and places a £20 note into his collecting tin. Moments later, WHITBREAD realises that he will not have enough cash to buy a computer game and returns to speak with GRATTON. He asks GRATTON for the money back but GRATTON refuses. WHITBREAD grabs hold of the collecting tin, removes the £20 and gives the tin back to GRATTON.

For the purposes of s. 5 of the Theft Act 1968, has WHITBREAD taken property 'belonging to another'?

A No, for although the money is no longer in WHITBREAD's direct control, he still retains a proprietary right or interest in the property.

B Yes, where money is given to charity collectors it becomes the property of the charitable trustees at the moment it goes into the collecting tin.

C No, as GRATTON is only the representative of the charity, 'ownership' of the money would remain with WHITBREAD until it is officially handed to the relevant charitable trustees.

D Yes, because you can steal property belonging to yourself. The money may be WHITBREAD's but it 'belongs' to GRATTON.

Question 10.8

DENYER opens a garden centre specialising in water features. One large fountain has a sign next to it that says '*Make a wish, all donations go to local charity.*' After a couple of months the garden centre is having financial problems. DENYER decides to collect the coins in the fountain and place the cash into the company bank account instead of giving it to charity. DENYER intends to replace the charity funds if her business survives the difficult period.

Has DENYER committed the offence of theft?

A Yes, DENYER has received and retained money to use in a specific way. She has contravened this obligation and is guilty of theft.

B No, as DENYER intends to replace the money she cannot commit the offence of theft.

C Yes, but only if she is unable to repay the money to the nominated charity.

D No, ownership of the money has been transferred to DENYER who has a moral and not a legal obligation to pass the money on to a local charity.

Question 10.9

PAREKH is a wages clerk working at a small insurance company and calculates the wages of all the staff, including his own. One day he is particularly busy and mistakenly adds £50 to his weekly wage. At the end of the week the additional money is paid into his bank account but PAREKH does not realise the extra payment was as a result of his error, thinking instead that it was payment for overtime he had worked. PAREKH's employer discovers the error and demands that PAREKH pay back the money; PAREKH refuses.

Considering s. 5 of the Theft Act 1968, does PAREKH commit theft?

A Yes, as PAREKH is under an obligation to return the money and an intention not to return it amounts to an intention to permanently deprive.

B No, an employee who is mistakenly credited with extra money in his/her bank account cannot be prosecuted for theft.

C Yes, in such circumstances an employee will be liable for stealing the extra money if he/she keeps it.

D No, as this section only applies where someone other than PAREKH has made a mistake.

Question 10.10

While visiting a council art gallery, POINTON removes a painting worth £30,000 from the premises. When he takes the painting, his intention is to return it provided the council make a £3,000 donation to a local charity. The incident receives a large amount of press coverage, which causes POINTON to panic. He returns the picture to the gallery the next day.

Considering the offence of theft only, which of the following statements is correct?

A Although POINTON does not intend the gallery to permanently lose the painting, he treats the painting as if it were his own and therefore commits theft.

B This is not theft as there is no intention to permanently deprive the gallery of the painting at the time of the appropriation.

C POINTON commits theft as he may not be able to return the painting in the circumstances he imagines and this amounts to treating the painting as his own.

D Theft cannot be committed in these circumstances as at no stage does POINTON intend to permanently deprive the gallery of the picture.

Question 10.11

QUILTEY is walking his dog in a park when he finds £300 in £10 notes on the footpath. QUILTEY believes that the person to whom the money belongs cannot be discovered by taking reasonable steps and decides to keep the money. The money was lost by GILL 20 minutes before QUILTEY found it. GILL reported the loss at a police station near to the park where the money was lost.

Is s. 2 of the Theft Act 1968 applicable in these circumstances?

A Yes, because QUILTEY has not taken reasonable steps to discover the person to whom the property belongs.

B No, and as s. 2 is not applicable, the issue of whether QUILTEY was dishonest or not will have to be decided by reference to the ruling in *R* v *Ghosh*.

C Yes, as it is QUILTEY's belief that is important, not the fact that he did or did not go on to take reasonable steps to find the owner of the property.

D No, as QUILTEY does not appropriate the property in the belief that he has a right in law to deprive a person of it.

Question 10.12

BEST becomes friendly with BROOK. BROOK is in her 70s and of limited intelligence. Over a period of time, BEST worms his way into BROOK's affections and persuades BROOK to provide him with cash from her bank account and after some six months, BROOK has given BEST £30,000. This is done with the consent of BROOK who has made an absolute gift of the money to BEST. BROOK's son finds out about BEST's activities and reports the matter to the police.

Considering the law with regard to 'appropriation', which of the following statements is correct?

A In a prosecution for theft it will be necessary to prove that the taking of the property was done without the owner's consent.

B BEST cannot appropriate property belonging to another because BROOK has made an absolute gift of the money to BEST.

C In these circumstances, it is immaterial whether the act of appropriation was done with BROOK's consent or authority.

D As BROOK consented to the appropriation, BEST does not commit the offence of theft.

Question 10.13

The term 'property' is defined under s. 4 of the Theft Act 1968.

Which of the following comments is correct with regard to that term?

A A person cannot steal land, or things forming part of land in any circumstances.

B A person's characteristics and their administrative data (such as a national insurance number) would constitute property.

C A trademark is 'property' and is capable of being stolen.

D Confidential information can be classed as property.

Question 10.14

The term 'belonging to another' is defined by s. 5 of the Theft Act 1968.

Which of the following statements is correct with regard to that term?

A Unless property is stolen from an individual who has possession or control over it, there can be no theft.

B In determining whether a person has 'possession' of property, the period of possession can be finite (i.e. for a given number of hours, days, etc.) or infinite.

C In a prosecution for theft it is necessary to show who owns the property.

D In proving theft, you do not need to show that the property belonged to another at the time of the appropriation.

Question 10.15

Section 176 of the Anti-social Behaviour, Crime and Policing Act 2014 inserts a new s. 22A into the Magistrates' Courts Act 1980, which provides that low-value shoplifting is to be a summary offence. However, if the value of the goods exceeds a certain amount this will not be the case.

What is that amount?

A £100 or less.

B £150 or less.

C £200 or less.

D £250 or less.

Question 10.16

BLEAZE and ROMFORD are out shopping in a town centre and are examining goods in a large but expensive department store. BLEAZE is interested in a T-shirt priced at £180 and tells ROMFORD he is going to steal it. ROMFORD tells BLEAZE that he will help him by acting as a look-out while the theft takes place. BLEAZE takes the T-shirt and the two leave the department store. Outside the store, they are detained by a store detective and the police are called to the scene. PC FORD arrests BLEAZE and ROMFORD on suspicion of theft and takes them to a designated police station.

Considering the law of theft, in particular that relating to low-value shoplifting (dealt with by s. 22A of the Magistrates' Courts Act 1980), which of the following comments is correct?

A ROMFORD has not committed an offence as you cannot aid the commission of a summary-only offence (such as low-value shoplifting).

B BLEAZE and ROMFORD could be dealt with by way of a fixed penalty for committing this theft offence.

C As low-value shoplifting is a summary-only offence, PC FORD could not use powers under s. 18 of the Police and Criminal Evidence Act 1984 to search the homes of BLEAZE and ROMFORD.

D If BLEAZE and ROMFORD plead guilty to this offence, they could not be sent to the Crown Court for trial or committed there for sentence.

ANSWERS

Answer 10.1

Answer **A** — Section 2 of the Theft Act 1968 provides three instances where appropriation of property will not be regarded as dishonest. This question centres on s. 2(1)(a), which states appropriation will not be dishonest 'if he appropriates the property in the belief that he has in law the right to deprive the other of it, on behalf of himself or of a third person'. The belief of the defendant need only be honest and not reasonable, therefore answer B is incorrect. The appropriation can take place on behalf of a third person, making answer C incorrect. Answer D is incorrect as it relates to the ruling in *R* v *Ghosh* [1982] QB 1053 and although relevant to the issue of dishonesty, it does not form any part of s. 2 of the Act.

Investigators' Manual, paras 2.1.3, 2.1.4

Answer 10.2

Answer **D** — Plainly, A is incorrect; to attribute dishonesty on the basis of the moral beliefs of the defendant would be unsound. The test is whether, according to the ordinary standards of reasonable and honest people, what was done was dishonest and if it was, whether the defendant realised, making answer B incorrect. Answer C is incorrect as the jury makes the decision as to whether the defendant was dishonest.

Investigators' Manual, para. 2.1.3

Answer 10.3

Answer **C** — Appropriation under s. 3 of the Theft Act 1968 is an assumption by a person of the rights of an owner and there is no requirement for a dishonest intention, making answer D incorrect. There have been a number of cases involving the swapping of price labels but after *R* v *Gomez* [1993] AC 442, the House of Lords concluded that the mere swapping of the price labels on goods amounted to an 'appropriation'; this eliminates answers A and B. This was the case regardless of any further intentions of the defendant.

Investigators' Manual, para. 2.1.5

Answer 10.4

Answer **B** — Answer A is incorrect because although the buyer of the car 'appropriates' property, this has been done in good faith and for value and, as per s. 3(2) of the Theft Act 1968, this will not amount to theft. Answer D is incorrect as although an appropriation has taken place it is not accompanied by circumstances of dishonesty as per s. 2(1)(c) of the Theft Act 1968. Answer C is incorrect as although stolen property can be 'appropriated', the same property cannot be stolen again by the same thief (*R* v *Gomez* [1993] AC 442). The same stated case dealt with answer B. It is immaterial that the owner of the property permits or consents to an appropriation; it is still theft.

Investigators' Manual, para. 2.1.5

Answer 10.5

Answer **C** — Under s. 4(2)(c) of the Theft Act 1968, a tenant can appropriate fixtures or structures let to be used with the land, i.e. the fireplace. This makes answer D incorrect. Answers A and B are incorrect as a tenant cannot steal things forming part of the land (the flowers) or the land itself (the topsoil) when he/she is in possession of the land.

Investigators' Manual, para. 2.1.6

Answer 10.6

Answer **C** — A person cannot steal a human body. Human bodies are not classed as property under the Theft Act 1968 (*Doodeward* v *Spence* (1908) 6 CLR 406) unless some work has been carried out on the body for preservation or for a scientific purpose. This makes answers A and B incorrect. This conclusion was reached in *R* v *Kelly* [1999] QB 621, where body parts taken from the Royal College of Surgeons were classed as stolen. This makes answer D incorrect.

Investigators' Manual, para. 2.1.7

Answer 10.7

Answer **B** — In *R* v *Dyke* [2002] Crim LR 153, it was stated that the moment money given by members of the public to charity collectors goes into the collecting tin, it becomes the property of the relevant charitable trustees. So once the money is in the tin, it no longer 'belongs' to WHITBREAD, making options A and C incorrect. Option D is also incorrect because, whilst you cannot steal your own property, the money does not belong to WHITBREAD.

Investigators' Manual, para. 2.1.8

Answer 10.8

Answer **A** — Section 5(3) of the Theft Act 1968 states that when a person receives property from another and is under an obligation to deal with that property in a particular way, the property shall be regarded (as against him) as belonging to the other. An 'obligation' is a legal one not a moral one. This makes answer D incorrect. Section 6(2) of the Theft Act makes it clear that regardless of an intention to repay, a person parting with property under a condition as to its return that may not be possible commits theft, making answers B and C incorrect.

Investigators' Manual, para. 2.1.9

Answer 10.9

Answer **D** — This section only applies where someone *other than the defendant* has made a mistake. For that reason answers A and C are incorrect. Answer B is incorrect as s. 5(4) explicitly covers this scenario should the error come from someone other than the defendant. If that were the case then PAREKH would commit theft.

Investigators' Manual, para. 2.1.9

Answer 10.10

Answer **A** — If there is an intention to permanently deprive at the time of the appropriation then an offence of theft will be committed. The intention to permanently deprive is defined in s. 6(1) of the Theft Act 1968 and states that a person who appropriates property without meaning the other to permanently lose it has this intention if their intent is to treat the thing as their own regardless of the other's rights. POINTON's intention to 'ransom' the painting (regardless of his motives) would be caught by this section, making answers B and D incorrect. Answer C is incorrect as it relates to s. 6(2) of the Theft Act 1968, where someone parts with property belonging to another under a condition as to its return which he may not be able to perform, and does not relate to this scenario.

Investigators' Manual, para. 2.1.11

Answer 10.11

Answer **C** — Section 2 of the Theft Act relates to dishonesty, in particular what is *not* dishonest rather than what is. There are several circumstances where a defendant will not be dishonest and one of those (s. 2(1)(a)) is where the person appropriates property in the belief that he has a right in law to deprive the other of it. There are three other circumstances including (s. 2(1)(c)) if the person appropriates the property in the belief that the person to whom the property belongs cannot be discovered by taking reasonable steps. This makes answer D incorrect as a belief in the right in law is not the only time a person will/will not be dishonest. It also makes answer B incorrect as the ruling in *R* v *Ghosh* is only used when s. 2 is not applicable or helpful and s. 2(1)(c) clearly relates to the circumstances of this question. Answer A is incorrect as it is the defendant's *belief* at the time of the appropriation that is important, not that the defendant went on to take reasonable steps to discover the person to whom the property belonged.

Investigators' Manual, paras 2.1.3, 2.1.4

Answer 10.12

Answer **C** — In a prosecution for theft it is unnecessary to prove that the taking was without the owner's consent (*Lawrence* v *Metropolitan Police Commissioner* [1972] AC 626), making answer A incorrect. It is immaterial whether the act of appropriation was done with the owner's consent or authority (*R* v *Gomez* [1993] AC 442), making answer D incorrect. In *R* v *Hinks* [2001] 2 AC 24, the court held that even though the complainant had made an absolute gift of property, retaining no proprietary interest in the property or any right to resume or recover it, an appropriation can still take place. This makes answer B incorrect.

Investigators' Manual, para. 2.1.5

Answer 10.13

Answer **C** — Answer A is incorrect as although a person cannot steal land *in general*, there are several circumstances under s. 4(2) of the Act that are exceptions to this rule. Answers B and D are incorrect as a person's characteristics and administrative data and confidential information (*Oxford* v *Moss* (1978) 68 Cr App R 183) are not intangible property for the purposes of the Theft Act 1968.

Investigators' Manual, paras 2.1.6, 2.1.7

Answer 10.14

Answer **B** — Answer A is incorrect as property can be stolen from a person who has a right or interest in that property. Answer C is incorrect as in a prosecution for theft it is not necessary to show who owns the property, only that it belongs to someone else other than the defendant. Answer D is incorrect as you *must show* that the property belonged to another at the time of the appropriation.

Investigators' Manual, para. 2.1.8

Answer 10.15

Answer **C** — Shoplifting is not a specific offence as such but constitutes theft under s. 1 of the Theft Act 1968; accordingly, s. 22A(3) of the Magistrates' Courts Act 1980 defines shoplifting for the purposes of this provision, which applies if the value of the stolen goods is £200 or less. This makes answers A, B and D incorrect.

Investigators' Manual, para. 2.1.8

Answer 10.16

Answer **D** — An offence of low-value shoplifting includes secondary offences such as aiding and abetting, meaning that answer A is incorrect. Answer B is incorrect as to be dealt with by way of a fixed penalty for theft, the value of the goods cannot exceed £100. Section 22A(6) provides that certain powers conferred by the Police and Criminal Evidence Act 1984 on the police and others in respect of indictable offences remain available in respect of low-value shoplifting, notwithstanding that it is reclassified as summary only. The powers concerned include a power of arrest exercisable by a person other than a constable (e.g. a store detective), powers enabling police officers to enter and search premises and vehicles in various circumstances for the purposes of searching for evidence in connection with an investigation or arresting individuals suspected of committing offences, and powers enabling a magistrate to authorise such entry and search. This means that answer C is incorrect. The effect of s. 22A is that offences of low-value shoplifting cannot be sent to the Crown Court for trial or committed there for sentence; they will attract a maximum penalty of six months' custody; and they will be brought within the procedure in s. 12 of the Magistrates' Courts Act 1980 that enables defendants in summary cases to be given the opportunity to plead guilty by post (correct answer D).

Investigators' Manual, para. 2.1.8

11 Burglary

QUESTIONS

Question 11.1

WILKIN is a tramp with a long record for burglary offences. He breaks into a garden shed but is arrested as he is leaving the shed with a mower in his hands. He tells the arresting officer that he was going to sell the mower to buy drink. In interview WILKIN states that initially, he never intended to take anything from the shed; stealing the mower was just an idea he had once he was inside. The reason he entered the shed was that he was looking for shelter.

What offence is WILKIN guilty of?

A As WILKIN was only looking for shelter, he commits theft (contrary to s. 1 of the Theft Act 1968) when he steals the mower.

B WILKIN commits burglary (contrary to s. 9(1)(a) of the Theft Act 1968) as soon as he enters the shed.

C WILKIN commits burglary (contrary to s. 9(1)(b) of the Theft Act 1968) when he steals the mower.

D WILKIN commits burglary (contrary to s. 9(1)(a) of the Theft Act 1968) when he steals the mower.

Question 11.2

CATER asks her neighbour, TEW, to look after her house while she is away on holiday. CATER gives TEW a key to her house and tells him he is welcome to go into the house and watch the satellite TV system, situated in the lounge, any time he likes while she is away. TEW decides to steal from the house and at 02.00 hrs one morning, while CATER is on holiday, he uses the key to get into CATER's house. He goes into the main bedroom and steals all of CATER's jewellery. TEW is aware that CATER would never have consented to this activity.

Which of the following statements is correct with regard to TEW?

A As CATER has given TEW permission to enter the premises, he is not a trespasser and in these circumstances would be guilty of theft rather than burglary.

B TEW is guilty of burglary but if the jewellery were in the same room as the satellite TV, then TEW would be guilty of theft alone.

C As TEW is the temporary owner of the property, he has a 'charge' on it and its contents and cannot be guilty of any offence in these circumstances.

D As TEW has gone beyond a condition of entry, he is a trespasser and would be guilty of burglary.

Question 11.3

HILLEN is the 'nominated driver' on a stag night. While he drinks orange juice all evening, his four friends get extremely drunk in a pub. All five decide to go to a nightclub and are all walking along a street when the four drunken men decide to drag HILLEN into a house for a joke. The four men kick open the door of a house and throw HILLEN into the hallway against his will. HILLEN gets up and decides that while he is in the house he may as well make it worth his while, intending to steal something from the house. He spots £50 on a table in the hallway, takes the money and leaves.

What offence does HILLEN commit?

A HILLEN commits burglary (contrary to s. 9(1)(a) of the Theft Act 1968) when he forms the intent to steal from the house.

B HILLEN commits theft (contrary to s. 1 of the Theft Act 1968) when he steals the money from the hallway.

C HILLEN commits burglary (contrary to s. 9(1)(b) of the Theft Act 1968) when he steals the money from the hallway.

D HILLEN commits burglary (contrary to s. 9(1)(b) of the Theft Act 1968) but would have a defence in these circumstances.

Question 11.4

HAYDEN goes into his local store to do some shopping. While he is walking around the shopping area he notices that the door to the staff room is ajar and that there is an open safe containing several bundles of cash inside it. HAYDEN decides to steal the cash and hides behind a large cardboard display in the corner of the shopping area, intending to come out when the shop is closed. The shop closes and HAYDEN comes out from behind the display. He walks across the shopping area to the staff room door and enters the staff room. Once inside the staff room he approaches the open safe and steals the cash contents. To get out, HAYDEN has to force a fire exit at the rear of the staff room.

At what stage does HAYDEN commit an offence of burglary?

A When he decides to steal the cash and hides behind the cardboard display.
B When he comes out from behind the display after the shop has closed.
C When he enters the staff room and approaches the safe.
D When he forces the fire exit to get out of the store.

Question 11.5

SOUTHALL decides to burgle a stately home. He visits the home during the day to look at the security arrangements and sees that apart from some security cameras there is a warning sign telling people to 'Beware of the Dog!' He returns later the same night to burgle the stately home. In his possession he has a piece of meat containing a large quantity of Valium (used to incapacitate any guard dog inside the home) and a screwdriver he intends to use to force a window and gain entry. SOUTHALL uses the screwdriver to force a window and enters the stately home with both the screwdriver and the meat in his possession.

Does SOUTHALL commit an aggravated burglary?

A No, in these circumstances neither of the articles in his possession relate to an aggravated burglary offence.
B Yes, but only in respect of the drugged meat. This would be classed as a 'weapon of offence' as it is designed to incapacitate.
C Yes, both items are classed as 'weapons of offence' in these circumstances. The drugged meat is designed to incapacitate and the screwdriver could be adapted to cause injury.
D No, although both items are 'weapons of offence', SOUTHALL would actually have to use one or both of them to cause injury or incapacitate before the full offence is committed.

Question 11.6

CRADDOCK intends to break into and steal from ELVIN's house. CRADDOCK knows that ELVIN is 80 years old but does not wish to take any chances and so before he goes to the house he decides to take a piece of cord with him to tie up ELVIN, should ELVIN be in. He breaks into the house through a ground floor window and enters the lounge of the house with the cord ready in his hands. He searches the lounge but finds nothing worth taking so he goes through the lounge door into the dining room. In the dining room is ELVIN who has come from his bedroom after hearing the noise of the break-in. CRADDOCK decides to steal from the dining room and ties ELVIN's hands with the cord before committing theft.

At what stage does CRADDOCK first commit the offence of aggravated burglary?

A When, before he goes to the house, he decides to take the piece of cord with him to tie up any occupants.

B When he enters the house after forcing the ground floor lounge window.

C When he enters the dining room (another part of the building).

D When he uses the cord to tie the hands of the occupant and commits theft.

Question 11.7

KYRIACOU has made a grappling hook that, if pushed through a letterbox, will enable her to take hold of letters from the floors of houses. She intends to take any money or valuable goods from the letters she manages to seize. She goes to a house and puts the grappling hook through the letterbox of a porch at the front of the house. Unfortunately for KYRIACOU the grappling hook is not long enough to reach some of the letters on the floor and she has to put her hand through the letterbox to enable the hook to reach the letters. She manages to hook the letters and pulls them through the letterbox.

Which of the following statements is correct?

A The front porch of a house would not be classed as a building for the purposes of burglary; KYRIACOU commits theft.

B When KYRIACOU uses the grappling hook she does not commit burglary. It is only when her hand goes through the letterbox that this offence is committed.

C These circumstances would not qualify as an 'effective and substantial' entry for the purposes of burglary; KYRIACOU has committed theft.

D Using the grappling hook as an extension of her body means that KYRIACOU has 'entered' premises and would be guilty of an offence of burglary.

Question 11.8

KEYS owns a builders' merchants and is owed £5,000 by BEATON. KEYS phones BEATON and demands the money; BEATON tells KEYS he will not pay a penny and that KEYS will have to take it from him. KEYS goes to BEATON's home and breaks in, intending to find some or all of the £5,000. KEYS's honest belief is that he is legally entitled to act in this way because of BEATON's debt. There is no money in the house and so he goes to the building site where BEATON is working. He enters an unfinished house and demands the money from BEATON. When BEATON refuses, KEYS assaults him, breaking BEATON's arm.

Which of the following statements is correct?

A KEYS only commits burglary when he breaks into BEATON's house with intent to steal.

B KEYS only commits burglary when he inflicts grievous bodily harm on BEATON.

C KEYS commits burglary when he breaks into BEATON's house and also when he inflicts grievous bodily harm on BEATON.

D At no stage does KEYS commit the offence of burglary.

Question 11.9

The GARTONs go on holiday for a week in a houseboat and constantly move around the country's canal system, never staying in one location for more than a day. They moor the boat and go to 'The Hen' pub for lunch. When they return to the boat some three hours later, they find that it has been broken into and a camera has been stolen.

Would the houseboat be classed as a 'building' for a burglary offence?

A Yes, the term 'building' would apply to an inhabited vessel and it would also apply when the person living in or on the vessel is not there as well as times when he/she is.

B No, the term 'building' should be given its everyday meaning as a structure of some permanence. As the houseboat is continually moored in different places it is not permanent and cannot be a 'building' for the purposes of burglary.

C No, a vehicle or vessel can only be a building if a person has a habitation in it. In these circumstances, the houseboat was empty when the offence took place and therefore it is not a 'building'.

D Yes, but the houseboat would be classed as an 'other building' rather than a 'dwelling' and as such the maximum sentence for this offence would be 10 years' imprisonment.

Question 11.10

LAMONT and HEWITSON break into a house intending to steal from it. They are stealing from the premises when the police arrive and both men are arrested. When

LAMONT is searched he is found to have a cutlery knife in his coat pocket. The arresting officer asks LAMONT why he has the knife and LAMONT replies, *'For self-defence because it's a dodgy area out there.'* HEWITSON had no idea that LAMONT had a knife in his possession.

Has an offence of aggravated burglary been committed?

A Yes, LAMONT commits the offence. HEWITSON does not as he would have to know of the existence of the cutlery knife and its purpose to be guilty of aggravated burglary.

B No, neither man commits the offence. LAMONT does not intend to use the cutlery knife in the course of the burglary and HEWITSON has no knowledge of its existence.

C Yes, both men commit the offence. The mere fact that LAMONT has a weapon of offence with him (the cutlery knife) is all the evidence that is required.

D No, the cutlery knife is not a weapon of offence because it is not an article made or adapted for use of causing injury or incapacitating a person.

Question 11.11

HULBERT breaks into a house using a screwdriver to force a downstairs window. He walks into the lounge and starts searching for items to steal. As he searches, the owner of the house, WEEDON, confronts him. HULBERT threatens WEEDON with the screwdriver, telling her to leave him alone or he will stab her with the screwdriver. WEEDON backs away from HULBERT into a hallway. HULBERT decides to rape WEEDON and follows her into the hallway, threatening her with the screwdriver as he does so. He rapes WEEDON in the hallway, then, worried about leaving a witness, he stabs WEEDON in the throat with the screwdriver causing her grievous bodily harm in the process. He returns to the lounge, steals some cash and leaves.

At what point does HULBERT first commit an aggravated burglary?

A When he threatens WEEDON with the screwdriver in the lounge.

B When he decides to rape WEEDON and follows her into the hallway.

C When he stabs WEEDON in the throat with the screwdriver.

D When he returns to the lounge and steals the cash.

Question 11.12

RULE and HOQUE intend to steal from O'HALLORAN's house. The two men go to the back garden of the house where RULE smashes a window to the kitchen. He makes so much noise that O'HALLORAN comes outside and challenges the two men. HOQUE instantly picks up a piece of wood from the back garden and starts to hit O'HALLORAN on the head with it, intending to cause grievous bodily harm to him. O'HALLORAN runs away from the house, followed by HOQUE who is still hitting him with the piece of wood. RULE climbs into the kitchen and steals cash from the house.

Have RULE and HOQUE committed an offence of aggravated burglary?

A Yes, both men commit the offence as a piece of wood can be a weapon of offence and its use in these circumstances has enabled entry to the premises.

B No, the piece of wood can never be an offensive weapon for the purposes of aggravated burglary.

C Yes, but only HOQUE commits the offence as he intends to cause O'HALLORAN grievous bodily harm.

D No, when the burglary is committed nobody actually enters the premises with a weapon of offence.

Question 11.13

DARE decides to steal from the offices of a printing firm owned by SHEA. Thinking there might be a security guard on the premises he takes a pair of handcuffs with him in case he needs to incapacitate the guard. At 05.00 hrs when DARE gets to the offices and is standing outside the premises, it becomes obvious that there is no security guard on duty so he throws the handcuffs away. He breaks into the offices and begins searching. Minutes later DARE is confronted by SHEA who has come to work early. In order to escape, DARE picks up a pair of scissors (not intending to steal them) and threatens SHEA to stay back or he will be stabbed. SHEA backs away from DARE. Still holding the scissors, DARE picks up a cash-box and makes off.

Which of the following statements is correct?

A As the handcuffs are designed to incapacitate, DARE would commit an offence of aggravated burglary when he goes to the offices intending to steal.

B DARE is guilty of burglary but not aggravated burglary. The handcuffs were disposed of prior to entry and the scissors are used only to assist in his escape.

C When DARE steals the cash-box he commits an offence of aggravated burglary.

D When DARE picks up the scissors and threatens SHEA he commits an offence of aggravated burglary.

Question 11.14

BUCKNALL visits GRETTON's house to install a new television. BUCKNALL arrives at GRETTON's house and is shown into the downstairs lounge where GRETTON wants the television fixed to the wall. GRETTON tells BUCKNALL that she is going out to visit a friend and that he should make his own way out when the television is fixed to the wall. While GRETTON is out, BUCKNALL decides to steal from GRETTON's house. He searches the downstairs lounge and finds £500 in a moneybox, which he takes. He decides to look around the rest of the house to see if there is anything else worth stealing and leaves the lounge and goes into the hallway. He enters a study situated off the hallway and once inside the study, steals a computer before leaving the house.

At what stage, if at all, does BUCKNALL commit burglary?

A When he takes £500 in cash from a money box in the lounge.
B When he goes into the hallway from the lounge.
C When he enters GRETTON's study and steals her computer.
D BUCKNALL does not commit burglary, as he is never a trespasser.

Question 11.15

LLOYD visits DERMOT's house to pick up a drill. DERMOT invites LLOYD into his house and asks him to wait in the hall while he fetches the drill. While waiting, LLOYD spots an envelope on the hall window ledge; he can see it contains cash.

LLOYD quickly picks up the envelope and puts it in his pocket. DERMOT returns with the drill, hands it to LLOYD and LLOYD leaves. The envelope contains £2,000. A few minutes later, DERMOT discovers the envelope has gone. He chases after LLOYD and accuses him of taking the envelope. LLOYD pushes DERMOT over and runs away.

With regard to the Theft Act 1968 only, what offence does LLOYD commit?

A LLOYD commits theft (contrary to s. 1 of the Theft Act 1968).
B LLOYD commits burglary (contrary to s. 9(1)(b) of the Theft Act 1968).
C LLOYD commits burglary (contrary to s. 9(1)(a) of the Theft Act 1968).
D LLOYD commits robbery (contrary to s. 8 of the Theft Act 1968).

Question 11.16

The offence of burglary (contrary to s. 9(1)(a) of the Theft Act 1968) can be committed in a variety of ways.

In which of the following situations has such an offence been committed?

A HEDGELAND breaks into a house intending to cause actual bodily harm against MOORE. MOORE is not in the house so HEDGELAND does not carry out the offence.

B PANG breaks into a garage intending to commit an offence of taking a conveyance (contrary to s. 12 of the Theft Act 1968).

C TAMM breaks into a warehouse intending to steal but finds nothing worth taking. Out of spite, TAMM turns on all the warehouse lights, committing an offence of abstracting electricity (contrary to s. 13 of the Theft Act 1968).

D YOUNGER breaks into a garden shed looking for shelter. Once inside he commits criminal damage (contrary to s. 1(1) of the Criminal Damage Act 1971) to several gardening tools stored inside the shed.

Question 11.17

LEAVY intends to break into a house to steal property. In his pocket he is carrying a screwdriver which he intends to use to cause injury against anyone who tries to prevent him from escaping. LEAVY forces a downstairs lounge window and enters the house. Once inside the lounge he steals several ornaments before being disturbed by the householder. LEAVY pulls out the screwdriver and threatens the householder, who is not afraid and approaches LEAVY. LEAVY stabs the householder causing him grievous bodily harm.

At what point, if at all, does LEAVY first commit an offence of aggravated burglary (contrary to s. 10 of the Theft Act 1968)?

A When he initially breaks into the house.

B When he actually steals the ornaments.

C When he stabs the householder, causing him grievous bodily harm.

D The offence of aggravated burglary is not committed in these circumstances.

Question 11.18

CALTHORPE is a homeless military veteran looking for somewhere to shelter for the night because he is cold. To protect himself from the elements, he breaks into a house owned by TAYLOR. Once inside the lounge of the house he turns on an electric fire to warm himself up. Several minutes later he hears a noise in the house and, thinking that someone is in the house, he picks up a hammer which is on a table in the lounge to protect himself by hitting anyone who confronts him (he does not intend to keep the hammer). He hears another noise and panics—he smashes a window in the lounge to escape, drops the hammer and runs away.

Considering the law in relation to burglary, which of the following comments is correct?

A CALTHORPE commits a burglary (under s. 9(1)(b) of the Theft Act 1968) when he turns the electric fire on.

B CALTHORPE commits an aggravated burglary (under s. 10 of the Theft Act 1968) when he picks up the hammer.

C CALTHORPE commits an aggravated burglary (under s. 10 of the Theft Act 1968) when he smashes the window.

D CALTHORPE does not commit a burglary offence in the circumstances described.

Question 11.19

MORROW owns a Bentley Continental GT car and keeps it locked in a large garage which is separated from his house by several metres. KOLB is a friend of MORROW's and has asked MORROW on several occasions if he can take the Bentley for a drive—MORROW has always refused as he thinks KOLB is a poor driver. MORROW goes on holiday and whilst he is away, KOLB breaks into the garage intending to take the Bentley out for a drive and then return it to the garage. Once inside the garage, KOLB realises he will not be able to get into the Bentley and in a fit of rage he scratches the side of the Bentley causing thousands of pounds of damage to the vehicle. He is about to leave when he sees an expensive toolkit in the garage and decides to make his venture worthwhile and steals the toolkit.

In relation to the offence of burglary under s. 9(1)(a) of the Theft Act 1968, which of the following statements is correct?

A KOLB commits the offence when he breaks into the garage intending to take the Bentley for a drive.

B KOLB commits the offence when he damages the Bentley.

C KOLB commits the offence when he steals the toolkit.

D KOLB does not commit the offence of s. 9(1)(a) burglary.

Question 11.20

GATE breaks into a warehouse intending to steal from the premises. As soon as he is inside the warehouse he sees an office which is actually within the warehouse itself. He thinks there will be property worth stealing in the office and breaks down the door to see what is inside. Whilst he is inside the office and searching for something to steal, he hears the sound of footsteps approaching him and he picks up a large carving knife from a shelf in the office. GATE does not want to keep the carving knife but thinks it will certainly deter anyone who challenges him whilst he is on the premises and if threatening someone with the carving knife is not enough, he decides he will use it on anyone who tries to stop him. A security guard enters the office and GATE points the carving knife at the security guard shouting *'Stay back or I'll stab you!'* The security guard takes no notice and approaches GATE. A struggle between GATE and the security guard takes place during which GATE stabs the security guard causing the security guard serious injury. GATE grabs hold of a laptop from the office, drops the carving knife and runs away.

At what point is the offence of aggravated burglary (contrary to s. 10 of the Theft Act 1968) first committed?

A When GATE picks up the carving knife.
B When GATE threatens the security guard.
C When GATE injures the security guard.
D When GATE steals the laptop.

Question 11.21

MILWARD is owed £500 by HARPER who has refused to pay MILWARD after repeated requests. MILWARD has run out of patience and decides he will get his money back by any means. HARPER lives in a motor home behind a farm so MILWARD visits the motor home and breaks open the door. He enters the motor home intending to 'rough up' HARPER (causing him relatively minor injury). He searches the motor home but HARPER is not there. MILWARD lashes out at a TV set in the motor home and smashes it in the process. He leaves the motor home and is walking away when he decides he will damage more of HARPER's property. He returns to the motor home, goes inside and smashes every electrical item inside.

At what stage, if at all, does MILWARD commit a burglary contrary to s. 9(1)(a) of the Theft Act 1968?

A When he enters the motor home intending to cause minor injury to HARPER.
B When he smashes the TV set in the motor home.
C When he enters the motor home intending to damage HARPER's property.
D The offence has not been committed as the activity took place inside a motor home and that is not a 'building'.

Question 11.22

STANLEY has had a number of arguments with his neighbour DREW about the noise her dog makes at all times of the day. One afternoon DREW's dog is barking loudly and STANLEY decides he has had enough. He goes round to DREW's house and breaks in by smashing the back door off its hinges intending the threaten DREW with violence if she does not sort her dog out. DREW is not inside the house but STANLEY can hear her dog barking in the kitchen. He returns to his own house, grabs hold of some masking tape and returns to DREW's house intending to wrap the masking tape around the mouth of the dog to shut it up. He enters the kitchen but the dog is so aggressive that he cannot get close to it. He picks up a large knife from the kitchen and stabs the dog, seriously injuring it in the process.

Which of the following comments is correct in respect of STANLEY's activity and the offence of burglary under the Theft Act 1968?

A STANLEY commits a s. 9(1)(a) burglary when he enters DREW's house intending to threaten her with violence.

B STANLEY commits a s. 10 aggravated burglary when he enters DREW's house with the masking tape.

C STANLEY commits a s. 10 aggravated burglary when he picks up the knife and seriously injures the dog.

D STANLEY has not committed an offence of burglary in these circumstances.

ANSWERS

Answer 11.1

Answer **C** — Breaking into the garden shed clearly makes WILKIN a trespasser for the purposes of the offence of burglary. However, his lack of intent to commit any of the ulterior offences of theft, grievous bodily harm or criminal damage when he entered the shed means that he cannot be guilty of an offence under s. 9(1)(a) of the Theft Act 1968, making B and D incorrect. Although WILKIN does commit theft, he has entered as a trespasser and stolen, falling into the category of a burglary under s. 9(1)(b) of the Theft Act 1968 and making answer C correct. Answer A is incorrect because committing a theft after entering as a trespasser makes WILKIN a burglar.

Investigators' Manual, paras 2.2.1 to 2.2.5

Answer 11.2

Answer **D** — Answer C is incorrect as looking after property in such a manner would not prohibit the person in 'charge' of the property being guilty of theft should they treat it as TEW has done. CATER's permission for TEW to enter was granted 'conditionally'; that is, to watch the satellite TV. This conditional permission has been violated and that violation turns TEW into a trespasser (*R* v *Jones and Smith* [1976] 3 All ER 54), making answer B incorrect. TEW's intention to steal from the premises from the outset and his entry as a trespasser makes him guilty of burglary under s. 9(1)(a) of the Theft Act 1968. Even if the jewellery were in the same room as the satellite TV, TEW is a trespasser with intent to steal the moment he enters the house; this makes answer A incorrect.

Investigators' Manual, para. 2.2.1

Answer 11.3

Answer **B** — Answers A, C and D are incorrect because HILLEN is never a trespasser for the purposes of burglary. A crime is committed when there is a meeting of *mens rea* with *actus reus* but that *actus reus* must be voluntary. HILLEN's entry to the house must be deliberate or reckless and so, as he was not responsible for being thrown into the house by his drunken friends, the *actus reus* of burglary must be eliminated. Once inside the house he decides to steal, therefore, HILLEN is now guilty of theft.

Investigators' Manual, para. 2.2.1

Answer 11.4

Answer **C** — Initially, HAYDEN is not a trespasser as he enters the shop as a genuine and honest customer and with the implied permission of the shop owner. Even when he decides to hide and steal, he remains in the part of the shop he has legitimate access to and is not a trespasser at this stage, making answer A incorrect. When the shop closes, he *does* become a trespasser. This is because, at that time, he had no right to be in the store. But although he is a trespasser, you must remember that in order for a burglary to be committed the person must *enter as a trespasser*—not become one by exceeding a condition of entry (and this is what has happened at this stage), making answer B incorrect. The offence of burglary would be committed when he moves into the staff room as at this point he *enters part of a building as a trespasser* with intent to steal, making answer D incorrect as a result.

Investigators' Manual, para. 2.2.5

Answer 11.5

Answer **A** — One way an aggravated burglary can be committed is when a person enters premises in possession of a weapon of offence. A screwdriver is not a weapon of offence 'per se' and SOUTHALL would have to intend for the screwdriver to be used as such for this item to fall into the category of offensive weapon. This makes answer C incorrect. Drugged meat to incapacitate a dog is not an offensive weapon as the weapon must be to incapacitate a person, making answer B incorrect. Answer D is incorrect as neither of the items is a weapon of offence.

Investigators' Manual, para. 2.3.1

Answer 11.6

Answer **B** — There are two questions to ask to obtain the correct answer to this question: (i) Is the cord a weapon of offence? (ii) What type of burglary is this? The piece of cord intended to tie up any occupants is a weapon of offence as it is intended to incapacitate a person. This is a burglary under s. 9(1)(a) of the Theft Act 1968 as CRADDOCK intends to break in and steal from the house and burglary is committed when he enters with that intent. Where these two points meet is where the aggravated burglary is first committed.

Investigators' Manual, para. 2.3.1

Answer 11.7

Answer **D** — Answer A is incorrect, as the front porch of a house would be classed as a building or part of a building. Although *R* v *Collins* [1973] QB 100 stated that entry must be 'effective and substantial', this ruling was altered by *R* v *Brown* [1985] Crim LR 212, CA, where it was stated that entry had only to be 'effective'. This does not mean that the defendant needs to get the whole of their body into premises and any part of the body would be sufficient, making answer C incorrect. A person may use an object as an extension of himself or herself to enter, which makes B incorrect.

Investigators' Manual, para. 2.2.1

Answer 11.8

Answer **B** — If KEYS honestly believes that he has a right in law to deprive a person of property then he is not dishonest and cannot commit theft. Therefore, if there is no theft, KEYS does not commit burglary at BEATON's house, making answers A and C incorrect. An unfinished house is a building for the purposes of burglary and KEYS has entered as a trespasser and committed grievous bodily harm, satisfying the requirements for an offence under s. 9(1)(b) of the Theft Act 1968, making answer D incorrect.

Investigators' Manual, paras 2.1.2, 2.2.1, 2.2.2, 2.2.5

Answer 11.9

Answer **A** — Section 9 of the Theft Act 1968 defines a building and states that the word 'building' applies to inhabited vehicles or vessels (the houseboat) and applies to those vehicles or vessels at times when they are unoccupied (when the GARTONs go for a meal).

Investigators' Manual, para. 2.2.2

Answer 11.10

Answer **A** — Answer D is incorrect as the definition of a weapon of offence is incomplete; you should add 'or intended by the person having it with him for such use'. On this basis, the knife will become a weapon of offence. The fact that LAMONT had the weapon of offence in his possession for some other purpose than to use during the course of the burglary is irrelevant. The harm this section aims to protect the public from is that a burglar may be tempted to use such a weapon to injure someone during a burglary, making answer B incorrect. Finally, answer C is incorrect as HEWITSON must know of the existence of the knife and, because it is not an offensive weapon per se, its purpose.

Investigators' Manual, para. 2.3.1

Answer 11.11

Answer **C** — The screwdriver is not a weapon of offence until HULBERT intends to use it to cause injury and this intention is accompanied by an offence under s. 9(1)(a) or (b) of the Theft Act 1968. When HULBERT threatens WEEDON with the screwdriver, it instantaneously changes from a screwdriver to a weapon of offence (think about the concept of 'instant arming') but while he remains in the lounge an aggravated burglary can only be committed if he commits or attempts to commit one of the offences under s. 9(1)(b) of the Theft Act 1968, i.e. theft or grievous bodily harm. It cannot be under s. 9(1)(a) at this moment as he has already entered the premises when the intention regarding the use of the screwdriver is formed. When HULBERT decides to rape WEEDON and moves from the lounge to the hall, he does not commit burglary as his intention is to commit an offence of rape—this is not a 'trigger' offence for the purposes of the s. 9(1)(a) offence. The offence of aggravated burglary is *first committed* when HULBERT stabs WEEDON, as at this point he has entered the hall as a trespasser and committed GBH.

Investigators' Manual, para. 2.3.1

Answer 11.12

Answer **D** — The inclusion of an article intended by a person to cause injury or incapacitate within the definition of a weapon of offence means that absolutely anything can instantaneously become a weapon of offence in the hands of the burglar, making answer B incorrect. This is a burglary under s. 9(1)(a) of the Theft Act 1968 and so to become an aggravated burglary the weapon of offence must be with the offender at the time of entry. This is not the case. The fact that entry has been gained because of the use of the piece of wood against O'HALLORAN is irrelevant; RULE is the only person entering the premises and he does not have any weapon at the time of entry, making answer A incorrect. HOQUE does not commit the offence as he never enters the premises, therefore answer C is incorrect.

Investigators' Manual, para. 2.3.1

Answer 11.13

Answer **C** — Although handcuffs are a weapon of offence, DARE disposes of them prior to entry and so cannot commit aggravated burglary because he does not have the weapon in his possession at the time of entry, making answer A incorrect. At this stage, DARE is guilty of burglary alone. When he picks up the scissors they become a weapon of offence, but a mere threat to use them does not make his burglary aggravated so answer D is incorrect. As DARE then commits a theft by stealing the cash-box he commits a burglary under s. 9(1)(b) and is in possession of an offensive weapon when he does so. This makes him guilty of aggravated burglary so answer B is incorrect.

Investigators' Manual, para. 2.3.1

Answer 11.14

Answer **B** — To work out when BUCKNALL commits burglary you must decide when he enters a building or part of a building as a trespasser. At point A, GRETTON has invited BUCKNALL into her lounge to install a TV. BUCKNALL has no intent to commit one of the trigger offences for burglary under s. 9(1)(a) (**DIT** — Damage, Inflicting GBH, Theft) so is not a trespasser for burglary under s. 9(1)(a) at this point. When GRETTON leaves, BUCKNALL decides to steal from the lounge and takes £500 from a moneybox. You could never say that GRETTON would be happy with such behaviour (she did not invite BUCKNALL into her house to steal)—BUCKNALL has gone beyond a condition of entry and would become a trespasser when he steals. However, this does not make him a burglar as he did not enter the lounge as a trespasser. When you are thinking about burglary, it is essential that the person concerned enters as a trespasser or the offence cannot be completed. At point A BUCKNALL is a thief, not a burglar. At point B BUCKNALL has moved from one part of a building to another (from the lounge into the hallway) with the intention to steal (s. 9(1)(a) burglary). He has gone beyond the conditional entry permission given by GRETTON and as a consequence he enters a part of a building as a trespasser. The fact that he enters with the intention of stealing is all that is required and it is immaterial whether he enters with the idea to steal if there is 'anything worth stealing' (*R* v *Walkington* [1979] 1 WLR 1169). As a consequence, answers C and D are incorrect.

Investigators' Manual, paras 2.2.1 to 2.2.5

Answer 11.15

Answer **A** — LLOYD cannot commit burglary because he never entered a building or part of a building as a trespasser. DERMOT invited him into his house and, when he entered, LLOYD had no criminal intentions, making answers B and C incorrect. No robbery has been committed because the force has been used after the property has been appropriated, making answer D incorrect.

Investigators' Manual, paras 2.1.2, 2.2.1 to 2.2.5, 2.4.1

Answer 11.16

Answer **C** — Answer A is incorrect as actual bodily harm is not a trigger offence for the purposes of s. 9(1)(a). Answer B is incorrect as an intent to steal will not include an intention to commit an offence of taking a conveyance (as there is no intent to permanently deprive). Answer D is incorrect as an offence of criminal damage is only relevant to an offence under s. 9(1)(a) of the Theft Act 1968. As YOUNGER did not *enter* with such an intent, there is no burglary. Answer C is a burglary as the offender breaks in with the intention of stealing. The fact that the offender goes on to commit an offence of abstracting electricity out of spite is immaterial.

Investigators' Manual, paras 2.2.1 to 2.2.5

Answer 11.17

Answer **A** — At point A LEAVY has committed a burglary contrary to s. 9(1)(a) of the Theft Act 1968 and has with him a weapon of offence (his intent to use it to cause injury makes it a weapon of offence), making this an aggravated burglary. It does not matter that he only intended to use it to assist in his escape.

Investigators' Manual, paras 2.3.1 to 2.3.2

Answer 11.18

Answer **D** — CALTHORPE enters the house as a trespasser but not for any purposes under s. 9(1)(a) of the Theft Act 1968. Once inside the lounge he could commit a burglary (under s. 9(1)(b) of the Act) if he stole or attempted to steal, committed or attempted to commit grievous bodily harm—he turns on an electric fire to warm himself up but this is not theft as electricity is not property so he does not commit a burglary under s. 9(1)(b) of the Act, making answer A incorrect. He hears a noise and picks up a hammer; however, he does not intend to steal it. This is not a burglary so he cannot commit an aggravated burglary at this stage, making answer B incorrect. When CALTHORPE smashes the window he commits criminal damage but this is not an offence of burglary under s. 9(1)(b) so, again, he does not commit aggravated burglary, making answer C incorrect. No burglary offence is committed by CALTHORPE (answer D is correct).

Investigators' Manual, paras 2.2.1 to 2.3.2

Answer 11.19

Answer **D** — A burglary under s. 9(1)(a) of the Theft Act 1968 is committed when a person enters a building or part of a building with the intention of stealing anything in the building or part of the building in question, of inflicting on any person therein any grievous bodily harm or of doing unlawful damage to the building or anything therein. When KOLB enters the garage he does not intend to steal the Bentley (he intends to commit an offence of taking a conveyance which does not include the element of permanent deprivation required for theft), making answer A incorrect. The only time a s. 9(1)(a) burglary can be committed is at the point of entry into the building or part of a building and so once KOLB is in the garage the time frame in which the offence can be committed has come and gone, meaning that answers B and C are incorrect. When KOLB damages the Bentley he commits criminal damage—when he steals the toolkit he commits a burglary under s. 9(1)(b) of the Act.

Investigators' Manual, paras 2.2.1 to 2.2.5

Answer 11.20

Answer **C** — An aggravated burglary occurs when a burglary (under s. 9(1)(a) or 9(1)(b)) is committed and at the time of that offence the offender has with them a weapon of offence, firearm, imitation firearm or explosive. A weapon of offence can be made, adapted or intended to cause injury and the carving knife would fall into the 'intended' category. But when GATE picks up the carving knife no burglary occurs as whilst he has a weapon of offence with him, he does not intend to keep it, making answer A incorrect. When GATE threatens the security guard, no burglary occurs (GATE could only commit a s. 9(1)(b) burglary in the office and he has not stolen/attempted to steal or inflicted/attempted to inflict grievous bodily harm upon a person), making answer B incorrect. When he injures the security guard he commits a s. 9(1)(b) burglary and at the time has a weapon of offence with him, meaning he commits aggravated burglary at this point. He also commits an aggravated burglary when he steals the laptop but he *first* committed the offence at point C, therefore making answer D incorrect.

Investigators' Manual, paras 2.2.1 to 2.3.2

Answer 11.21

Answer **C** — A burglary under s. 9(1)(a) of the Theft Act 1968 is committed when a person enters a building or part of a building with the intention of stealing anything in the building or part of the building in question, of inflicting on any person therein any grievous bodily harm or of doing unlawful damage to the building or anything therein. An inhabited motor home would be classed as a 'building', making answer D incorrect. Answer A is incorrect as when MILWARD first enters the motor home he does not have one of the states of mind required to commit an offence under s. 9(1)(a). The s. 9(1)(a) offence is committed on *entry only* so when damage is caused *after* entry it would not amount to a burglary, making answer B incorrect. When MILWARD leaves then re-enters the motor home intending to commit criminal damage, the offence is committed (answer C).

Investigators' Manual, paras 2.2.1 to 2.2.3

Answer 11.22

Answer **D** — A burglary under s. 9(1)(a) of the Theft Act 1968 is committed when a person enters a building or part of a building with the intention of stealing anything in the building or part of the building in question, of inflicting on any person therein any grievous bodily harm or of doing unlawful damage to the building or anything therein. When STANLEY enters the house he has none of these intentions, making answer A incorrect. He does not have any of these intentions when he returns to the house with the masking tape, making answer B incorrect. Inside the kitchen he can only commit a s. 9(1)(b) burglary if he stole or attempted to steal, committed or attempted to commit grievous bodily harm—he does not do so when he seriously injures the dog, meaning that answer C is incorrect. No burglary is committed by STANLEY (answer D is correct).

Investigators' Manual, paras 2.2.1 to 2.3.2

12 Robbery

QUESTIONS

Question 12.1

CREW, MUSGROVE and BYER play cards together on a regular basis. As a result, BYER falls into debt, owing CREW and MUSGROVE £500 each. One evening, BYER is drinking in a bar when CREW and MUSGROVE approach him. CREW places the tip of a knife against BYER's face and MUSGROVE says, *'Give us all you have or your face might not have a future.'* BYER hands over his wallet and all his gold jewellery. CREW and MUSGROVE believe they are legally entitled to the property but realise they are not entitled to use force to get it.

Which of the following statements is correct with regard to the offence of robbery (contrary to s. 8 of the Theft Act 1968)?

A CREW and MUSGROVE commit robbery. It does not matter that they believe in a right to take the property; they have used force in order to obtain it.

B The beliefs of CREW and MUSGROVE are immaterial as such a gambling debt amounts to a moral obligation to repay the money. This is a robbery.

C There is no dishonesty by CREW or MUSGROVE and as a robbery involves theft and therefore no dishonesty is present, the offence of robbery is incomplete.

D Only CREW is guilty of robbery as he is the only person actually using force against BYER.

Question 12.2

ASGHAR and CULLEM are pickpockets. On a train station platform ASGHAR nudges into GLENN, knocking him off-balance and into CULLEM, who steals a wallet from inside GLENN's jacket. GLENN realises the wallet has been stolen and tells ASGHAR and CULLEM he is going to inform the police. CULLEM produces a flick-knife and threatens GLENN with it, telling him to keep quiet or he will be stabbed.

At what point, if at all, has the full offence of robbery been committed?

A When ASGHAR nudges into GLENN knocking him off-balance.

B When CULLEM steals the wallet from inside GLENN's jacket.

C When CULLEM threatens GLENN with the flick-knife.

D At no time has an offence of robbery has been committed.

Question 12.3

DEIGHTON is part of a football crowd who become involved in a street brawl with a group of rival supporters. During the course of the fight, DEIGHTON punches and kicks WATTON to the floor, knocking WATTON unconscious. Even though WATTON is unconscious and can offer DEIGHTON no resistance, DEIGHTON continues to punch WATTON about the head and face with his right fist for pure sadistic pleasure. At the same time he removes WATTON's wallet with his left hand.

Has DEIGHTON committed robbery?

A Yes, as DEIGHTON has used force on WATTON immediately before a theft was committed.

B No, WATTON was unconscious during the theft so DEIGHTON cannot put or seek to put him in fear of being then and there subjected to force.

C Yes, at the time the theft takes place, DEIGHTON has used force against WATTON.

D No, DEIGHTON's use of force against WATTON was not in order to commit theft.

Question 12.4

The police receive information that ROCK is planning to steal the takings from a shop owned by MAN. MAN wishes to help and volunteers to run the shop on his own at the time of the offence as part of a trap laid by the police. Three police officers are waiting in a small room behind the till when ROCK enters the shop. ROCK produces a toy pistol and points it at MAN, demanding the takings. Although MAN hands over some cash from the till, he does not believe he will be subjected to force because there are police officers nearby and he realises the gun is a fake.

Which of the following statements is correct with regard to these circumstances?

A The force used during a robbery should at least amount to an assault. As MAN does not apprehend the immediate infliction of force there can be no robbery.

B This is not a robbery as the police were nearby and MAN realised the gun was a fake. Therefore, MAN cannot fear that ROCK would be able to use force on him or even threaten to do so.

C ROCK's state of mind is irrelevant to the offence of robbery. Whether ROCK intended to put MAN in fear of force being used or not is an objective decision to be made by a jury.

D The fact that MAN could have successfully resisted if he wished is immaterial. The offence of robbery is committed because ROCK seeks to put MAN in fear of being subjected to force.

Question 12.5

HONEYBOURNE owns and operates a hot dog stand and has had a particularly good day's business at a music festival. As he is counting his takings, he is approached by ORDISH who produces an imitation firearm and says, *'Hand over the money!'* ORDISH intends HONEYBOURNE to believe the gun is real and that he will be shot if he does not do as ORDISH demands. HONEYBOURNE does not believe he will be subjected to force as he used to be in the army and realises that the gun is not real. He laughs at ORDISH and tells him if he wants to rob people he should get a real gun. ORDISH flees empty-handed.

Which of the following statements is correct?

A This is not an offence of robbery because ORDISH did not actually use force against HONEYBOURNE.

B An offence of robbery has not been committed because ORDISH has not actually stolen the takings.

C As HONEYBOURNE realised the gun was a fake and did not fear that he would be subjected to force, an offence of robbery is not committed.

D Robbery has not been committed because ORDISH did not verbally threaten HONEYBOURNE with violence.

Question 12.6

TI FRAY has several reports on her desk. All the reports have been recorded as offences of robbery (contrary to s. 8 of the Theft Act 1968). However, only one of the reports is actually an offence of robbery.

Which one of the following is actually an offence of robbery?

A ROSE was leaving work when an offender demanded her watch or he would beat her up when she left work the next day. ROSE handed over her watch.

B DREW was detained for robbery after he punched his employer and took £100 from his employer's pocket. DREW states that he honestly believed he was legally entitled to the money as his employer had not paid him for a month.

C WARD intended to put GREY in fear of being then and there subjected to force and demanded GREY hand over her purse. GREY was not frightened but felt sorry for WARD and handed him her purse.

D PHIN (a pickpocket) was in the process of stealing a wallet from MONK while on a train when the train jolted and PHIN accidentally collided with MONK. In the process of the collision between the two, PHIN stole MONK's wallet.

Question 12.7

CARMEN approaches GREEN who is sitting in the cab of his HGV. The HGV load is several hundred thousand pounds of cigarettes. CARMEN opens the passenger door and gets into the vehicle. He tells GREEN to hand over the keys to the vehicle or *'the next time I see you I will shoot you'*. GREEN refuses to do so. CARMEN then produces a photograph of GREEN's wife and tells GREEN that unless he hands the keys to the HGV over to him, GREEN's wife will be beaten up. GREEN does not believe CARMEN and refuses. CARMEN produces a mobile phone which shows live pictures of GREEN's living room (a hundred miles away from GREEN's present location). GREEN can see that his wife is in the process of being assaulted by CARMEN's associate. CARMEN once again demands the keys and tells GREEN the assault will continue if he does not give in. At this point GREEN hands over the keys and gets out of the cab of the HGV. CARMEN drives off with the load of cigarettes.

At what point, if at all, is an offence in respect of robbery (contrary to s. 8 of the Theft Act 1968) actually committed?

A When CARMEN threatens to shoot GREEN the next time he sees him.

B When CARMEN threatens GREEN's wife.

C When CARMEN shows GREEN pictures of his wife being assaulted.

D When CARMEN drives off with the load of cigarettes.

Question 12.8

Late one evening whilst going home, JOHNSON is walking down the road when he sees NICKLIN walking towards him. JOHNSON decides that he is going to rape NICKLIN and approaches her and punches her in the face. The force of the blow knocks her to the ground and as she hits the pavement her purse falls out of her bag. Instead of raping NICKLIN, he takes the purse. JOHNSON runs off and continues his journey home. As he crosses a car park he sees MURRAY who he knows used to work in a garage. JOHNSON approaches MURRAY and pulls a knife on him and says *'When I come into the garage where you work tomorrow I want a full tank of petrol for free in my car understood?'* When JOHNSON goes to the garage the next day MURRAY is not working so he has to pay for his petrol.

Which of the following statements is correct with regard to offences committed by JOHNSON?

A The offences against NICKLIN are theft and assault; the offence against MURRAY is blackmail.

B The offence against NICKLIN is robbery and the offence against MURRAY is blackmail.

C The offences against NICKLIN are theft and assault; the offence against MURRAY is attempted robbery.

D The offence against NICKLIN is robbery; the offence against MURRAY is attempted blackmail.

ANSWERS

Answer 12.1

Answer **C** — One of the essential elements of an offence of robbery is that there must be a theft. Theft in robbery is the same as s. 1 of the Theft Act 1968 and the elements of dishonesty under s. 2 will therefore apply. The honest belief of CREW and MUSGROVE means that they are not dishonest. This principle stems from *R* v *Robinson* [1977] Crim LR 173, CA, where it was held that all the defendant had to show was an honest belief in the entitlement to the property and not an honest belief in an entitlement to take it in the way he did. The fact that the requirement to repay the gambling debt is a moral obligation does not affect the situation.

Investigators' Manual, para. 2.4.1

Answer 12.2

Answer **B** — A theft has taken place and, immediately before the theft, force has been used, making answer D incorrect. When CULLEM threatens GLENN with a flick-knife it is not in order to steal but to deter him from reporting the matter, making answer C incorrect. When force is used, no theft has taken place and so the full offence is incomplete, making answer A incorrect, although this may be an attempted robbery. Although the use of force in nudging into GLENN may appear minimal it is nevertheless a use of force (*R* v *Dawson and James* (1976) 64 Cr App R 170).

Investigators' Manual, para. 2.4.1

Answer 12.3

Answer **D** — An offence of robbery is committed when the offender not only uses force against the victim immediately before or at the time of stealing but also *in order to do so*. Therefore, if the violence has no connection with the offence of theft and is effectively an unnecessary and sadistic activity, it is not a robbery. Answer A is incorrect as the force used is because of a fight and not in order to commit theft. Answer C is incorrect for the same reason. Answer B is incorrect as the definition also includes the direct application of force as a means of committing the offence as well as the threat of its use.

Investigators' Manual, para. 2.4.1

Answer 12.4

Answer **D** — There is no requirement that the force used during a robbery should amount to an assault, making answer A incorrect. The fact that the victim does not resist or is unafraid because of the surrounding circumstances is of no consequence; the offence is still committed, so answer B is incorrect. It is enough that the offender puts or seeks to put the victim in fear of force being used at that time and so the state of mind of the offender is significant. It is not an objective decision made by the jury and so answer C is incorrect.

Investigators' Manual, para. 2.4.1

Answer 12.5

Answer **B** — Although many robbery offences will involve the use of force, the offence can just as easily be committed without it by the use of a threat, i.e. the defendant puts or seeks to put any person in fear of being then and there subjected to force, therefore answer A is incorrect. Putting a person in such fear does not require a verbal threat of violence as actions (pointing an imitation firearm at the intended victim) can satisfy this part of the offence, making answer D incorrect. The fact that the victim is not in fear of the threat is immaterial as it is the intention of the defendant that is important, making answer C incorrect. There is no offence of robbery in these circumstances as there was no actual theft; this is an *attempted* robbery.

Investigators' Manual, para. 2.4.1

Answer 12.6

Answer **C** — Answer A is incorrect as the force must be used or threatened 'immediately before or at the time' of the theft. Here force is threatened to be used the next day. Answer B is incorrect as to have a robbery there must be a theft. If one of the theft elements is missing (here there is no dishonesty), then there is no theft and therefore no robbery. Answer D is incorrect as the accidental application of force is not willed by the offender, i.e. there is no voluntary conduct and therefore no *actus reus*. The fact that GREY (in answer C) is not actually in fear does not matter—it is the intent of the offender that is all important.

Investigators' Manual, paras 2.5.1 to 2.5.4

Answer 12.7

Answer **D** — A robbery is committed *when a person steals* and immediately before or at the time of doing so, and in order to do so, uses force on any person or puts or seeks to put any person in fear of being then and there subjected to force. For the full offence to be committed there must be a theft and until that takes place there is no robbery.

Investigators' Manual, para. 2.4.1

Answer 12.8

Answer **A** — The force used against NICKLIN was not used in order to facilitate an offence of theft so NICKLIN is not the victim of a robbery, ruling out answers B and D. The threat to use force against MURRAY is not one that is 'there and then' so this is not robbery either, although it is an offence of blackmail as once the unwarranted demand is made, the offence is complete, making answer C incorrect.

Investigators' Manual, paras 2.4.1 to 2.5.3

13 Blackmail

QUESTIONS

Question 13.1

LONGSTAFF needs money to fund his drug habit. He waits in the car park of a supermarket and watches McCOY park her car and enter the supermarket with her three-month-old daughter. LONGSTAFF follows McCOY into the store. While McCOY is shopping, LONGSTAFF approaches her and tells her that it is dangerous to park where she has. He demands that she hand over her purse or he will wait by her car and stab her and her daughter when they return to the car. McCOY hands over her purse and LONGSTAFF runs away.

At what stage, if at all, is the offence of blackmail committed?

A When LONGSTAFF tells McCOY that it is dangerous to park where she has.

B When LONGSTAFF makes the demand for the purse.

C When McCOY hands over her purse to LONGSTAFF.

D No offence of blackmail is committed; this is a robbery.

Question 13.2

GARWOOD has placed a large bet on the outcome of a local Sunday league football match. Two days before the match is due to take place he finds out that the team he has backed have lost four of their star players after they were involved in a car accident. Worried that he will lose his money, GARWOOD approaches the referee of the match. GARWOOD tells the referee, *'If you don't call off the game my friends will rape your wife.'* The referee takes no notice of GARWOOD and two days later the game goes ahead. GARWOOD loses his bet.

Considering the offence of blackmail (contrary to s. 21 of the Theft Act 1968) only, which of the following statements is true?

A GARWOOD does not commit the offence because he did not 'gain' any money.

B GARWOOD does not commit the offence because the threat is that his friends rather than GARWOOD would rape the referee's wife.

C As the game went ahead, GARWOOD commits an offence of attempted blackmail.

D In these circumstances GARWOOD commits the offence as he intended to keep what he already had (his original bet).

Question 13.3

GILCHRIST has just started a new job at a bank when she is approached by BAXTER, who tells her that he knows she used to be a prostitute and that if she does not have sexual intercourse with his friend, HUMPHRIES, he will inform the bank manager and she will probably be sacked. GILCHRIST reluctantly agrees to BAXTER's demand and has sexual intercourse with HUMPHRIES.

Is this an offence of blackmail (contrary to s. 21 of the Theft Act 1968)?

A Yes, because BAXTER makes the unwarranted demand with a view to gaining a benefit for another.

B No, because 'gain' is to be construed as extending only to a gain in money or other property.

C Yes, as a 'gain' refers to anything at all and not necessarily something with a monetary value.

D No, because BAXTER did not make the demand with a view to gain for himself.

Question 13.4

BRIDALE, FORD and HILL all work at the same office. BRIDALE and FORD are having an affair and need somewhere that they can meet and have sex. BRIDALE approaches HILL and tells him that unless he hands over the keys to his flat and leaves the flat for one night a week, he (BRIDALE) will inform the management that HILL has been stealing from the tills. HILL believes that BRIDALE will carry out his threat and does as BRIDALE demands.

Would this constitute an offence of blackmail (contrary to s. 21 of the Theft Act 1968)?

A Yes, as the gain and loss of property can be temporary.

B No, because BRIDALE did not threaten HILL with any form of violence.

C Yes, but only because HILL actually believes BRIDALE will carry out his threat.

D No, as the gain and loss must both be of a permanent nature.

Question 13.5

GILPIN is a keen golfer and has entered a competition he believes he can win if he uses a high quality set of golf clubs. EGAN (GILPIN's friend) believes the same and approaches CORK (who works as a shop assistant in a golf shop) and asks if he can hire a set of clubs from the shop for GILPIN to use. CORK refuses. EGAN then tells CORK that he will tell CORK's employers that he has been stealing from the till if he does not allow him to use the clubs for free. CORK gives EGAN the clubs and after GILPIN wins the competition, EGAN returns them to CORK.

With regard to the offence of blackmail, which of the following statements is correct?

A EGAN does not commit the offence because 'gain' and 'loss' in blackmail only relate to money.

B The offence has not been committed because EGAN has made the demand with a view to gain for GILPIN.

C EGAN does not commit the offence because the 'gain' he has made is not permanent.

D In these circumstances, EGAN has committed the offence.

Question 13.6

SCHULTEN approaches WARNER in the street. SCHULTEN tells WARNER that he has been watching him and knows that WARNER has a nine-year-old son. Intending to make money from WARNER, SCHULTEN tells WARNER that unless WARNER pays him £20,000 the following day, he will kidnap WARNER's son and subject the boy to a serious sexual assault. WARNER does not believe SCHULTEN and tells him to go away and that the money will never be paid to him.

Considering the offence of blackmail (contrary to s. 21 of the Theft Act 1968), which of the following statements is correct?

A Blackmail has not been committed because there has been no offence of theft.

B An offence of blackmail has been committed by SCHULTEN the moment he makes the demand of WARNER.

C Blackmail has not been committed because WARNER did not believe SCHULTEN.

D These circumstances would constitute an offence of attempted blackmail.

ANSWERS

Answer 13.1

Answer **B** — The offence of blackmail is committed when the demand with menaces is made as the offence of blackmail is aimed at the making of the demands rather than the consequences of them. Answers A and C are incorrect because at point A no demand has been made, although this would form part of the menace. At point C the offence has already been committed. Answer D is incorrect, as although blackmail and robbery are closely linked, a robbery cannot occur where the threat to use force is not immediately before or at the time of the theft.

Investigators' Manual, paras 2.5.1 to 2.5.4

Answer 13.2

Answer **D** — There is no such offence as 'attempted blackmail', making answer C incorrect. It is immaterial whether the menaces relate to action to be taken by the person making the demand, making answer B incorrect. 'Gain' for the purposes of blackmail includes a gain by keeping what one has, making answer A incorrect.

Investigators' Manual, paras 2.5.1 to 2.5.3

Answer 13.3

Answer **B** — The demand can be made with a view to gain for another, making answer D incorrect. The 'gain' must be in money or other property, making answers A and C incorrect.

Investigators' Manual, para. 2.5.1

Answer 13.4

Answer **A** — Answer B is incorrect as there is no requirement for violence to form any part of the demand with menaces. Answer C is incorrect as there is no need for the victim of the offence to actually believe the threat by the offender (even if the victim did not believe the threat, the offence would be committed). The gain or loss in blackmail can be in money or in other property (the flat) and this gain and loss can be either permanent or temporary. HILL has lost his flat for one evening a week—the temporary loss of property, making answer D incorrect and answer A correct in the process.

Investigators' Manual, paras 2.5.1 to 2.5.3

Answer 13.5

Answer **D** — A 'gain' and 'loss' relate to money and other property, making answer A incorrect. Answer B is incorrect because the demand can be made with a view to gain for 'himself or another'. Answer C is incorrect as the gain need not be permanent.

Investigators' Manual, paras 2.5.1 to 2.5.4

Answer 13.6

Answer **B** — An offence of blackmail is committed the moment a person makes the demand with menaces. This makes it almost impossible to have an offence of attempted blackmail, making answer D incorrect. Answer A is incorrect as there is no requirement for a theft to take place for the offence of blackmail to be complete. Whether the person to whom the demand with menaces is made actually believes the demand and/or reacts to it is surplus to requirements for the offence to be committed, therefore answer C is incorrect.

Investigators' Manual, paras 2.5.1 to 2.5.4

14 Fraud

QUESTIONS

Question 14.1

Section 1 of the Fraud Act 2006 creates three different ways in which an offence of fraud can be committed.

Which of the following conditions is one of those fraud offences?

A Fraud by impersonation of an individual.

B Fraud by failing to disclose information.

C Fraud by data theft.

D Fraud by communication deception.

Question 14.2

THORP steals BING's wallet, which contains a store card for 'Callows Auto Parts' store in BING's name. THORP decides to use the store card to obtain a large quantity of car tools from the store for his own use. THORP goes into the store and puts £800 worth of car tools into his shopping trolley and takes them to the till. Intending to fool the cashier into thinking the card is his, THORP hands over BING's card in payment but does not say anything to the cashier. The cashier is not fooled by THORP and realises that the card does not belong to THORP as he has seen the real owner, BING, in the store on several previous occasions. However, the cashier is not at all concerned by THORP's behaviour and asks him to sign for the card payment which THORP does. THORP leaves the store with the power tools.

Considering the offence of fraud by false representation (contrary to s. 2 of the Fraud Act 2006), which of the following statements is correct?

A THORP has not committed the offence in these circumstances because he did not use any words to represent that the credit card belonged to him.

B The offence has not been committed because the cashier was not fooled into thinking that THORP was in fact BING.

C The offence has been committed. By handing the card to the cashier THORP represents that he has authority to use it for that transaction. It does not matter that the cashier is not deceived or that words were not used.

D The offence has not been committed as fraud by false representation relates to a 'gain' for another and in these circumstances the gain is directly for the benefit of THORP.

Question 14.3

TIs VENABLES and YOUNG are taking the National Investigators' Examination and are testing each other on the law contained in the Fraud Act 2006. The officers make several remarks relating to the Fraud Act, in particular about the offence of fraud by false representation (s. 2 of the Act). However, only one of those remarks is correct.

Which remark is correct?

A TI VENABLES states that the 'dishonesty' referred to in the offence of fraud by false representation is the same as the 'dishonesty' referred to in s. 2 of the Theft Act 1968.

B TI YOUNG states that the 'gain and loss' referred to in the offence of fraud by false representation must actually take place for the offence to be complete.

C TI VENABLES states that a false representation carried out by post would only be complete when the letter was received by the intended victim.

D TI YOUNG states that if a person makes an untrue statement in the honest belief that it is in fact true, they could not commit the offence.

Question 14.4

VANDER sends out a large number of e-mails purporting to represent a well-known bank in the hope that people receiving the e-mail will send him their bank account details. VANDER intends to use any details he receives to remove money from his victims' bank accounts and place it into his own account. IBBET is deceived by the e-mail and sends VANDER a return e-mail containing all of his bank account details. VANDER telephones an automated banking facility at IBBET's bank and transfers the entire contents of IBBET's account into his own.

At what stage, if any, does VANDER first commit the offence of fraud by false representation (contrary to s. 2 of the Fraud Act 2006)?

A When he sends out the bulk e-mails purporting to represent a well-known bank.

B When he receives the return e-mail from IBBET, providing him with his bank account details.

C When he telephones the automated banking facility and removes money from IBBET's account.

D The offence is not committed in these circumstances.

Question 14.5

PURDY is a solicitor who has a written contract with SORRELL to look after her property portfolio and the money that is earned from it, as SORRELL owns 30 houses and does not have the time to administer them herself. PURDY and SORRELL have an argument during which SORRELL insults PURDY. PURDY is extremely offended by SORRELL and to get revenge he does not tell SORRELL when several of her tenants fail to pay their rent. As a consequence of PURDY's inaction, SORRELL loses several thousand pounds in rent.

Would this constitute an offence under s. 3 of the Fraud Act 2006?

A Yes, as PURDY would be under a legal duty to disclose the information to SORRELL.

B No, because the relationship between PURDY and SORRELL is not a fiduciary one.

C Yes, but only because the contract between PURDY and SORRELL was written.

D No, because PURDY acted in order to cause a loss to SORRELL rather than make a gain for himself.

Question 14.6

NEWBURY works for a printing company and is responsible for marketing the company and securing new contracts. NEWBURY is working on obtaining a major contract that will provide the company with £10 million worth of business when he is approached by the owner of a rival firm. The owner of the rival firm tells NEWBURY that if he allows his company to win the battle for the printing contract then he will hire NEWBURY as the General Manager and give him a pay rise worth £50K a year. NEWBURY agrees and as a result he fails to take up the chance of the contract, allowing the rival company to take it up at the expense of his current employer.

Considering offences under the Fraud Act 2006 only, what offence, if any, does NEWBURY commit?

A Fraud by false representation (contrary to s. 2 of the Fraud Act 2006).

B Fraud by failing to disclose information (contrary to s. 3 of the Fraud Act 2006).

C Fraud by abuse of position (contrary to s. 4 of the Fraud Act 2006).

D NEWBURY does not commit any offence in these circumstances.

Question 14.7

COXSEY is a career criminal who specialises in offences of fraud. He has a large amount of material at his disposal in order to commit these offences, which he keeps at various locations. The police raid COXSEY's home address and arrest him for fraud-related offences. In the searches that follow his arrest the police find a 'phishing' kit in a bedroom at his home address (which COXSEY used last week to carry out an offence of fraud by false representation (contrary to s. 2 of the Fraud Act 2006)). In COXSEY's car, which was parked on the front drive of his home address, they find several blank credit cards (which COXSEY later states he was going to use to commit offences of fraud by false representation (contrary to s. 2 of the Fraud Act 2006)) and in a store room rented by COXSEY but several miles away from his home address, they find several hundred blank bank statements (which COXSEY states he was looking after for a friend who was going to use them to commit fraud-related offences).

In relation to which items does COXSEY commit the offence of possession or control of articles for use in frauds (contrary to s. 6 of the Fraud Act 2006)?

A The 'phishing' kit and the blank credit cards only.

B The blank credit cards only.

C The blank bank statements only.

D The blank credit cards and the blank bank statements only.

Question 14.8

ASTBURY works for a credit card company. He is short of money and decides to supplement his income by selling a list of other people's credit card details that he has downloaded from the company computer onto a CD-ROM. He takes the CD-ROM to FOXLEY whom he knows commits offences of fraud and sells the CD-ROM to him. During the sale of the CD-ROM, ASTBURY offers to supply and sell FOXLEY 1,000 blank credit cards (even though he does not actually have possession of the cards). FOXLEY agrees to buy the cards and gives ASTBURY £500 for the CD-ROM and £500 for the blank credit cards.

With regard to the offence of making or supplying articles for use in frauds (contrary to s. 7 of the Fraud Act 2006), which of the following comments is true?

A ASTBURY commits the offence but only in respect of the CD-ROM containing lists of other people's credit card details.

B ASTBURY does not commit the offence as a CD-ROM containing other people's credit card details is not an 'article' and making an offer to supply requires the offender to be in possession of the article concerned.

C ASTBURY commits the offence but only in respect of the offer to supply the 1,000 credit cards to FOXLEY.

D ASTBURY commits the offence in respect of the CD-ROM and the offer to supply the 1,000 credit cards to FOXLEY.

Question 14.9

HANCOCK is a volunteer worker. He visits the homes of senior citizens and carries out a variety of maintenance work on their houses; he does not charge anyone for the work he carries out. MORGAN, a 35-year-old, is not very good at 'Do-it-Yourself' and so contacts HANCOCK. MORGAN lies to HANCOCK and tells him that her 85-year-old grandmother requires some repair work to be carried out on her roof and gives HANCOCK her own home address as the location for the work. MORGAN lives alone and would not be entitled to HANCOCK's help unless she was over 65 years of age. HANCOCK believes MORGAN and agrees to complete the work. He visits MORGAN's house and carries out the roof repair at no cost to MORGAN.

Has MORGAN committed the offence of obtaining services dishonestly (contrary to s. 11 of the Fraud Act 2006)?

A Yes, as the fraud used by MORGAN has caused HANCOCK to provide services that MORGAN would not normally be entitled to.

B No, obtaining services dishonestly can only be committed where the service should be paid for. As HANCOCK provided the services for free the offence is not committed.

C Yes, as soon as HANCOCK agrees to carry out the work the offence is committed.

D No, providing maintenance work for free would not fall within the definition of a 'service' for the purposes of this offence.

Question 14.10

MALIN is interested in buying TBT Ltd (a company producing and distributing soft furnishings around the United Kingdom). He makes his interest known to FLYNN who is the owner of the company. The company is not performing too well at the moment and has just made a loss because a major customer owing thousands of pounds to TBT Ltd went bust. FLYNN decides that he will not enter this loss in the company account books to make TBT Ltd a more attractive proposition to purchase. He also rips out several pages from the account books and destroys them with the idea of, once again, making the company look financially sound. MALIN examines the company accounts but decides not to buy TBT Ltd after all (the company accounts have no bearing on this decision).

Considering the offence of false accounting only (contrary to s. 17 of the Theft Act 1968), which of the following comments is correct?

A The offence is first committed when FLYNN omits to include details in the accounts about his loss.

B The offence is first committed when FLYNN rips out and destroys several pages from the account books.

C The offence is first committed when MALIN examines the accounts.

D The offence has not been committed in these circumstances.

Question 14.11

ROMFORD has an expensive gambling habit and wants to reduce the amount he spends on everyday items so that he can increase the amount he gambles. He makes a number of false £20 notes which he intends to spend on food at local supermarkets. The fact is that the forged notes are terrible and would never fool anyone—they are so bad that even ROMFORD realises that they will never fool anyone and so he leaves them in his house and never uses them. ROMFORD is arrested for an unconnected matter and the forged £20 notes are discovered during a search of his house. ROMFORD is questioned regarding the forged notes and the officer in the case, TI GRANE, is considering the offence of making a false instrument with intent (contrary to s. 1 of the Forgery and Counterfeiting Act 1981).

Why would such a charge be inappropriate?

A Because the forged notes were discovered at ROMFORD's home address.

B Because ROMFORD never actually tried to make use of the forged £20 notes.

C Because currency notes are not classed as an 'instrument'.

D Because ROMFORD made the forged notes for his own use rather than for another person's use.

Question 14.12

GOUGH is friendly with TYLER as the two men drink in the same pub. GOUGH is well known for making up stories about his life to try and impress people and one day he tells TYLER that he is a qualified accountant. TYLER has heard about GOUGH's 'tall stories' and asks him to prove it. GOUGH tells TYLER he will and that evening he forges an award from the Institute of Chartered Accountants in England and Wales stating that he is a qualified accountant. GOUGH visits the pub the next day and shows TYLER the award. TYLER is a little gullible and believes that the award is real which is exactly what GOUGH wanted. Unexpectedly, TYLER then asks GOUGH what he should do with £5,000 he has in a savings account. GOUGH has no idea what to say and, as a guess, tells TYLER to invest in gold. GOUGH thinks TYLER is only enquiring about what to do with the money but TYLER was so impressed with GOUGH's false award certificate that he invests in gold which, unfortunately for TYLER, drops in price so that his investment is worth £500.

Considering offences in relation to making and using a false instrument with intent (contrary to ss. 1 and 3 of the Forgery and Counterfeiting Act 1981), which of the following comments is correct?

A GOUGH does not commit the offence under s. 1 of the Act but does commit the offence under s. 3.

B GOUGH commits the offences under ss. 1 and 3 of the Act.

C GOUGH commits the offence under s. 1 but not under s. 3 of the Act.

D GOUGH does not commit either offence.

ANSWERS

Answer 14.1

Answer **B** — Fraud by failing to disclose information is an offence created by virtue of s. 1(2)(b) of the Fraud Act 2006. Answers A, C and D are all fabricated.

Investigators' Manual, para. 2.6.2

Answer 14.2

Answer **C** — The fact that THORP has not actually said anything in order to accomplish the offence makes no difference. The offence can be committed by a representation that is express or *implied* and is communicated by words or *conduct*. THORP's conduct would suffice, making answer A incorrect. Answer B is incorrect as whether the cashier was fooled by THORP is immaterial. What matters is that THORP makes a representation knowing that it is false, or might be. Answer D is incorrect as the 'gain' for this offence can be for the individual or another.

Investigators' Manual, para. 2.6.3

Answer 14.3

Answer **D** — The 'dishonesty' referred to in the offence of fraud by false representation is as per the test in *R* v *Ghosh* [1982] QB 1053, making answer A incorrect. Answer B is incorrect as the 'gain and loss' does not actually have to take place. Answer C is incorrect as a false representation carried out by post would be complete when the letter is posted.

Investigators' Manual, para. 2.6.3

Answer 14.4

Answer **A** — The practice of 'phishing' is covered by the Fraud Act 2006. The offence would be committed when VANDER initially sends out the e-mail falsely representing that he is from a well-known bank.

Investigators' Manual, para. 2.6.3

Answer 14.5

Answer **A** — A fiduciary relationship is one relating to the responsibility of looking after someone else's money in a correct way. Looking after SORRELL's property portfolio would be such a relationship, making answer B incorrect. The offence under s. 3 (fraud by failing to disclose information) is committed when a person has a legal duty to disclose information. Such a duty can arise from oral or written contracts, making answer C incorrect. Answer D is incorrect as the harm caused by failing to disclose such information is either to make a gain or cause a loss to another (see s. 3(b) of the Act).

Investigators' Manual, para. 2.6.4

Answer 14.6

Answer **C** — This is one of the examples provided in your Manual as to how an offence under s. 4 of the Fraud Act 2006 (fraud by abuse of position) may be committed. The crux of the offence is the abuse of a position of trust and while this may relate to the positive action of the defendant, it can also relate to omission.

Investigators' Manual, para. 2.6.5

Answer 14.7

Answer **D** — The offence of possession of articles for use in frauds relates to items that will be used in the *future* to commit such offences. This removes the 'phishing' kit from the equation as it was used last week to commit an offence and therefore answer A is incorrect. The offence is committed by having possession or *control* over items (covering both the blank credit cards and blank bank statements) not only for the defendant's own use but also for use by another to commit offences of fraud, which means that both the blank credit cards and blank bank statements would be covered, making answers B and C incorrect.

Investigators' Manual, para. 2.6.7

Answer 14.8

Answer **D** — Section 8 of the Fraud Act 2006 deals with the term 'article' and this will encompass programs or data held in electronic form (such as a CD-ROM containing other people's credit card details). Making and selling such an item would be caught by the offence, making answers B and C incorrect in the process. Making an offer to supply an article for use in frauds is similar to the concept of making an offer to supply a drug, i.e. it does not matter whether you actually have the goods; what matters is you made the offer. This makes answer A incorrect.

Investigators' Manual, paras 2.6.7, 2.6.8

Answer 14.9

Answer **B** — Answer A is incorrect as unless the services are provided on the basis that they are chargeable then, regardless of the behaviour of the defendant, the offence cannot be committed. Services provided for free are not covered by the Act. Answer C is further incorrect as the offence of obtaining services dishonestly is a result crime and requires the actual obtaining of the service before it is complete. Answer D is incorrect as the term 'service' has not been defined by the Act.

Investigators' Manual, para. 2.6.9

Answer 14.10

Answer **A** — The offence can be committed in a variety of ways such as destroying, defacing, concealing or falsifying records or documents required for an accounting purpose. It can be committed by omission so in failing to enter the loss the *actus reus* of the offence is complete. The mental element includes 'with a view to gain for himself or another' and will not require the gain to be made, just that the person does something with that possibility in their mind. When FLYNN omits to put that loss in the account book, this state of mind exists and he commits the offence at point A.

Investigators' Manual, para. 2.6.10

Answer 14.11

Answer **C** — Section 8 of the Forgery and Counterfeiting Act 1981 defines an 'instrument' for the purposes of the offence under s. 1 of the Act. Section 8(2) states that a currency note (e.g. the forged £20 note) is not an instrument for the purposes of the Act, making answers A, B and D incorrect.

Investigators' Manual, para. 2.6.11.1

Answer 14.12

Answer **D** — Both offences involve the offender making (s. 1) or using (s. 3) a false instrument *with the intent* that it will induce somebody to accept it as genuine, and by reason of so accepting it to do or not to do some act to his own or any other person's prejudice. This was never GOUGH's intention when he made the false award so he does not commit the offence under s. 1 (meaning that answers B and C are incorrect) and the same would apply to the offence under s. 3 (meaning that answer A is incorrect).

Investigators' Manual, paras 2.6.11.1 to 2.6.11.4

15 Handling, Buying Scrap Metal for Cash and the Proceeds of Crime Act 2002

QUESTIONS

Question 15.1

FENSHAW is a collector of rare records. He visits a car-boot sale to see if there are any bargains available. While browsing at a stall run by REAY, he spots a record that he knows would cost over £1,000 from his normal reputable source. He asks REAY how much the record costs and REAY tells him he can buy the record for £30. FENSHAW remarks that this is a bargain, to which REAY replies '*Easy come and easy go.*' FENSHAW buys the record.

If FENSHAW were later arrested for handling stolen goods, what state of mind would be required for a prosecution to succeed?

A FENSHAW would have to know or believe the record to be stolen goods.
B FENSHAW would have to presume that the record was stolen goods.
C FENSHAW would have to think it probable that the record was stolen goods.
D FENSHAW would have to suspect that the record was stolen goods.

Question 15.2

GOODCHILD steals a car from TURVEY and sells it to CLIFF for £2,000. This is a cheap price for the car and although CLIFF is suspicious of GOODCHILD, she buys the car nevertheless. CLIFF drives the car for several days and eventually finds papers in the car belonging to TURVEY. CLIFF telephones TURVEY, who tells her that the car is stolen. CLIFF quickly hangs up and retains the car for two days while she decides what she will do. Realising that she may lose the car if she returns it to TURVEY, CLIFF sells the car to MARTINEZ for £500.

At what stage, if at all, does CLIFF commit the offence of handling stolen goods (contrary to s. 22 of the Theft Act 1968)?

A When CLIFF buys the car for £2,000 from GOODCHILD.

B When CLIFF retains the car knowing it is stolen.

C When CLIFF sells the car to MARTINEZ.

D CLIFF does not commit the offence in these circumstances.

Question 15.3

VENN breaks into a house and steals a quantity of jewellery. He takes the jewellery to AUSTEN and tells him about the burglary. AUSTEN gives VENN £100 for the jewellery. VENN uses the money to buy a games console. AUSTEN exchanges the jewellery for two tickets to a football match. He keeps one ticket for his own use and gives the other to PEERS as a birthday present. PEERS knows nothing about the origin of the ticket.

Which of the following statements correctly identifies 'stolen goods' from this scenario for the purposes of the offence of handling stolen goods?

A Only the £100 given to VENN and the games console he buys with the money would be 'stolen goods'.

B Only the jewellery (in the hands of AUSTEN alone) would be 'stolen goods'.

C All of the property except for the ticket in the hands of PEERS would be 'stolen goods'.

D Only the jewellery and both tickets in the hands of AUSTEN would be 'stolen goods'.

Question 15.4

GREEN orders a computer from a company owned by FORD. FORD dispatches the computer using a postal firm but the computer is stolen in transit. Two months later, SMITH is arrested in possession of the computer and is charged with an offence of handling stolen goods. The prosecution wish to serve a statutory declaration on SMITH under s. 27 of the Theft Act 1968 as proof that the computer was stolen.

Which of the following statements is correct?

A Only GREEN can make the declaration and a copy of it must be given to SMITH at least three days before the trial.

B Either GREEN or FORD can make the declaration and a copy of it must be given to SMITH at least seven days before the trial.

C Only FORD can make the declaration and this must be given to SMITH at least 14 days before the trial.

D Only GREEN can make the declaration, a copy of which must be given to SMITH at least 21 days before the trial.

Question 15.5

POPPITT contacts HUNN and tells him that he plans to steal a lorry full of designer clothes. HUNN tells POPPITT that he will store the goods after the theft and then sell them on for a share of the proceeds that will go to POPPITT.

Which of the following statements is correct with regard to the offence of handling stolen goods?

A Even though HUNN's actions are merely preparatory to the receiving of stolen goods, he commits the offence as he has arranged to receive them.

B HUNN commits an offence of handling stolen goods as the act of receiving does not require the physical reception of the goods.

C HUNN does not commit an offence of handling stolen goods in these circumstances.

D HUNN commits the offence of handling stolen goods as he has arranged to act for the benefit of another.

Question 15.6

DEAKIN has been charged with offences of handling stolen goods and theft. DEAKIN has a previous conviction for handing stolen goods that is six years old and a previous conviction for theft that is four years old.

Would the prosecution be able to use s. 27 of the Theft Act 1968 to prove that DEAKIN knew or believed the goods to be stolen goods?

A No, as both convictions are over 12 months old.

B Yes, but only in relation to the conviction for theft.

C No, as DEAKIN has been charged with theft as well as handling stolen goods.

D Yes, both previous convictions could be used.

Question 15.7

BARSTOW is a well-known handler of stolen goods. The police carry out a raid on his home address and find a large amount of property that they believe is associated with BARSTOW's criminal activity. Included in this property is a £30,000 sports car that BARSTOW bought with the proceeds of his handling enterprises, a painting by a local artist valued at £1,000 (BARSTOW actually bought the painting for cash, half of which was from a legitimate source, the other half from his handling offences) and a Rolex watch which BARSTOW had been given by a criminal associate. BARSTOW suspects that the watch is stolen but does not know for sure.

Which of these items, if any, would be covered by the term 'criminal property' under the Proceeds of Crime Act 2002?

A The £30,000 sports car only.

B The £30,000 sports car and the painting only.

C The £30,000 sports car, the painting and the Rolex watch.

D None of the items mentioned would be covered as the Proceeds of Crime Act relates to money only.

Question 15.8

MUTCH is a thief and steals several widescreen TV sets from a retail outlet. MUTCH alters the serial numbers and several other identification marks on the televisions to disguise them and make them look legitimate when he comes to sell them. Before he can actually sell them, MUTCH is arrested for the theft and the property is recovered from his home address.

Has MUTCH committed the offence of concealing criminal property (contrary to s. 327 of the Proceeds of Crime Act 2002)?

A No, because MUTCH is the original thief and cannot commit this offence as a consequence.

B Yes, as he has disguised criminal property.

C No, because he has not actually sold the property or exchanged it for other goods.

D Yes, as long as it can be shown that he intended to sell the goods outside the United Kingdom.

Question 15.9

STEWARD has been charged with an offence of handling stolen goods. The prosecution wish to use s. 27(3) of the Theft Act 1968 to show STEWARD's previous misconduct. STEWARD has a previous conviction for handling stolen goods that is eight years old and a previous conviction for theft that is four years old.

Which of the following statements is true?

A Provided that seven days' notice in writing has been given to STEWARD of the intention to prove the convictions, both convictions would be admissible.

B Provided that three days' notice in writing has been given to STEWARD of the intention to prove the conviction, the handling stolen goods conviction would be admissible.

C Provided that seven days' notice in writing has been given to STEWARD of the intention to prove the conviction, the theft conviction would be admissible.

D Provided that three days' notice in writing has been given to STEWARD of the intention to prove the convictions, both convictions would be admissible.

Question 15.10

ASTON is a career criminal involved in serious and high-value robbery offences. He carries out a robbery on a van carrying gold bullion and manages to get away with the contents of the van. To ship the gold abroad, he takes the gold to PULCHER and instructs PULCHER to melt the gold, turn into Eiffel Tower-shaped paperweights and ship it abroad to France—PULCHER is well aware of where the gold has come from. ASTON promises to pay PULCHER a hefty fee from the sale of the gold as and when he finally disposes of it abroad. PULCHER does as ASTON asks and six months later he receives a bank transfer from ASTON for £50,000.

Considering only the offence of acquisition, use and possession of criminal property (contrary to s. 329 of the Proceeds of Crime Act 2002), when does PULCHER first commit the offence?

A When he takes possession of the gold bullion from ASTON.

B When he melts the gold bullion down.

C When he ships the gold abroad.

D When he receives the £50,000 from ASTON.

Question 15.11

KELLY works as an accountant and is struggling with significant debts. He tells his supervisor, BROWN, about his debt situation and BROWN tells KELLY that he can help him. KELLY handles accounts for THOMAS who BROWN knows is a drug dealer looking to launder money through his accounts. BROWN speaks to THOMAS who agrees to pay off KELLY's debts if KELLY helps him to launder some of his drug money.

BROWN approaches KELLY and puts the deal to him. KELLY is not certain but suspects where the money originates from but is desperate and agrees to do as requested. Before any transfer of funds takes place, THOMAS is arrested in connection with supplying controlled drugs.

Considering only the offence of arrangements in relation to criminal property (contrary to s. 328 of the Proceeds of Crime Act 2002), which of the following comments is correct?

A The offence has not been committed by KELLY as no transfer of funds ever took place.

B The offence has been committed but only by KELLY.

C The offence has not been committed by KELLY as he only suspects that the money is drug-related funds.

D The offence has been committed by KELLY and by BROWN.

Question 15.12

MASSA steals a large amount of copper signal cabling from the side of a railway line and visits 'Scrap It!', a scrap metal dealership owned by BROOKE. MASSA goes into the office of the company where BROOKE is talking to SMITH (who is the site manager at the scrapyard) and tells BROOKE how much copper he has and offers the copper to BROOKE for £3,000. SMITH states that it is only worth £2,000 and BROOKE, listening to SMITH, tells MASSA that rather than pay MASSA £3,000, he will give MASSA a Ford Fiesta motor vehicle worth £2,200 for the copper—MASSA agrees and the exchange takes place later that afternoon at the scrapyard.

Who, if anyone, commits the offence of buying scrap metal for cash (contrary to s. 12 of the Scrap Metal Dealers Act 2013)?

A BROOKE only.

B BROOKE and SMITH.

C BROOKE, SMITH and MASSA.

D The offence has not been committed in these circumstances.

Question 15.13

Section 12 of the Scrap Metal Dealers Act 2013 makes it an offence to buy scrap metal for cash.

Which of the following comments correctly describes the mode of trial and sentence for this offence?

A It is summary only and punishable by a fine.

B It is summary only and punishable by six months' imprisonment and/or a fine.

C It is triable either way and punishable by a maximum term of three years' imprisonment.

D It is triable either way and punishable by a maximum term of five years' imprisonment and/or a fine.

ANSWERS

Answer 15.1

Answer **A** — Section 22 of the Theft Act 1968 states that a person can only handle stolen goods if he/she *'knows or believes'* the goods to be stolen. Any other state of mind, including suspicion, will not suffice, making answers B, C and D incorrect.

Investigators' Manual, paras 2.7.1 to 2.7.8

Answer 15.2

Answer **D** — CLIFF must know or believe the goods to be stolen and mere suspicion will not suffice, making answer A incorrect. To commit an offence of handling stolen goods, the retention, removal, disposal or realisation must be by or for the benefit of *another*. Retaining the car and then disposing of it is only done for the benefit of CLIFF so the offence is not made out, making answers B and C incorrect.

Investigators' Manual, paras 2.7.1, 2.7.7

Answer 15.3

Answer **C** — 'Stolen goods' under s. 24 of the Theft Act 1968 are those that directly or indirectly represent the stolen goods in the hands of the thief or the handler, or the original stolen goods themselves. The jewellery in the hands of VENN would be considered as stolen goods as he is the original thief. The £100 given to VENN and the games console he buys with the money indirectly represent the stolen goods in the hands of the thief. The jewellery in the hands of AUSTEN is the original stolen goods in the hands of the handler. The tickets exchanged for the jewellery indirectly represent the stolen goods in the hands of the handler. The ticket passed on to PEERS ceases to be 'stolen goods' as PEERS is in innocent possession of the ticket and has no idea as to its origin. Therefore, answers A, B and D are incorrect.

Investigators' Manual, para. 2.7.2

Answer 15.4

Answer **B** — Section 27 of the Theft Act 1968 allows a declaration of proof that goods were stolen to be made in proceedings for any theft or handling stolen goods from that theft. The declaration can be made by the person who dispatched the goods (FORD) or the person who failed to receive the goods (GREEN) and is admissible if a copy of the statement is given to the person charged (SMITH) at least seven days before the hearing or trial. This makes answers A, C and D incorrect.

Investigators' Manual, para. 2.7.4

Answer 15.5

Answer **C** — Although the conduct mentioned in answers A, B and D would qualify as activities associated with the offence of handling stolen goods, the offence will only be committed if the goods are stolen. If the goods have yet to be stolen, as in this case, then the offence is not committed.

Investigators' Manual, para. 2.7.1

Answer 15.6

Answer **C** — Section 27 of the Act can be used to prove that the defendant knew or believed the goods to be stolen goods if he: (i) had in his possession, or has undertaken or assisted in the retention, removal, disposal or realisation of, stolen goods from any theft taking place not earlier than 12 months before the offence charged; and (ii) evidence that he has within five years preceding the date of the offence charged been convicted of theft or of handling stolen goods. Therefore the conviction for handling stolen goods cannot be used, making answer D incorrect. Answer A is incorrect in relation to the time limits regarding the previous convictions. The prosecution may only use s. 27 if the defendant is being proceeded against in relation to a charge of handling stolen goods *alone* and not any other offence. As DEAKIN has been charged with theft in addition to handling stolen goods, the power under s. 27 cannot be used, making answer B incorrect.

Investigators' Manual, para. 2.7.8

Answer 15.7

Answer **C** — The term 'criminal property' relates to property that:

(a) constitutes a person's benefit from criminal conduct or represents such a benefit (in whole or in part and whether directly or indirectly); and
(b) the alleged offender knows or suspects that it constitutes or represents such a benefit.

It is not limited to money only, making answer D incorrect. The 'benefit' of BARSTOW's criminal activity is the sports car, the painting (even though half of the painting's purchase price came from a legitimate source) and the Rolex watch. In respect of the watch, the defendant need only suspect that the property constitutes or represents such a benefit.

Investigators' Manual, para. 2.9.3

Answer 15.8

Answer **B** — Answer A is incorrect as whereas handling only occurs 'otherwise than in the course of stealing' and 'by or for the benefit of another', the offence under s. 327 can potentially be committed *during the commission of an offence* and *for the benefit of the thief*. On a literal reading of s. 327, a thief who conceals, disguises or sells property that he has just stolen may thereby commit offences under that section because the definition of criminal property applies to the laundering of an offender's own proceeds of crime as well as those of someone else. The property need not be moved outside the United Kingdom, making answer D incorrect. The offence is committed if a person:

(a) conceals criminal property;
(b) disguises criminal property;
(c) converts criminal property;
(d) transfers criminal property;
(e) removes criminal property from England and Wales and Scotland or from Northern Ireland.

MUTCH therefore commits the offence when he disguises the TV sets.

Investigators' Manual, para. 2.9.4

Answer 15.9

Answer **C** — Seven days' notice in writing must be given to the defendant that the prosecution intend to prove previous convictions, making answers B and D incorrect. The defendant's previous convictions can be for theft or handling stolen goods; however, the conviction for the offence must be in the five years preceding the date of the offence charged. Therefore the handling conviction would not be admissible, making answer A incorrect.

Investigators' Manual, para. 2.7.8

Answer 15.10

Answer **A** — The offence under s. 329 is committed when a person acquires, uses or has possession of 'criminal property'. The gold bullion is most certainly criminal property so as soon as PULCHER takes possession of the gold bullion the offence is committed.

Investigators' Manual, paras 2.9.2 to 2.9.3, 2.9.6

Answer 15.11

Answer **D** — A person commits an offence under s. 328 of the Proceeds of Crime Act 2002 if he/she enters into or becomes concerned in an arrangement which he/she knows or suspects facilitates (by whatever means) the acquisition, retention, use or control of criminal property by or on behalf of another person. The fact that no transfer of funds ever took place is immaterial, making answer A incorrect. Answer C is incorrect as *suspicion* as to the nature of the criminal property will be enough. Answer B is incorrect as KELLY has entered into an arrangement and BROWN is concerned in the arrangement.

Investigators' Manual, para. 2.9.5

Answer 15.12

Answer **B** — Section 12 of the Scrap Metal Dealers Act 2013 states that a scrap metal dealer must not pay for scrap metal except by cheque (which is not transferable) or by an electronic transfer of funds. 'Paying' includes paying in kind with goods or services, so the offer of the Ford Fiesta would be covered. The person(s) who can commit the offence are:

- the scrap metal dealer (BROOKE);
- if the payment is made at the site, the site manager (SMITH);
- any person who makes the payment acting for the dealer.

This means that BROOKE and SMITH would commit the offence—MASSA would not. This makes answers A, C and D incorrect.

Investigators' Manual, para. 2.8.1

Answer 15.13

Answer **A** — The offence is a summary-only offence and is punishable by a fine.

Investigators' Manual, para. 2.8.1

16 Criminal Damage

QUESTIONS

Question 16.1

HARDCASTLE assists his wife in her job as a warden of a block of flats for pensioners. HARDCASTLE's wife constantly complains about the poor condition of the fire alarm and worries that if it is not changed the pensioners' lives will be in danger and there might be a large amount of damage caused to the flats if there is a fire. To demonstrate to the owner of the flats that the fire alarm is defective and needs changing, HARDCASTLE sets fire to some bedding in one of the flats. Eventually, the fire alarm activates and the fire is put out. HARDCASTLE is arrested for arson.

Would HARDCASTLE be able to claim that he had a lawful excuse to commit criminal damage?

A Yes, because the damage was caused in order to protect the property.

B No, because what has been done by HARDCASTLE is not done in order to protect property.

C Yes, because the damage was caused in order to protect the lives of the pensioners.

D No, because the element of 'lawful excuse' does not apply to offences of arson.

Question 16.2

WATE is a vicar who wishes to protest against Great Britain's involvement in military operations in the Middle East. He visits the Houses of Parliament and, as a sign of his disapproval of the military activities, he writes a quotation from the Bible in ink on a pillar outside the main door to the building. He honestly believes what he has done is morally right.

Considering the offence of criminal damage (contrary to s. 1(1) of the Criminal Damage Act 1971), which of the following statements is correct?

A WATE would have a defence if he claims he had damaged the property as a reasonable means of protecting other property located in Afghanistan from being damaged by warfare.

B WATE would have a defence if he claimed that he was carrying out God's instructions and therefore had a lawful excuse based on his belief that God was entitled to consent to such damage.

C WATE has not committed criminal damage. It is immaterial whether his beliefs for causing criminal damage were justified; what matters is that the beliefs were honestly held.

D WATE is guilty of criminal damage because it has been held that a belief in The Almighty's consent is not a lawful excuse and that such conduct would be too remote from any need to protect property in Afghanistan.

Question 16.3

DYKE has a long-standing disagreement with MONK over who owns a section of land that lies between their respective houses. One evening, after DYKE has been drinking at his local pub, he decides to get revenge on MONK and walks up the drive of MONK's house intent on damaging MONK's property.

At what point does DYKE first commit an offence of criminal damage?

A As DYKE enters the driveway he stamps on and destroys some flowers that are growing wild at the entrance to the drive.

B DYKE passes a garden shed owned by MONK and, although he knows it will easily be washed off, he smears the word 'Wanker' in mud across the shed.

C DYKE picks up a large container of black paint and pours this over MONK's front lawn.

D DYKE approaches a chicken coop and reaches inside. He picks up a chicken and breaks its legs.

Question 16.4

FALLON is homeless and searching for somewhere to sleep for the night. He breaks into an abandoned detached house and, using some old furniture for fuel, sets a fire that quickly burns out of control, destroying part of the house. FALLON only escapes with his life because of the rapid attendance of the fire brigade. Because of the gap between the neighbouring houses there is no likelihood that the fire will spread to any other buildings.

Would FALLON be liable for an offence under s. 1(2) of the Criminal Damage Act 1971?

A Yes, because of FALLON's actions he recklessly endangered his own life.

B No, because FALLON did not intend to endanger his own or any other person's life.

C Yes, what matters is the potential for damage and danger created by FALLON's conduct.

D No, because the fire brigade attended and because of the gap between the houses, there was no actual danger to life.

Question 16.5

MAYHEW breaks off his engagement to CUTHBERT, who takes the news badly. CUTHBERT is desperate to rekindle the relationship and phones MAYHEW telling him that unless the two of them get back together, she will steal his car, set it alight and burn herself alive in it. CUTHBERT does not intend to carry out her threat but does intend for MAYHEW to believe her. Unknown to CUTHBERT, MAYHEW has sold his car and so does not actually fear that the threat will be carried out.

Which of the following statements is correct with regard to a threat to destroy or damage property under s. 2 of the Criminal Damage Act 1971?

A CUTHBERT is not guilty of the offence because MAYHEW has sold his car and therefore knows that the threat is incapable of being carried out.

B The offence is not committed because CUTHBERT has not threatened to destroy or damage her own property.

C The offence is not committed because CUTHBERT never intended to carry out her threat.

D CUTHBERT has committed the offence because her intention was to make MAYHEW fear that the threat would be carried out.

Question 16.6

FISHER argues with NEGUS and decides that he will take revenge on him by pouring a container of paint stripper over NEGUS's car. FISHER does not have any paint stripper and so visits a garage owned by SMITH and asks if he will provide him with the paint stripper. When SMITH asks why FISHER wants it, FISHER tells him of his plan. SMITH tells FISHER that the paint stripper is at the back of his garage and advises FISHER to wait for a week before he actually commits the criminal damage so that

NEGUS will not suspect that FISHER is responsible. FISHER collects the paint stripper and tells SMITH that he will take his advice.

Considering the offence of having articles with intent to destroy or damage property (s. 3 of the Criminal Damage Act 1971) only, which of the following statements is correct?

A In these circumstances, both SMITH and FISHER would commit the offence.

B Only SMITH commits this offence as FISHER is not the owner of the paint stripper and therefore cannot have custody or control over it.

C Only FISHER commits the offence as he is the only person who actually has physical possession of the paint stripper.

D Neither SMITH nor FISHER commits the offence as the criminal damage will take place at some time in the future.

ANSWERS

Answer 16.1

Answer **B** — Answer D is incorrect as the element of lawful excuse is contained within the s. 1(2) offence. Section 5(2) of the Criminal Damage Act 1971 gives the circumstances when a person may have a lawful excuse to damage or destroy property. This must involve an *immediate* need for the action taken in order to protect the property and also that the means adopted were reasonable having regard to the circumstances. In this question, HARDCASTLE's activities would not fall into either of the last two categories and the element of 'lawful excuse' would not be satisfied, making answers A and C incorrect (action taken in order to draw attention to a defective fire alarm and not done in order to protect property would not be a 'lawful excuse').

Investigators' Manual, para. 2.10.2.6

Answer 16.2

Answer **D** — This question is based on the case of *Blake* v *DPP* [1993] Crim LR 586. Although the two defences under s. 5(2)(a) and (b) both involve the honestly held belief of the defendant, it does not mean that *any* honestly held belief will suffice, making answer C incorrect. *Blake* protested against Great Britain's involvement in the Gulf War and damaged a pillar outside the Houses of Parliament. His defence was as per answers A and B and the Divisional Court's response was as per answer D.

Investigators' Manual, para. 2.10.2.6

Answer 16.3

Answer **B** — Under s. 10 of the Criminal Damage Act 1971, flowers growing wild on any land would not be classed as property making answer A incorrect. The items referred to in options B, C and D would all be classed as property; land can be subject to criminal damage along with wild creatures that are ordinarily kept in captivity or have been reduced into possession (the chickens). There is no requirement that criminal damage be associated with an economic loss. It has been held by the Divisional Court that graffiti smeared in mud, even though it is easily washed off, can amount to criminal damage (*Roe* v *Kingerlee* [1986] Crim LR 735). Therefore, the offence is first committed at point B.

Investigators' Manual, para. 2.10.2.2

Answer 16.4

Answer **C** — The aggravated form of criminal damage can only be committed if the life endangered is someone else's other than the defendant's, making answers A and B incorrect. Answer B is further incorrect as the offence can be committed recklessly. Answer D is incorrect, as it does not matter that there was no *actual* danger to life. What is relevant is the *potential danger* to life.

Investigators' Manual, para. 2.10.3

Answer 16.5

Answer **D** — The central element for the commission of this offence is that the defendant *intended* the complainant to fear that the threat would be carried out. That threat can be to destroy or damage property belonging to that or another person or to destroy or damage his/her own property in a way that will endanger the life of that other or a third person, making answer B incorrect. The fact that CUTHBERT never intended to carry out her threat or that the threat is incapable of being carried out makes no difference, making answers A and C incorrect.

Investigators' Manual, para. 2.10.5

Answer 16.6

Answer **A** — The offence under s. 3 of the Act is committed when an individual has anything in his *custody or control* intending without lawful excuse to *use it* or *cause or permit another to use it* to destroy or damage property belonging to another or to destroy or damage his own or another's property in such a way that he knows is likely to endanger the life of some other person. It is not necessary to be the owner of the item in order to commit this offence, making answer B incorrect. Neither is it necessary to actually have physical possession of the item, making answer C incorrect. The fact that the damage is planned for a week's time is immaterial as it is the intention of the parties that is relevant for this offence, making answer D incorrect.

Investigators' Manual, para. 2.10.6

PART THREE

Assaults, Drugs, Firearms and Gun Crime

17 Homicide

QUESTIONS

Question 17.1

FOZIA despises her husband, ALI. For years, ALI has subjected FOZIA to repeated physical and verbal abuse, making her life a misery. One night FOZIA is severely beaten by ALI. The attack proves to be 'the last straw' for FOZIA. After the attack FOZIA decides that enough is enough and plans to kill ALI. She waits for him to fall asleep and attacks him with a claw hammer. She strikes ALI five times about the head, causing serious injuries but not, as she intended, ALI's death.

Which of the following statements is correct?

A FOZIA has committed an attempted murder but because she suffered abuse over a prolonged period, she may raise the 'special defence' of loss of control.

B FOZIA has committed an attempted murder and would be able to use any of the 'special defences' provided by the Homicide Act 1957 or by the Coroners and Justice Act 2009.

C FOZIA's intention to kill ALI provides the *mens rea* needed to support a charge of attempted murder but she would not be able to use any 'special defences'.

D FOZIA has committed an attempted murder but could raise diminished responsibility as a defence if she can prove she was suffering from 'battered wives' syndrome'.

Question 17.2

PIGGOT and LAY both own burger bars. They pitch next to each other in a prime location on a bridge over a subway near a football ground on match days. The subway is a well-used route to the football ground by pedestrians; a fact that both PIGGOT and LAY are fully aware of. The pair become involved in an argument about stealing trade from each other and PIGGOT, in a fit of rage, picks up a tray of canned drinks from the counter of LAY's burger bar and throws the tray over the bridge. The tray of drinks strikes YEO, who is walking along the subway to the match, and kills him.

Does PIGGOT commit the offence of manslaughter by unlawful act?

A Yes, as long as PIGGOT foresaw the risk of somebody being harmed.

B No, as PIGGOT does not have the *mens rea* for assault.

C Yes, the risk of someone being harmed will be judged objectively.

D No, as PIGGOT's initial action was not directed or aimed at a person.

Question 17.3

CHALLINOR and BARNSLEY, both British citizens, are on holiday in Cuba (a country not forming part of the Commonwealth). The two men are having dinner when an argument takes place over who will pay for the meal. CHALLINOR loses his temper, picks up a steak knife from the table and stabs BARNSLEY in the chest. BARNSLEY immediately dies from his injuries.

Could CHALLINOR be tried in this country for the offence of murder?

A No, as the offence was committed outside the jurisdiction of the English courts CHALLINOR would have to be tried in Cuba under Cuban law.

B Yes, any British citizen who commits a murder anywhere in the world may be tried in England and Wales.

C No, the Offences Against the Person Act 1861 makes it clear that such offences may only be tried in this country if the act is committed in a country belonging to the Commonwealth.

D Yes, but this is only because both CHALLINOR and BARNSLEY are British citizens.

Question 17.4

STEWARD is seven months pregnant when MORRELL, her boyfriend, finds out that she has had an affair and the child may not be his. MORRELL attacks STEWARD intending to cause her serious harm. He stabs her in the stomach and, in the process of doing so, not only seriously injures STEWARD but also injures the unborn child. STEWARD is rushed to hospital where, as a result of the attack, she prematurely gives birth. The child is born alive but subsequently dies three days after the incident from the injuries received from being stabbed whilst in STEWARD's womb.

Considering the law regarding murder and manslaughter only, what is MORRELL's criminal liability regarding the child?

A In these circumstances, MORRELL has no criminal liability regarding the child.
B MORRELL can only face criminal charges relating to the child if he intended to kill STEWARD.
C As MORRELL intended to cause serious harm to STEWARD, he is guilty of the murder of the child.
D MORRELL's intention to cause serious injury to STEWARD may support a charge of manslaughter of the child.

Question 17.5

BUSHELL is involved in a fight with GREY. BUSHELL intends to cause grievous bodily harm to GREY and does so. BUSHELL is arrested and convicted for a s. 18 wounding (contrary to the Offences Against the Person Act 1861) and receives a 15-year jail sentence. Two years after the attack, GREY dies as a direct consequence of the injuries received during the fight with BUSHELL.

With regard to the law relating to murder, which of the following statements is correct?

A BUSHELL cannot be charged with the murder of GREY as the *mens rea* needed for a murder conviction is the intention to kill only.
B As BUSHELL has already been convicted in circumstances connected with the death of GREY, the consent of the Attorney General is needed before bringing a prosecution.
C If convicted of murder, BUSHELL must be sentenced to life imprisonment unless there are exceptional circumstances surrounding the case.
D BUSHELL cannot be charged with murder as he has already been convicted of an offence committed under the circumstances connected with the death.

Question 17.6

APPLETON is employed by Jays Heating Ltd to fit a central heating system in CURTIS's house. The company director, HUNTER, failed to check whether APPLETON had any formal qualifications to fit the system; APPLETON does not. As a consequence he fails to connect a vital part of the central heating system. The result of this failure is that CURTIS dies from leaking fumes. Sergeant JENNINGS investigates the incident.

Which of the following comments is correct?

A In these circumstances APPLETON could be guilty of manslaughter by gross negligence.

B Whether a defendant's conduct amounts to gross negligence is a question of law which falls to the trial judge to decide.

C APPLETON must have committed an unlawful act in order to be successfully prosecuted for an offence of manslaughter by gross negligence.

D Jays Heating Ltd could not be prosecuted for an offence of manslaughter by gross negligence unless the company director (HUNTER) was physically responsible for the central heating system failure.

Question 17.7

DCs MORA, PERCOX, RUSSELL and POOLE are seconded to a murder enquiry and are discussing the offence. During their discussion, several statements are made regarding the offence of murder.

Which one of their statements is correct?

A DC MORA states that if a victim of an alleged murder dies more than a year and a day after receiving their injury, then the consent of the Attorney General is required before bringing a prosecution.

B DC PERCOX states that a defendant who successfully advances the defence of 'loss of control' will be acquitted of the offence of murder and found guilty of involuntary manslaughter.

C DC RUSSELL states that in order to prove an offence of murder, the prosecution must show some degree of premeditation on the part of the defendant.

D DC POOLE states that the term 'unlawful killing' includes occasions where someone fails to act after creating a situation of danger.

Question 17.8

Section 5 of the Domestic Violence, Crime and Victims Act 2004 creates an offence of causing or allowing a child or vulnerable adult to die or suffer serious physical harm.

What does the term 'child' mean for the purposes of this offence?

A A 'child' is a person under the age of 10.

B A 'child' is a person under the age of 14.

C A 'child' is a person under the age of 16.

D A 'child' is a person under the age of 18.

ANSWERS

Answer 17.1

Answer **C** — FOZIA's *mens rea* to kill ALI is the only state of mind that would support a charge of attempted murder. Regardless of the motives FOZIA has to commit the offence, she does not kill ALI and would, therefore, only be liable for that offence. The 'special defences' of diminished responsibility, loss of control and suicide pact are only available to a defendant who is responsible for murder, making answers A, B and D incorrect.

Investigators' Manual, paras 3.1.2, 3.1.3, 3.1.3.1, 3.1.3.2

Answer 17.2

Answer **C** — This is an offence of manslaughter by an unlawful act. To prove the offence there must be: (i) an inherently unlawful act by the defendant; (ii) evidence that the act involved the risk of somebody being harmed (a risk that will be judged objectively, making answer A incorrect); and (iii) proof that the defendant had the required *mens rea* for the unlawful act which leads to the death of the victim. The unlawful act does not have to be aimed or directed against a person; it can be aimed at property, making answer D incorrect. Answer B is incorrect for the same reason; the *mens rea* required is for the specific act carried out by the defendant, in this case, theft of the tray of drinks and not necessarily the offence of assault.

Investigators' Manual, paras 3.1.4, 3.1.4.1

Answer 17.3

Answer **B** — Under the provisions of s. 9 of the Offences Against the Person Act 1861, any British citizen who commits a murder anywhere in the world may be tried in England or Wales. Jurisdiction is not an issue, making answer A incorrect. Whether the country where the offence took place is a part of the Commonwealth or not makes no difference, so answer C is incorrect. The only issue relating to country of origin is if the defendant, not the victim, is a British citizen, making answer D incorrect.

Investigators' Manual, para. 3.1.2

Answer 17.4

Answer **D** — This is a complex area of the law touching on the doctrine of transferred *mens rea*. The answer also depends on the state of mind of the offender. If, as in this case, the defendant only intends to cause serious harm to the mother and as a result of the attack the baby dies after being born, then it is possible, after the ruling in *Attorney General's Reference (No. 3 of 1994)* [1998] AC 245, to charge the defendant with manslaughter. If the defendant intended to kill the mother then this intention could be sufficient to bring a charge of murder.

Investigators' Manual, para. 3.1.2

Answer 17.5

Answer **B** — Answer A is incorrect as the *mens rea* for murder is an intention to kill or an intention to cause grievous bodily harm. Answer C is incorrect as the sentence for murder is a mandatory life sentence regardless of the surrounding circumstances. If a defendant has already been convicted of an offence relating to the incident that causes the eventual death of the victim it will not prevent a charge of murder being made against the defendant. The consent of the Attorney General is required for such action (s. 2(2)(a) of the Law Reform (Year and a Day Rule) Act 1996), making answer D incorrect and answer B correct.

Investigators' Manual, paras 3.1.2, 3.1.2.1, 3.1.2.2

Answer 17.6

Answer **A** — Whether a defendant's conduct amounts to gross negligence is a question for the jury to decide, not the judge, making answer B incorrect. An unlawful act is not required for a person to be prosecuted for the offence of manslaughter by gross negligence, making answer C incorrect. Answer D is incorrect as it does not matter whether HUNTER was physically responsible for the central heating system failure; it is not possible to bring proceedings for gross negligent manslaughter against a company or other organisation to which the offence under the Corporate Manslaughter and Corporate Homicide Act 2007 applies (s. 20 of the Corporate Manslaughter and Corporate Homicide Act 2007).

Investigators' Manual, paras 3.1.4, 3.1.4.1, 3.1.4.2

Answer 17.7

Answer **D** — Statement A is incorrect as the consent of the Attorney General is only required if the victim dies more than three years after receiving their injury or if the defendant has already been convicted of an offence committed under the circumstances connected with the death. Statement B is incorrect as a successful special defence plea reduces the offence from murder to *voluntary* manslaughter. Statement C is incorrect as premeditation is not required to prove an offence of murder.

Investigators' Manual, paras 3.1.2, 3.1.3

Answer 17.8

Answer **C** — For the purposes of an offence under s. 5 of the Act, a 'child' is a person under the age of 16.

Investigators' Manual, para. 3.1.6

18 Non-fatal Offences against the Person

QUESTIONS

Question 18.1

GUNNING is walking his dog in a park. Although he knows his dog is bad-tempered there is nobody else in the park and so he lets his dog off its lead and allows it to run free. Just after GUNNING lets his dog free, O'HARE walks into the park. Because GUNNING has omitted to keep his dog on the lead, the dog runs towards O'HARE. O'HARE is frightened of the dog and believes it will bite him. GUNNING runs up to his dog and puts it back on the lead. O'HARE says, *'You bloody idiot, if your dog wasn't with you I'd kick your head in!'* GUNNING is annoyed by the comment and lets his dog off the lead again saying, *'Bite him boy!'* The dog bites O'HARE.

At what point, if at all, is an assault committed?

A When, because of GUNNING's omission, his dog causes O'HARE to believe he will be bitten.

B When O'HARE threatens GUNNING.

C When GUNNING sets his dog on O'HARE.

D An assault has not taken place in these circumstances.

Question 18.2

ILLINGWORTH makes a series of telephone calls to FENNEL over a period of several days. One day, he makes 14 phone calls within a one-hour period. When FENNEL answers the phone, ILLINGWORTH remains silent, sometimes for several minutes. FENNEL suffers psychiatric harm as a result.

Which of the following comments is true?

A ILLINGWORTH could only be charged with a s. 47 assault (contrary to the Offences Against the Person Act 1861), as psychiatric injuries can never amount to a s. 20 assault (contrary to the Offences Against the Person Act 1861).

B No assault is committed because 'silence' would not constitute the *actus reus* of an assault.

C ILLINGWORTH could be charged with a s. 20 assault (contrary to the Offences Against the Person Act 1861) as serious or really serious harm includes psychiatric injury.

D In these circumstances no assault is committed as the victim and the defendant are not face to face when the threats take place.

Question 18.3

LAKER is a prostitute. She is contacted by SAINSBURY, a sadomasochist, who tells her that he wishes to beat her for his sexual gratification. LAKER agrees to SAINSBURY's offer and meets him in a hotel room where, during sexual intercourse, SAINSBURY punches LAKER in the face and breaks two of her front teeth. A member of staff at the hotel hears LAKER crying out and calls the police, who arrive just as SAINSBURY is paying LAKER for her services.

Considering the issues in relation to 'consent', which of the following statements is correct?

A LAKER has consented to the use of force so any assault and battery committed on her person is lawful and as a consequence no offence is committed.

B All assaults that result in more than transient harm will be unlawful unless there is good reason for allowing the plea of 'consent'.

C Consensual activity between LAKER and SAINSBURY would not be classed as a matter for criminal investigation.

D The European Court of Human Rights has held that consensual sadomasochistic injuries may not justifiably be made the subject of criminal law.

Question 18.4

ELVIN is a store detective who witnesses YEUNG stealing a bottle of whisky from a supermarket. ELVIN arrests YEUNG outside the supermarket, at which point YEUNG punches ELVIN in the face and runs off. ELVIN chases after YEUNG and catches her 200 metres away where the two begin fighting. GILLIGAN sees the struggle and believes that ELVIN is trying to rob YEUNG. GILLIGAN punches ELVIN in the face and as a result YEUNG manages to escape.

Who, if anyone, has committed the offence of assault with intent to resist arrest (contrary to s. 38 of the Offences Against the Person Act 1861)?

A Only YEUNG commits the offence.

B Only GILLIGAN commits the offence as he is preventing the lawful apprehension of another.

C Both YEUNG and GILLIGAN commit the offence.

D Neither YEUNG nor GILLIGAN commits the offence because ELVIN is not a police officer.

Question 18.5

BARTLEY and FABWELL play for rival Sunday League football teams. They are drinking in the same pub on the Saturday evening before the two teams meet in a grudge match. BARTLEY shouts over to FABWELL, *'You're gonna get your legs broken tomorrow!'* FABWELL replies by shouting *'And if you weren't with all your mates you'd get your legs broken now!'* BARTLEY walks over to FABWELL and says, *'If you don't leave this pub right now, you're gonna get a kicking!'*

At what point, if at all, is an assault committed?

A When BARTLEY shouts over to FABWELL *'You're gonna get your legs broken tomorrow!'*

B When FABWELL shouts at BARTLEY *'And if you weren't with all your mates you'd get your legs broken now!'*

C When BARTLEY walks over to FABWELL and says, *'If you don't leave this pub right now, you're gonna get a kicking!'*

D No offence of assault is committed in these circumstances.

Question 18.6

GAUNT is looking after his two children (aged 12 and 14). The two children are behaving badly and while play fighting with each other they topple into a TV set, smashing it in the process. GAUNT is extremely angry and hits both children. The blows result in the 12-year-old child receiving injuries that would qualify as a s. 39 battery (contrary to s. 39 of the Criminal Justice Act 1988) and the 14-year-old child receiving injuries that would qualify as a s. 47 assault (contrary to s. 47 of the Offences Against the Person Act 1861). The children complain to the police about the assaults.

Considering the general issue of lawful chastisement and the Children Act 2004, which of the following statements is true?

A GAUNT commits an offence in respect of both assaults but could use the defence of 'lawful chastisement' in respect of the s. 39 assault against the 12-year-old child.

B The Children Act 2004 is only relevant to the 12-year-old child. GAUNT commits an offence in respect of this child only.

C The Children Act 2004 will allow GAUNT to justify both assaults as they constitute reasonable punishment.

D GAUNT commits an offence with regard to the s. 47 assault on the 14-year-old child only.

Question 18.7

PC COPPLE is dealing with an incident where several assaults and public order offences were committed. The officer is considering the possibility of charging several of the participants in the disorder with the offence of obstruct police (contrary to s. 89 of the Police Act 1996) and approaches you for some advice on the matter. The officer tells you that during the incident HARTELL was spoken to by the police but refused to answer any questions, NORRIS stood in the doorway of a house and blocked police access to the premises for several minutes, STANSFIELD made a telephone call on his mobile phone providing a false location of the disorder to the police resulting in other officers attending the incorrect address several streets away from the incident and CARTER stood in his doorway several feet from the incident and did nothing to assist the police when the disorder began. All three were later arrested for assaults.

Which of the following comments is correct?

A Obstruct police requires some sort of physical opposition so the only person who commits the offence is NORRIS.

B NORRIS and STANSFIELD commit the offence, HARTELL does not. CARTER would only commit the offence if he were under some duty towards the police to assist them.

C All four commit the offence of obstruct police in these circumstances.

D HARTELL, NORRIS and STANSFIELD commit the offence.

Question 18.8

BALDWIN hates HIGGS as the two have had numerous fights with each other. BALDWIN is drinking in his local pub when he sees ROBERTS, a friend of HIGGS, walk into the pub. BALDWIN approaches ROBERTS and says, '*Next week I'm getting a gun and I'm gonna use it to kill HIGGS*.' BALDWIN does not intend ROBERTS to believe the threat will be carried out; he just enjoys intimidating HIGGS's friends. ROBERTS believes BALDWIN and passes the threat on to HIGGS, who does not fear the threat at all.

Why has no offence of making a threat to kill (s. 16 of the Offences Against the Person Act 1861) been committed?

A Because BALDWIN has made a threat to kill another person at some time in the future.

B Because the person to whom the threat is directed (HIGGS) does not fear that the threat would be carried out.

C Because the threat has been made to a third party (ROBERTS), rather than the person to whom the threat is directed.

D Because the person making the threat does not do so with the intention that the person receiving it (ROBERTS) would fear it would be carried out.

Question 18.9

GLANVILLE is having a bonfire party but does not invite HOCKLEY. HOCKLEY feels insulted and so, when GLANVILLE is out, he places a small gas canister at the base of the bonfire believing that when it is lit the canister will explode and put the bonfire out. HOCKLEY believes that this is perfectly safe although there is a very minor chance that the explosion may hurt someone. During the party, the bonfire is lit and five minutes later the canister explodes. The gas canister hits GLANVILLE in the temple, causing him to lose consciousness.

Which of the following statements is true regarding HOCKLEY's liability for an offence of assault?

A HOCKLEY is not liable because for an assault to be committed, force must be applied directly. The placing of the canister in the bonfire is an indirect application of force.

B HOCKLEY is liable for an offence as he foresees the possibility of someone being hurt but nevertheless goes on to take the risk.

C HOCKLEY is not liable because he must actually intend to cause harm to some person when placing the canister in the bonfire.

D HOCKLEY is liable because the risk of the canister exploding and causing harm would have been obvious to any reasonable person.

Question 18.10

CATON steals a car and is pursued by PC STONE, who is driving a police livery vehicle. CATON drives into a cul-de-sac and is followed by the officer. CATON realises that there is no way out of the cul-de-sac and that he will be arrested if he does not ram PC STONE's vehicle. Intending to escape and avoid arrest, CATON drives into the officer's car. CATON realises that this may cause some harm to PC STONE. The resulting crash causes multiple cuts to PC STONE's face, requiring 100 stitches. CATON is caught several minutes later.

With regard to assaults under the Offences Against the Person Act 1861, which of the following statements is correct?

A In these circumstances, CATON has 'inflicted' the injury and so the appropriate offence would be one of a s. 20 wounding.

B CATON commits s. 20 wounding, as there was no intent to wound the officer.

C CATON's actions were malicious and carried out in order to resist arrest. This means that he commits s. 18 wounding.

D CATON's actions would not provide the evidence required for a successful prosecution under s. 18 or 20 of the Offences Against the Person Act.

Question 18.11

BROSTER puts a letter through FELLOWS's front door intending that when FELLOWS reads the letter he will fear immediate unlawful violence. To create that fear, BROSTER has written words in the letter containing numerous threats of unlawful personal violence that will take place a minute or two after FELLOWS reads the letter. FELLOWS reads the letter and as a consequence he believes that he is going to be immediately assaulted.

Would BROSTER's activities constitute an assault?

A No, because FELLOWS cannot fear immediate personal violence.

B Yes, as long as the force or violence apprehended by FELLOWS is a certainty.

C No, words, whether said or written, can never amount to an assault.

D Yes, where the words threatening immediate unlawful force come in the form of a letter, an assault may have been committed.

Question 18.12

STANFORD and HARTELL are neighbours who have had a long-standing dispute over car parking outside their respective houses. One afternoon, STANFORD parks his car directly outside HARTELL's house. HARTELL sees this and, grabbing hold of an imitation pistol, he runs outside and confronts STANFORD. Intending to make STANFORD believe he will be subject to immediate unlawful violence, HARTELL points the imitation pistol at STANFORD and says, *'If you don't move your car, I'll shoot you!'* HARTELL believes the threat and moves his car.

Considering the offences of assault and battery only (under s. 39 of the Criminal Justice Act 1988), which of the following comments is true?

A STANFORD's actions would constitute a 'battery'.

B STANFORD does not commit an assault as this is a conditional threat.

C STANFORD has committed an offence of 'assault'.

D STANFORD does not commit an assault as he cannot physically harm HARTELL with an imitation pistol.

ANSWERS

Answer 18.1

Answer **C** — Answer A is incorrect, as an assault cannot be committed by an omission. When O'HARE threatens to assault GUNNING it is a conditional threat; the assault will not be committed because of the presence of the dog and, therefore, GUNNING cannot fear immediate application of force. An assault is committed at point C because the 'indirect' application of force (via the dog) qualifies as an assault.

Investigators' Manual, paras 3.2.2, 3.2.3, 3.2.4

Answer 18.2

Answer **C** — In *R* v *Ireland* [1998] AC 147, it was held that telephone calls to a victim, followed by silences, could amount to an assault. This makes answers B and D incorrect. The harm caused in *R* v *Ireland* was psychiatric harm and the offender was charged and convicted of a s. 47 assault. This does not mean that psychiatric harm caused to the victim will limit the charge to a s. 47 assault only; there is nothing to stop an offence of s. 20 assault being committed when the harm is of a psychiatric nature, making answer A incorrect.

Investigators' Manual, paras 3.2.2.3, 3.2.12

Answer 18.3

Answer **B** — A person may consent to the use of force on their person but that does not mean that a person causing the injury will be able to use 'consent' as a defence against a charge relating to assaults, making answer A incorrect. Whether the defence has any merit will often depend on the circumstances and the degree of harm caused. There are several cases that relate to this proposition, the most notable being *R* v *Brown* [1994] 1 AC 212. In this case, the House of Lords followed a policy decision that mirrors answer B. In *R* v *Wilson* (1996) 2 Cr App R 241, the court held that consensual activity between husband and wife is not a matter for criminal investigation, although this would depend on the degree of harm caused, making answer C incorrect. The European Court of Human Rights considered the case of *R* v *Brown* (mentioned previously) and held that it could justifiably be made the subject of criminal investigation on the grounds of 'protection of health' and that investigation and prosecution of such activity did not infringe the Article 8 rights to private life.

Investigators' Manual, paras 3.2.5, 3.2.6, 3.2.7

Answer 18.4

Answer **A** — This offence applies to arrests made by several groups of people including store detectives, making answer D incorrect. To commit the offence the offender must assault any person knowing that the person assaulted was trying to make or help in an arrest. This knowledge is not present in GILLIGAN's mind, making answers B and C incorrect.

Investigators' Manual, para. 3.2.14.1

Answer 18.5

Answer **C** — No offence is committed at point A because the threat does not involve immediacy, i.e. the threat is to assault the next day. Point B is a conditional threat meaning that no assault will take place because BARTLEY has his friends with him. At point C an assault is committed because this is an immediate threat conditional upon some real circumstance. If FABWELL does not leave the pub he will be assaulted. This makes answer D incorrect.

Investigators' Manual, para. 3.2.2.4

Answer 18.6

Answer **A** — The Children Act 2004 applies to persons under 18 years of age, making answer B incorrect. The Children Act 2004 states that a battery of a person under 18 cannot be justified on the ground that it constituted reasonable punishment in relation to an offence of s. 47, 18 or 20 of the Offences Against the Person Act 1861, making answer C incorrect. However, where an assault amounting to an offence of s. 39 of the Criminal Justice Act 1988 is committed, although this is still an offence (making answer D incorrect) the defence of lawful chastisement is available.

Investigators' Manual, para. 3.2.8

Answer 18.7

Answer **B** — HARTELL's refusal to answer police questions is not obstruction, making answers C and D incorrect. Although obstruct police may involve some sort of physical opposition (NORRIS), it can also be committed by making it more difficult for a constable to carry out his/her duty (STANSFIELD), making answer A incorrect. Obstruction can be caused by omission (CARTER) but only where the defendant was already under some duty towards the police or the officer.

Investigators' Manual, para. 3.2.14.3

Answer 18.8

Answer **D** — The offence of making a threat to kill can only be committed if it can be shown that the threat was made with the *intention* that *the person receiving it* would fear it would be carried out. It is the *intention* of the person who makes the threat that is important in this offence. It is immaterial that the threat to kill is a threat to kill another in the future, making answer A incorrect. It is also immaterial that the person to whom the threat is directed does not believe the threat and that that threat has been made via a third party, making answers B and C incorrect.

Investigators' Manual, para. 3.2.15

Answer 18.9

Answer **B** — An assault can be committed by the direct or indirect application of force, making answer A incorrect. The state of mind required for the offence to be complete is that the defendant either intended to cause harm or subjective recklessness as to that consequence, making answer C incorrect. Subjective recklessness involves the belief of the person committing the offence, not the objective view of a reasonable person, making answer D incorrect.

Investigators' Manual, paras 3.2.2, 3.2.3

Answer 18.10

Answer **C** — Whilst there is no intention to wound, CATON's actions are 'malicious'. Maliciousness means that the defendant must realise that there is a risk of some harm being caused to the victim. The defendant does not need to foresee the degree of harm that is eventually caused, only that his/her behaviour may bring about some harm to the victim. When the harm is caused with *intent* to *resist or prevent lawful apprehension* (arrest), the s. 18 grievous bodily harm/wounding offence is made out. This makes answers A, B and D incorrect.

Investigators' Manual, paras 3.2.12, 3.2.13

Answer 18.11

Answer **D** — Answer A is incorrect as, in *R* v *Ireland* [1998] AC 147, the House of Lords suggested that a threat to cause violence 'in a minute or two' might be enough to qualify as an assault. The force or violence apprehended by the victim does not have to be a 'certainty'. Causing fear of some possible violence can be enough (*R* v *Ireland*), making answer B incorrect. Words can amount to an assault provided they are accompanied by the required *mens rea*, making answer C incorrect. In *R* v *Constanza* [1997] 2 Cr App R 492, it was held by the Court of Appeal that where the words threatening immediate unlawful force come in the form of letters, an assault may have been committed.

Investigators' Manual, para. 3.2.2.2

Answer 18.12

Answer **C** — A 'battery' is the actual application of force requiring some degree of contact; there has been no such contact so answer A is incorrect. Answer D is incorrect as even though the pistol is an imitation and incapable of firing it is the intention of the defendant coupled with the belief of the victim that is important. These circumstances would constitute an assault (answer C). Answer B is incorrect as this *is not* a conditional threat. A conditional threat would be something like STANFORD approaching HARTELL and pointing the pistol at him and saying, *'If you ever park your car outside my house I'll shoot you!'* The threat in the question is different as it is an immediate threat conditional upon some real circumstance—move your car or else!

Investigators' Manual, paras 3.2.2, 3.2.3

19 Child Abduction, False Imprisonment and Kidnap

QUESTIONS

Question 19.1

HILL has separated from his common-law wife, YEO. There is a 15-year-old child by this relationship and the two have an informal understanding that HILL will have the child at weekends and YEO will have the child during the week. On Tuesday afternoon, YEO comes to your police station to report an offence of child abduction. She tells you that she has received a telephone call from HILL telling her he has taken the child to Germany and will not be back for two more weeks. HILL stated he had attempted to contact YEO but had been unable to communicate with her. YEO wants HILL arrested and charged with the offence of child abduction (contrary to s. 1 of the Child Abduction Act 1984).

What will you tell her?

A HILL has not committed an offence under this legislation as it only applies to a child under the age of 14.

B HILL has committed the offence but he may be able to avail himself of a defence to the charge in these circumstances.

C HILL has not committed the offence as the child has been taken out of the United Kingdom for less than one month.

D HILL has committed the offence but the consent of the Attorney General is required before a charge of child abduction is brought.

Question 19.2

HAYMAN (aged 16 years) and NICHOLL (aged 13 years) are in a park when they are approached by EAMES (aged 30 years). EAMES tells them that he has just had his bike stolen and asks them if they would help him look for it. This is not true as EAMES's real motive is to attack the boys and sexually assault them at the first opportunity. Both boys willingly agree to EAMES's request and walk towards some nearby bushes where EAMES claims he left the bike. After walking some 30 metres with EAMES, the boys have second thoughts and run off.

Has EAMES committed an offence of child abduction (contrary to s. 2 of the Child Abduction Act 1984)?

A Yes, but only in relation to NICHOLL.
B No, because both HAYMAN and NICHOLL consented to go with EAMES.
C Yes, both HAYMAN and NICHOLL are covered by the legislation.
D No, neither of the boys has been removed from the lawful control of any person.

Question 19.3

SMITH is selling her house to GLYNN and the two have verbally agreed a price. Before any contracts are signed, SMITH has her house revalued and discovers that she can obtain another £20,000 should she put it back up for sale. In view of this, SMITH contacts GLYNN to ask for more money. GLYNN is outraged and goes to SMITH's house. SMITH lets GLYNN into her house but when he becomes abusive she demands he leave; he refuses. SMITH then tries to leave the house but GLYNN stops her by telling her that she is not leaving until she signs a contract agreeing to sell at the lower price. SMITH begins to cry and several minutes later GLYNN decides to leave.

Considering the offence of false imprisonment only, which of the following statements is correct?

A The offence is not committed because SMITH has not been physically detained.
B The offence will only be committed if GLYNN intends to restrain SMITH's movements.
C Keeping SMITH in her home for however short a time may amount to false imprisonment.
D Common law states that false imprisonment cannot be committed in the home of the complainant.

Question 19.4

MARSTON is part of a religious commune. UNWIN believes that MARSTON is in danger as the commune will ask MARSTON to turn all her property over to them. UNWIN decides that she will return MARSTON to her parents' home by whatever means are necessary. UNWIN visits the commune and finds MARSTON. She asks MARSTON to walk with her while they discuss her situation and MARSTON agrees. MARSTON refuses to return with UNWIN, who then lies to MARSTON stating that MARSTON's mother is seriously ill and that she must come with her. MARSTON agrees and begins walking with UNWIN. Several minutes later, MARSTON asks for proof of her mother's illness from UNWIN who, at this point, physically drags MARSTON along for several metres before she lets her go.

At what point, if at all, does UNWIN first commit the offence of kidnap?

A When UNWIN initially begins walking with MARSTON intending to return her by whatever means necessary.

B When she lies to MARSTON about her mother and MARSTON walks with her for several minutes.

C When UNWIN uses physical force to drag MARSTON for several metres.

D UNWIN does not commit the offence because she has a lawful excuse to carry away MARSTON.

Question 19.5

POTTS and OLDFIELD lived together as common-law husband and wife but the relationship has ended. There were two children by this relationship, ANN (aged 12 years) and MARTIN (aged 16 years). Both children now live with their mother (OLDFIELD), who has lawful custody of the children. One evening, POTTS visits his children. While OLDFIELD goes out shopping, POTTS persuades the two children to go on holiday with him to Spain for two weeks. The children agree and all three leave for Spain without the consent of OLDFIELD.

Would this constitute an offence of child abduction (contrary to s. 1 of the Child Abduction Act 1984)?

A No, as POTTS has taken the children outside the United Kingdom for less than one month.

B Yes, but only in relation to ANN.

C No, because POTTS is the father of both children.

D Yes, in relation to ANN and MARTIN.

Question 19.6

RICKWOOD works in a high security building where all the doors to the section where he works are controlled electronically. BRADISH approaches the control panel for the door locks and turns it off. This causes all of the doors in RICKWOOD's section of the building to lock shut. BRADISH believes that someone may have been locked in the building as a consequence of his actions but is not sure. As a result, RICKWOOD is locked in his section for 20 minutes until the door locks are released.

Which of the following statements is correct with regard to the offence of false imprisonment?

A RICKWOOD would have to be detained for several hours before a charge of false imprisonment would be appropriate.

B The offence is not committed because BRADISH did not actually intend anyone's freedom to be restrained.

C The fact that BRADISH was reckless as to whether anyone would be locked in means the offence is committed.

D BRADISH will only be found guilty of the offence if a jury consider his actions were reckless.

ANSWERS

Answer 19.1

Answer **B** — This legislation applies to children under the age of 16, making answer A incorrect. A person would not commit an offence if they took a child out of the United Kingdom for less than a month *and* they are a person in whose favour there is a residence order in force with respect to the child. In this case there is an informal arrangement, making answer C incorrect. Although HILL commits the offence, it is the consent of the Director of Public Prosecutions that is required before bringing a charge under this legislation. HILL may be able to avail himself of the defence under s. 1(5)(b) of the Act, i.e. that he has taken all reasonable steps to communicate with YEO but has been unable to communicate with her.

Investigators' Manual, paras 3.3.1, 3.3.2

Answer 19.2

Answer **A** — The legislation covers children under the age of 16 years, making answer C incorrect. The fact that the boys consented to go with EAMES is irrelevant, making answer B incorrect. The Act talks about the taking or detaining of a child and this includes keeping a child where they are found or inducing the child to remain with the defendant or another person. Effectively, this taking or keeping is complete when the defendant substitutes his/her authority or will for that of the person in lawful control of the child and in this example the substitution takes place when EAMES walks with the boys towards the bushes (*R* v *Leather* (1993) 98 Cr App R 179). Therefore, answer D is incorrect.

Investigators' Manual, para. 3.3.3

Answer 19.3

Answer **C** — There is no requirement for the detaining of a person to be carried out by a physical action, just that their movement be restrained; this may be achieved by words alone, making answer A incorrect. The mental element required to commit this offence was stated in *R* v *Rahman* (1985) 81 Cr App R 349 as being 'the unlawful and intentional or reckless restraint of a victim's movement from a particular place' so the offence can be committed recklessly, making answer B incorrect. The 'particular place' can be absolutely anywhere and this includes a victim's own house, making answer D incorrect.

Investigators' Manual, para. 3.4

Answer 19.4

Answer **B** — The offence of kidnap is the unlawful taking or carrying away of one person by another by force or fraud (*R* v *D* [1984] AC 778). At point A UNWIN's intentions are to remove MARSTON by any means; however, MARSTON has voluntarily consented to walk with UNWIN and no fraud or force is used. At point B the offence is committed as UNWIN has used a fraud to move MARSTON from one point to another; distance is no object. Although a 'lawful excuse' would provide UNWIN with a defence to the charge, a concern for finances or a moral or spiritual concern would not suffice; there must be a necessity recognised as law (*R* v *Henman* [1987] Crim LR 333, CA), making answer D incorrect.

Investigators' Manual, para. 3.5

Answer 19.5

Answer **B** — This offence can be committed by any person listed under s. 1(2) of the Act who is connected to the child/children. The Act states that a person is connected with a child (at s. 1(2)(b)) in the case of a child whose parents were not married to each other at the time of his birth, if there are reasonable grounds for believing that he is the father of the child, i.e. POTTS. However, just because POTTS is the father of the children does not afford him immunity from this offence, making answer C incorrect. The offence can only be committed in relation to a child under the age of 16 so it cannot be committed in relation to MARTIN, making answer D incorrect. The fact that POTTS has taken the children outside the United Kingdom for less than one month is immaterial. The time factor is only relevant if there is a residence order in existence in favour of POTTS (and there is not); what is relevant is that POTTS has taken ANN outside the United Kingdom without the consent of OLDFIELD, making answer A incorrect.

Investigators' Manual, para. 3.3.1

Answer 19.6

Answer **C** — Detention for however short a period may amount to false imprisonment, making answer A incorrect. The state of mind required for this offence is 'subjective recklessness' making answers B and D incorrect.

Investigators' Manual, para. 3.4

20 Public Order and Racially, Religiously Aggravated and Homophobic Offences

QUESTIONS

Question 20.1

WIDDOWS, WARD and SLEWS visit a nightclub and get extremely drunk. As a result of their drunken behaviour they are thrown out of the club. They decide to get revenge on the doorman of the club and wait for him in a nearby deserted alley. When the doorman leaves the club, WIDDOWS, WARD and SLEWS approach him and tell him that they are going to '*cut his eyes out*'. The doorman laughs at all three and has no fear whatsoever for his personal safety. The three continue making threats and are arrested shortly afterwards.

Do WIDDOWS, WARD and SLEWS commit violent disorder (contrary to s. 2 of the Public Order Act 1986)?

A Yes, all three men had the required 'common purpose' necessary. If this element were not present in the actions of the three men then no offence of violent disorder would take place.

B No, the Public Order Act 1986 specifically caters for the effects of 'drunkenness' and the three would be able to state their awareness was impaired and use the defence.

C Yes, the fact that the doorman was not frightened of the three men makes no difference. It is not necessary to prove that a person of reasonable firmness was actually caused to fear for their safety.

D No, the doorman would be classed as a person of reasonable firmness and he must fear for his personal safety. As he does not, the offence is incomplete.

Question 20.2

MALKIN has a long-running dispute with his neighbour, HOLLYOAKE. After a heated argument one evening MALKIN decides to get revenge on HOLLYOAKE by smashing a greenhouse in HOLLYOAKE's back garden. MALKIN stands in his own back garden and uses a mobile phone to call his neighbour. When HOLLYOAKE answers the phone MALKIN says, *'Look out of your back window.'* HOLLYOAKE looks out of the window and as he does so, MALKIN leans over the garden fence separating the two houses and smashes several panes of greenhouse glass with a hammer.

Does MALKIN commit an affray (contrary to s. 3 of the Public Order Act 1986)?

A Yes, the threat is accompanied by actions (MALKIN smashed the panes of glass).
B No, HOLLYOAKE is inside a dwelling when the threat is made to him.
C Yes, this offence can be committed in private as well as public places.
D No, affray does not include conduct towards property.

Question 20.3

ASPINALL is unemployed and desperately needs cash. He is given £25 by POWELL to hand out leaflets to members of the public. POWELL promises ASPINALL that if he hands out all the leaflets he will receive a further £25. The leaflets contain material on white supremacy movements and are intended to stir up racial hatred against black people. ASPINALL is aware of the content of the leaflets and their purpose but only wants to distribute them to receive payment from POWELL and begins distributing the leaflets to members of the public.

With regard to s. 19 of the Public Order Act 1986 only, which of the following statements is correct?

A This offence can only be committed in a public place.
B Although ASPINALL commits the offence, he would be able to claim a defence under s. 19, as he did not intend to stir up racial hatred.
C ASPINALL does not commit the offence because he did not publish the written material.
D ASPINALL commits the offence as having regard to all the circumstances racial hatred is likely to be stirred up.

Question 20.4

OLLERTON and KHAN are neighbours and are in dispute over the boundary between their respective back gardens. One evening, OLLERTON comes home to find that KHAN has erected a fence between the two gardens. OLLERTON loses her temper and begins to break the fence. As OLLERTON is breaking the fence, KHAN comes out into the back garden. Motivated by frustration over the fence and also her intense hostility to Muslims, OLLERTON says to KHAN, *'How dare you put up a fence, you Muslim pig.'* KHAN is not upset by OLLERTON's comments, as he is not a Muslim.

Would this offence of criminal damage be 'racially aggravated' under s. 28 of the Crime and Disorder Act 1998?

A Yes, as it is immaterial whether OLLERTON's hostility is also based, to any extent, on any other factor.

B No, because KHAN is not personally upset by the situation.

C Yes, but only because the words uttered were said during the commission of the offence.

D No, as 'simple' criminal damage (under s. 1(1) of the Criminal Damage Act 1971) is not capable of being 'aggravated' under the Crime and Disorder Act 1998.

Question 20.5

CROW is walking along a street past a pub that is frequented by members of the gay community. As he passes the front door of the pub, PEEL and SINCLAIR walk out arm in arm and kissing each other (PEEL and SINCLAIR are both male). CROW sees this and exclaims, *'God almighty, you people utterly sicken me!'* PEEL responds, *'What is your problem?'* CROW replies, *'You two, you pair of nancy queer boys.'* PEEL and SINCLAIR are both offended by this abusive and insulting behaviour and tell CROW to leave them alone. CROW responds by saying, *'Fuck off now or I'll kick the shit out of both of you'* intending to make the two men think they are going to be assaulted.

Considering offences relating to hatred on the grounds of sexual orientation, which of the following statements is correct?

A CROW first commits an offence when he tells PEEL and SINCLAIR they sicken him.

B CROW first commits an offence when he is abusive about PEEL and SINCLAIR.

C CROW first commits the offence when he threatens PEEL and SINCLAIR with violence.

D CROW does not commit an offence in this scenario.

ANSWERS

Answer 20.1

Answer **C** — Answer A is incorrect as there is no requirement for a 'common purpose' for the offence of violent disorder to be committed. Section 6 of the Public Order Act 1986 does cater for the effects of drunkenness, but unless the intoxication is as a result of drugs taken in the course of medical treatment or it is not self-induced, the defendant will be deemed to be aware of his/her activities as if he/she were sober, making answer B incorrect. The fact that the doorman is not in fear is irrelevant; the person of reasonable firmness need not be present at the scene and so answer D is incorrect.

Investigators' Manual, paras 3.6.2, 3.6.3

Answer 20.2

Answer **D** — An affray cannot be committed when the conduct of the defendant is directed towards property alone. This is specifically mentioned in s. 8 of the Act, where it is stated that 'violence means any violent conduct *except in the context of affray*, it includes violent conduct towards *property* as well as violent conduct towards persons'.

Investigators' Manual, para. 3.6.4

Answer 20.3

Answer **D** — Section 19 of the Public Order Act 1986 deals with the publishing or distribution of written material with intent to stir up racial hatred. Answer A is incorrect as this offence can be committed in public or in private. Answer B is incorrect as although there is a defence to this offence, it is only available if the person can show that they were unaware of the content of the material and did not suspect and had no reason to suspect that it was threatening, abusive or insulting. Answer C is incorrect as the offence can be committed by distribution to the public or a section of the public, as well as by publication to that group.

Investigators' Manual, paras 3.7.13, 3.7.13.1

Answer 20.4

Answer **A** — Section 28(3) of the Crime and Disorder Act 1998 states that it is immaterial whether or not the offender's hostility is also based, to any extent, on any other factor (correct answer A). Answer B is incorrect as the Administrative Court has held that the victim's own perception of the words used was irrelevant, as was the fact that the victim was not personally upset by the situation (*DPP* v *Woods* [2002] EWHC Admin 85). Answer C is incorrect as a racially aggravated offence can take place *immediately before, at the time of committing an offence or after committing the offence.* Answer D is incorrect as s. 1(1) 'simple' damage is capable of being an 'aggravated' offence under the Crime and Disorder Act 1998.

Investigators' Manual, paras 3.7.1, 3.7.2

Answer 20.5

Answer **D** — Section 74 of and sch. 16 to the Criminal Justice and Immigration Act 2008 extended the offences of inciting hatred on racial or religious grounds to cover hatred against people on the grounds of sexual orientation. However, these sexual orientation offences can only be committed by an offender who carries out activity with the intention of stirring up such hatred—that was not CROW's intention at any point, making answers A, B and C incorrect.

Investigators' Manual, para. 3.7.16

21 Misuse of Drugs

QUESTIONS

Question 21.1

TURVEY has just lost his job and is finding money hard to come by. RANDELL feels sorry for TURVEY and gives him a packet of ten cigarettes that also contains a small amount of cocaine. TURVEY knows nothing about the cocaine inside the packet of cigarettes. Several hours later, TURVEY is stopped by PC MAIR, who discovers the cocaine inside the cigarette packet.

Which of the following statements is correct with regard to TURVEY?

A Provided TURVEY has physical control of the cigarettes and knows of their presence he has 'possession' of the drug.

B The only requirement for 'possession' is that TURVEY had the drug in his physical control.

C To show that TURVEY has 'possession' of the drug you must show that he actually knew that what he possessed was cocaine.

D TURVEY cannot be in 'possession' of the cocaine because he does not know of its existence.

Question 21.2

WILLSON is the landlord of a flat rented out to BOWN. WILLSON is aware of the fact that BOWN is cultivating several cannabis plants in the flat. BOWN goes on holiday and asks MELLING to water his plants until he returns. MELLING has no idea that the 'plants' are cannabis plants and is watering them when the police execute a warrant at the premises.

Apart from BOWN, who, if either, commits the offence of cultivation of cannabis (contrary to s. 6 of the Misuse of Drugs Act 1971)?

A Only WILLSON, as the landlord, commits the offence.
B Only MELLING commits the offence.
C Both WILLSON and MELLING commit the offence.
D Neither WILLSON nor MELLING commit the offence.

Question 21.3

You are taking part in a drugs operation. The subjects of the operation are MENSAH and ROWLES, both well-known drug dealers. MENSAH arrives at the car park of a local pub and begins to deal. Shortly afterwards, ROWLES arrives driving a van. You and your colleagues carry out the operation and MENSAH and ROWLES are detained in the car park. In ROWLES's van is £20,000 worth of heroin. ROWLES states that the heroin belongs to MENSAH, that he was going to return it to him and he was only looking after it for £100 while MENSAH dealt the drug.

What offence(s) under the Misuse of Drugs Act 1971 does ROWLES commit?
A Possession of a controlled drug (contrary to s. 5(2)) only.
B Supplying a controlled drug (contrary to s. 4(3)) only.
C Possession of a controlled drug (contrary to s. 5(2)) and possession with intent to supply a controlled drug (contrary to s. 5(3)) only.
D Possession with intent to supply (contrary to s. 5(3)) and supplying a controlled drug (contrary to s. 4(3)).

Question 21.4

It is SHANAHAN's birthday and he gets drunk with some friends at a pub. On his way home McFADDEN stops him. SHANAHAN knows McFADDEN is a drug dealer. McFADDEN asks SHANAHAN to drop an envelope at an address and gives SHANAHAN £100 to deliver it. Because SHANAHAN is drunk he has no reason to suspect the envelope contains drugs and accepts the offer. SHANAHAN is approaching the delivery address when he is arrested for possessing a controlled drug (which was inside the envelope) with intent to supply.

Would SHANAHAN have any defence under s. 28(2) of the Misuse of Drugs Act 1971?
A Yes, in these circumstances SHANAHAN's 'reason to suspect' was impaired by his drunken condition and because the 'reason to suspect' is judged subjectively he will be able to use a defence.
B No, the fact that SHANAHAN was drunk is irrelevant. He knew McFADDEN was a drug dealer and should have suspected that the envelope contains drugs because of the large reward for delivering it.

C Yes, SHANAHAN could state that he neither knew nor suspected that the envelope contained a controlled drug and that he neither knew nor suspected that he was supplying it to another.

D No, this section only provides a defence to the offence of unlawful possession of a controlled drug.

Question 21.5

DC BAUGH is working undercover in an area well known for the sale and distribution of controlled drugs. She is approached by CREIGHTON, who is considering robbing DC BAUGH. To find out if DC BAUGH has any money and is worth robbing, CREIGHTON offers to supply some cocaine to her for £200. CREIGHTON does not have any cocaine and has no intention of supplying DC BAUGH with the drug.

Which of the following statements is correct?

A CREIGHTON commits an offence (under s. 4(3) of the Misuse of Drugs Act 1971) when he offers to supply a controlled drug to DC BAUGH.

B No offence is committed by CREIGHTON, as he did not possess the cocaine to make good on his offer to DC BAUGH.

C CREIGHTON is not guilty of an offence, as he had no intention of supplying the drug to DC BAUGH.

D As CREIGHTON made his offer to an undercover police officer, he can claim that the offer to supply was not a 'real' offer.

Question 21.6

MOSTAFA is convicted of an offence of supplying a controlled drug (contrary to s. 4(3) of the Misuse of Drugs Act 1971) and is sentenced to five years' imprisonment for the offence.

Considering the law with regard to travel restriction orders (under the Criminal Justice and Police Act 2001), which of the following statements is correct?

A This offence of supplying a controlled drug is not covered by the legislation in relation to travel restriction orders.

B The minimum period for such an order is four years.

C MOSTAFA must surrender his UK passport as part of the order.

D If an order was made then MOSTAFA may apply to the court that made the restriction order to have it revoked or suspended.

Question 21.7

GRAPNELL is subject to a travel restriction order under the Criminal Justice and Police Act 2001. A rival gang of drug dealers kidnaps him outside his home address in London. The gang drives GRAPNELL to Scotland and then takes him to Northern Ireland. From Northern Ireland the gang takes GRAPNELL to France.

At what stage, if at all, does GRAPNELL commit an offence of contravening the travel restriction order?

A When he enters Scotland.
B When he enters Northern Ireland.
C When he enters France.
D The offence is not committed.

Question 21.8

One of the main practical effects of being able to identify the classification of a controlled drug is to determine the mode of trial and sentencing powers of the court.

Which of the following drugs would be classified as Class B?

A Heroin.
B 'Magic mushrooms' (containing psilocin).
C Methadone.
D Codeine.

Question 21.9

CUTLER and HAVELIN are both drug addicts who use heroin on a regular basis. They obtain some heroin and HAVELIN obtains two items, a tourniquet and a hypodermic syringe, to assist in the administration of the drug. HAVELIN offers to supply both articles to CUTLER so that he can administer the drug to himself.

With which, if any, of the two items would HAVELIN commit the offence of supplying articles for administering or preparing controlled drugs (contrary to s. 9A of the Misuse of Drugs Act 1971)?

A The tourniquet only.
B The hypodermic syringe only.
C The tourniquet and the hypodermic syringe.
D Neither of the two items.

Question 21.10

MIRZA owns a café that is managed by NORTHALL. The café is regularly frequented by a group of teenagers who smoke cannabis inside the café. NORTHALL is fully aware that the teenagers use controlled drugs in the café but does not know what drug they use and as the teenagers are such good customers he decides to ignore their activities. MIRZA has no idea that the teenagers even use the café let alone smoke cannabis on the premises.

With regard to the offence of being the occupier or manager of premises and permitting drug use (contrary to s. 8 of the Misuse of Drugs Act 1971), which of the following statements is correct?

A Neither MIRZA nor NORTHALL would commit the offence because smoking cannabis or cannabis resin is not covered by this particular piece of legislation.

B The fact that MIRZA does not know the teenagers smoke drugs in the café is immaterial; this is an offence of strict liability and as the café owner he commits the offence.

C NORTHALL commits the offence but would only be found guilty if the prosecution could show that he knew what type of drugs were being used by the teenagers.

D MIRZA does not commit the offence because he does not know that the teenagers are smoking cannabis in his café.

Question 21.11

DC PHILLIPS (in plain clothes) has been taking a witness statement and is walking back to her car when she sees BOND and FARMER acting suspiciously. BOND is talking to FARMER, who is sitting in a car and smoking. DC PHILLIPS approaches the two and as she does so she smells what she thinks is cannabis being smoked. She suspects that the two men are committing offences contrary to the Misuse of Drugs Act 1971 and that she will find drugs on their persons and in the car.

With regard to the power of entry, search and seizure under s. 23 of the Misuse of Drugs Act 1971, which of the following comments is correct?

A DC PHILLIPS cannot exercise powers under s. 23 unless she is in uniform.

B DC PHILLIPS can search both BOND and FARMER and also search the car FARMER is sitting in.

C The power cannot be exercised unless DC PHILLIPS reasonably believes that offences contrary to the Act are being committed.

D DC PHILLIPS can search BOND and FARMER but not FARMER's car.

Question 21.12

The Home Secretary has the power, under the Misuse of Drugs Act 1971, to make any drug subject to temporary control. On 10th April 2015 the drug Ethylphenidate, which has been marketed as an alternative to cocaine and is often referred to as 'Gogaine' or 'Burst', was made subject to such an order. DC GAD is on plain clothes patrol when he sees FURMAN and CLAY walking towards him. FURMAN is holding a bright red packet labelled 'Gogaine'. As the officer draws level with FURMAN, FURMAN says to CLAY, *'Here, you try some, you're going to love this high!'* and hands the packet to CLAY.

Which of the following comments is correct in relation to the law surrounding such temporary control and the powers of DC GAD?

A CLAY has committed an offence merely by being in possession of a drug that is subject to a temporary class order.

B A temporary drug class order comes into immediate effect when it is made and lasts for up to 24 months.

C DC GAD could not search FURMAN or CLAY using his powers under s. 23 of the Misuse of Drugs Act 1971.

D FURMAN has committed an offence by supplying a controlled drug to CLAY.

Question 21.13

DC LONGWELL receives information about a house owned by MALLORY being used to manufacture a variety of drugs. The officer applies for a warrant to search the premises under s. 23 of the Misuse of Drugs Act 1971 and the application is granted.

How long will such a warrant last?

A It lasts for a period of one month from the date of issue.

B It lasts for a period of two months from the date of issue.

C It lasts for a period of three months from the date of issue.

D It lasts for a period of four months from the date of issue.

Question 21.14

DC SAFFORD is in plain clothes and is standing on a street corner carrying out authorised surveillance activities in an area well known for the supply and use of drugs. EMERSON approaches the officer thinking that DC SAFFORD is a drugs dealer and asks the officer to supply him with some heroin.

Considering only the Misuse of Drugs Act 1971, what offence, if any, has EMERSON committed?

A EMERSON has not committed an offence under the Misuse of Drugs Act 1971 as asking someone to supply you with a controlled drug is not an offence known to law.

B EMERSON commits an offence under s. 4(3) of the Act as he is 'concerned' in the supply of a controlled drug.

C EMERSON has committed the offence of 'incitement' under s. 19 of the Act.

D EMERSON has not committed an offence under the Misuse of Drugs Act 1971 as DC SAFFORD is an undercover police officer and there was no possibility of the officer actually being induced to commit the offence.

ANSWERS

Answer 21.1

Answer **A** — This question does not ask if TURVEY has committed an offence, merely if he satisfies what the law requires for 'possession' of the drug. In order to be in possession of anything, the common law requires physical control of the object plus knowledge that it contains something, making answers B and C incorrect. The fact that TURVEY does not know of the existence of the cocaine within the cigarette packet may afford him a defence to a charge of possession but he still 'possesses' the drug, making answer D incorrect.

Investigators' Manual, paras 3.8.3, 3.8.3.1 to 3.8.3.7

Answer 21.2

Answer **B** — Although WILLSON knows of the existence of the cannabis plants, this does not mean that he commits the offence. For the offence to be committed you must show some element of attention to the plant by the defendant, making answers A and C incorrect. The element of attention could be watering the plant. In proving the offence it is only necessary to show that the plant is of the genus *Cannabis* and that the defendant cultivated it; it is not necessary to show that the defendant knew it to be a cannabis plant (*R* v *Champ* (1981) 73 Cr App R 367), making answer D incorrect.

Investigators' Manual, para. 3.8.8

Answer 21.3

Answer **C** — This question is as per the circumstances in *R* v *Maginnis* [1987] AC 303. Clearly, ROWLES is in possession of a controlled drug, ruling out answers B and D. To 'supply' something, the person who you are giving the item to must obtain some benefit from it. If ROWLES had given the drugs to MENSAH, MENSAH would have benefitted as he could sell the drugs so if that transaction had taken place, ROWLES would have 'supplied' MENSAH. However, he did not so there cannot be an actual 'supply'. As ROWLES intended to give the drugs to MENSAH in these circumstances there is an offence of possession with intent to supply, meaning answer A is incorrect.

Investigators' Manual, paras 3.8.4, 3.8.5

Answer 21.4

Answer **B** — Section 28 provides a defence for several offences under the Act, one of those being possession with intent to supply, making answer D incorrect. The fact that SHANAHAN knew McFADDEN as a drugs dealer and was paid a large amount of money to deliver the envelope would negate any defence he may attempt to raise as he should have 'reason to suspect' the envelope contained drugs in these circumstances, making answer C incorrect. The 'reason to suspect' is judged objectively (*R* v *Young* [1984] 1 WLR 654) so where a 'reason to suspect' is not apparent because the defendant is too intoxicated to see it, the defence will not apply, making answer A incorrect.

Investigators' Manual, paras 3.8.9, 3.8.9.1 to 3.8.9.3

Answer 21.5

Answer **A** — The offence under s. 4(3) states that it is an offence to supply or offer to supply a controlled drug. The offence is complete when the offer is made. It is irrelevant whether or not the defendant actually has the means to meet the offer or even intends to carry it out (*R* v *Goodard* [1992] Crim LR 588), making answers B and C incorrect. If the offer was made to an undercover police officer the offence is still committed (*R* v *Kray*, 10 November 1998, unreported).

Investigators' Manual, paras 3.8.4, 3.8.4.1, 3.8.4.2

Answer 21.6

Answer **D** — The offences that are covered by travel restriction orders include the supply of controlled drugs, making answer A incorrect. Answer B is incorrect as the minimum period for such an order is two years (s. 33(3)). Answer C is incorrect as an offender *may* be required to surrender his/her UK passport as part of the order.

Investigators' Manual, para. 3.8.16

Answer 21.7

Answer **C** — The offence is committed when the person subject to the order leaves the United Kingdom. It is immaterial that GRAPNELL has been kidnapped, as the conduct of the defendant does not have to be voluntary.

Investigators' Manual, para. 3.8.16

Answer 21.8

Answer **D** — Answers A, B and C are all Class A drugs.

Investigators' Manual, para. 3.8.2

Answer 21.9

Answer **A** — Hypodermic syringes, or parts of them, are not covered by this offence (s. 9A(2)), making answers B and C incorrect. The tourniquet would be covered as this offence deals with 'articles' used in the administration or preparation of drugs to 'himself or another', making answer D incorrect.

Investigators' Manual, para. 3.8.6

Answer 21.10

Answer **D** — Cannabis and cannabis resin are covered by this offence (s. 8(d)), making answer A incorrect. This offence can only be committed if the occupier or person concerned in the management of the premises *knowingly* permits the use of drugs in the prescribed manner. This is not an offence of strict liability and so answer B is also incorrect. It is not necessary to show that the defendant knew exactly what drugs were being produced, supplied, etc.; only that they were 'controlled drugs' (*R* v *Bett* [1999] 1 All ER 600), making answer C incorrect.

Investigators' Manual, para. 3.8.11

Answer 21.11

Answer **B** — The power under s. 23 is exercisable by a constable who does not have to be in uniform and who has *reasonable grounds to suspect* that a person is in possession of a controlled drug in contravention of the Act, making answers A and C incorrect. Answer D is incorrect as the Act provides the power to search and detain persons and any vehicle or vessel in which the constable suspects that the drug may be found.

Investigators' Manual, paras 3.8.17, 3.8.17.1, 3.8.17.2

Answer 21.12

Answer **D** — The Home Secretary has the power, under the Misuse of Drugs Act 1971, to make any drug subject to temporary control. The order will come into immediate effect and will last for up to 12 months, subject to Parliament agreeing to it within 40 sitting days of the order being made, making answer B incorrect. Such a drug will be referred to as a 'temporary class drug' and will be a 'controlled drug' for the purposes of the Misuse of Drugs Act 1971, and other legislation such as the Proceeds of Crime Act 2002, unless otherwise stated. With the *exception of the possession offence*, all the offences under the Misuse of Drugs Act will apply, including possession in connection with an offence or prohibition, under ss. 3, 4 and 5(3) of the Act, i.e. possession with intent to supply. So CLAY would not commit an offence but FURMAN would (making answer A incorrect). Simple possession of a temporary class drug is not an offence under the 1971 Act; however, law enforcement officers have been given the following powers to enable them to take action to prevent possible harm to the individual:

- search and detain a person (or vehicle etc.) where there are reasonable grounds to suspect that the person is in possession of a temporary class drug;
- seize, detain and dispose of a suspected temporary class drug;
- arrest or charge a person who commits the offence of intentionally obstructing an enforcement officer in the exercise of their powers.

This makes answer C incorrect (in s. 23 note that the powers are available to a constable 'who has reasonable grounds to suspect that any person is in possession of a controlled drug in contravention of this Act or of any regulations or *orders*').

Investigators' Manual, paras 3.8.2.1, 3.8.17.1

Answer 21.13

Answer **A** — A warrant issued under s. 23 of the Act lasts for a period of *one month* from the date of issue.

Investigators' Manual, para. 3.8.17.1

Answer 21.14

Answer **C** — The Misuse of Drugs Act 1971, s. 19 states:

> It is an offence for a person to incite another to commit an offence under any other provision of this Act.

So answer A is incorrect as this offence has been committed by EMERSON. Asking to be supplied with drugs is not an offence under s. 4(3) making answer B incorrect. A person inciting an undercover police officer may commit an offence under s. 19 even though there was no possibility of the officer actually being induced to commit the offence (*DPP* v *Armstrong* [2000] Crim LR 379), making answer D incorrect.

Investigators' Manual, para. 3.8.14

22 Firearms and Gun Crime

QUESTIONS

Question 22.1

NIELSEN is the owner of a slaughterhouse and is licensed under s. 10 of the Firearms Act 1968 to possess slaughtering instruments. One of the instruments that he keeps for this purpose is a hand-held electric 'stun gun'. The stun gun develops a fault and is beyond repair but rather than throw it away, NIELSEN takes the broken stun gun to his home address. He intends to keep it in a display cabinet to show his friends the sort of instruments he uses at work.

Considering only the offence of possessing a prohibited weapon contrary to s. 5 of the Firearms Act 1968, which of the following statements is true?

A NIELSEN commits the offence as the stun gun is a prohibited weapon and he has it in his possession away from his place of work.

B No offence is committed because NIELSEN is a licensed slaughterer and s. 10 of the Act allows him to possess the stun gun.

C As NIELSEN only intends to keep the stun gun as a display item the offence would not be committed.

D NIELSEN cannot commit this offence because an electric stun gun is only a prohibited weapon as long as it can discharge an electric current.

Question 22.2

CALVER buys an antique vase from LAVERICK for £15,000 and, although LAVERICK has asked for the money several times, CALVER has always refused to pay it. LAVERICK goes to CALVER's home address and demands payment. The two have an argument during which CALVER tells LAVERICK that he will never pay him. LAVERICK puts his hands behind his back and onto an imitation 9 mm Beretta pistol. He tells CALVER that he has a gun and that if CALVER does not pay him he will be shot and killed.

Why is no offence under s. 16 of the Firearms Act 1968 committed?

A No offence is committed because LAVERICK has not actually endangered CALVER's life.

B No offence is committed because the threat is a conditional one.

C No offence is committed because the threat is made with an imitation firearm.

D No offence is committed because the firearm was never produced or shown to CALVER.

Question 22.3

PC SHANKS carries out a s. 1 PACE search on YOUNIS, who has been found trespassing in a building. In the course of the search, PC SHANKS finds an imitation pistol in YOUNIS's back pocket. She seizes the pistol and arrests YOUNIS for an offence under s. 20(1) of the Firearms Act 1968 (trespassing with a firearm in a building). YOUNIS struggles with the officer and punches her in the face attempting to prevent PC SHANKS from making the arrest. YOUNIS manages to take hold of the imitation pistol and points it at the officer, telling her to leave him alone. YOUNIS then strikes PC SHANKS in the face with the butt of the pistol.

At what stage, if at all, does YOUNIS commit an offence under s. 17 of the Firearms Act (using a firearm to resist arrest)?

A When he initially struggles with PC SHANKS and punches her in the face.

B When he takes hold of the imitation pistol and points it at PC SHANKS.

C When he strikes PC SHANKS in the face with the butt of the pistol.

D The offence under s. 17 of the Act is not committed.

Question 22.4

WHITHAM assaults GORMLEY, breaking GORMLEY's wrist during the attack. GORMLEY reports the assault to DC BUTTERS who visits WHITHAM's home address two days after the original assault. WHITHAM invites the officer into his house and into the lounge, where DC BUTTERS arrests WHITHAM for a s. 20 grievous bodily harm (contrary to the Offences Against the Person Act 1861). As the arrest is made, DC BUTTERS sees an imitation Magnum 44 on a lounge table.

Is WHITHAM liable for an offence of possessing a firearm while being arrested for a sch. 1 offence?

A No, because a s. 20 grievous bodily harm is not a sch. 1 offence.

B Yes, but only if WHITHAM is found guilty of the s. 20 assault.

C No, as WHITHAM must actually have the weapon in his physical possession.

D Yes, it is immaterial that the weapon is an imitation firearm.

Question 22.5

You arrest CHU for an offence of robbery and he is later sentenced to a term of imprisonment for three years.

When, if ever, would CHU be able to legally possess a firearm without committing an offence under s. 21 of the Firearms Act 1968?

A CHU must not have a firearm in his possession at any time before the end of a three-year period beginning on the date of his release.

B CHU must not have a firearm in his possession at any time before the end of a five-year period beginning on the date of his release.

C CHU must not have a firearm in his possession at any time before the end of a seven-year period beginning from the date of his release.

D CHU must not, at any time, have a firearm in his possession.

Question 22.6

MILLER discovers that PALFREY has been having an affair with his wife. He finds PALFREY drinking in a pub and approaches him. MILLER is holding several fingers inside his jacket and points them at PALFREY saying, *'Stand still or I'll blow you away.'* MILLER intends PALFREY to believe he has a firearm. PALFREY believes MILLER and stands still. MILLER picks up a glass from the bar, breaks it and pushes it into PALFREY's neck intending to and actually causing grievous bodily harm to PALFREY (a s. 18 offence under the Offences Against the Person Act 1861).

Is MILLER guilty of possessing a firearm while committing a sch. 1 offence (contrary to s. 17(2) of the Firearms Act 1968)?

A No, sch. 1 does not extend to causing grievous bodily harm with intent under s. 18 of the Offences Against the Person Act 1861.

B Yes, the offence can be committed when in possession of an imitation firearm and MILLER's fingers would represent an imitation firearm.

C No, MILLER must be in possession of a firearm as opposed to an imitation firearm.

D Yes, as long as MILLER is subsequently convicted of the offence of causing grievous bodily harm with intent.

Question 22.7

KING and HUNSTONE are both released from prison on the same day. KING had been sentenced to four years' imprisonment for an offence of robbery and HUNSTONE had been sentenced to 12 months' imprisonment for an offence of burglary.

According to s. 21 of the Firearms Act 1968, when, if ever, can KING and HUNSTONE lawfully possess a firearm?

A KING and HUNSTONE can never lawfully possess a firearm.

B KING can never lawfully possess a firearm; HUNSTONE can lawfully possess a firearm five years after his release.

C KING can lawfully possess a firearm five years after his release; HUNSTONE can lawfully possess a firearm three years after his release.

D KING can lawfully possess a firearm three years after his release; HUNSTONE can lawfully possess a firearm one year after his release.

Question 22.8

The Firearms Act 1968 contains certain offences dealing with the shortening and conversion of firearms. Section 4(1) of the Act deals with the offence of shortening the barrel of a shotgun.

With regard to the offences under s. 4(1), which of the following comments is correct?

A The maximum sentence for this offence is 10 years' imprisonment on indictment.

B The offence is committed when the barrel of a shotgun is shortened to a length of less than 24 inches.

C Registered firearms dealers are not excluded from committing this offence.

D The offence is committed when the barrel of a shotgun is shortened to a length of less than 28 inches.

ANSWERS

Answer 22.1

Answer **A** — Answer D is incorrect as an electric stun gun has been held to be a prohibited weapon as it discharges an electrical current (*Flack* v *Baldry* [1988] 1 WLR 393) and it continues to be a prohibited weapon even if it is not working (*R* v *Brown*, The Times, 27 March 1992). The test as to whether a weapon is prohibited or not is purely objective and is not affected by the intentions of the defendant (*R* v *Law* [1999] Crim LR 837), making answer C incorrect. Although s. 10 of the Act allows licensed slaughterers to possess such items, this is only applicable when the weapon is possessed in any slaughterhouse or knackers' yard in which the person is employed and if this condition is not met, then the exemption will not apply. This makes answer B incorrect.

Investigators' Manual, paras 3.9.4, 3.9.4.1, 3.9.8

Answer 22.2

Answer **C** — The intention does not have to be an immediate one and it may be conditional (*R* v *Bentham* [1973] QB 357), making answer B incorrect. There is no need for the firearm to be produced or shown to another, making answer D incorrect. This is an offence of intent and it is not required that the life of another be endangered, only that the intent to do so exists, making answer A incorrect. The offence cannot be committed using an imitation firearm.

Investigators' Manual, para. 3.9.10.1

Answer 22.3

Answer **B** — It is an offence for a person *to make any use whatsoever* of a firearm or imitation firearm with intent to resist or prevent the lawful arrest or detention of himself or another.

Investigators' Manual, paras 3.9.10.2, 3.9.10.3

Answer 22.4

Answer **D** — Section 20 assaults are covered by sch. 1 to the Act, making answer A incorrect. There is no need for the defendant to be subsequently convicted of the sch. 1 offence. All that is needed is to prove that he/she had the weapon in his/her possession at the time of his/her arrest for the offence (*R* v *Nelson (Damien)* [2000] QB 55), making answer B incorrect. With regard to possession, you need to prove that the person was in possession of the firearm but not that they actually had it with them (*R* v *North* [2001] Crim LR 746), making answer C incorrect.

Investigators' Manual, para. 3.9.10.5

Answer 22.5

Answer **D** — A person who has been sentenced to custody for life or to preventive detention, imprisonment, corrective training, youth custody or detention in a young offender institution for three years or more must not, at any time, have a firearm or ammunition in his/her possession.

Investigators' Manual, para. 3.9.11

Answer 22.6

Answer **A** — Answer B is incorrect as although the offence can be committed with an imitation firearm, 'fingers' have been held not to constitute an imitation firearm (*R* v *Bentham* [2005] 1 WLR 1057). Answer C is therefore incorrect as the offence can be committed with an imitation firearm. Answer D is incorrect as there is no need for the defendant to be subsequently convicted of the sch. 1 offence (*R* v *Nelson (Damien)* [2000] 3 WLR 300).

Investigators' Manual, paras 3.9.2.4, 3.9.10.5

Answer 22.7

Answer **B** — A person sentenced to three plus years' imprisonment can never lawfully possess a firearm; a person sentenced to three plus months' imprisonment *but less than three years*, can possess a firearm five years after the date of their release.

Investigators' Manual, para. 3.9.11

Answer 22.8

Answer **B** — The maximum sentence on indictment for this offence is five years' imprisonment, making answer A incorrect. Registered firearms dealers are exempted from this offence, making answer C incorrect. The offence is committed when the barrel of a shotgun is shortened to a length of less than 24 inches, making answer D incorrect.

Investigators' Manual, para. 3.9.6.2

23 Terrorism and Associated Offences

QUESTIONS

Question 23.1

Section 1 of the Terrorism Act 2000 provides a definition of the term 'terrorism'.

According to that definition, which of the following comments is correct?

A The definition limits 'terrorism' to the use or threat of action inside the United Kingdom.

B 'Terrorism' is limited to circumstances where the action of an individual or group endangers a person's life, other than that of the person committing the action.

C Actions designed to seriously interfere or disrupt an electronic system are not covered by the definition.

D 'Terrorism' incorporates the use or threat of action where the use or threat is made for the purpose of advancing a racial cause.

Question 23.2

MASON holds extreme views about the Muslim faith and strongly believes that the activities of al-Qaeda (a proscribed organisation under Part II of the Terrorism Act 2000) are fully justified. He visits a mosque to attempt to rally support for the al-Qaeda cause. MASON stands outside the Mosque and puts on an armband that has the words 'al-Qaeda member' written on it (MASON is not a member of al-Qaeda). Several people approach MASON and speak to him, during which time MASON invites them to support the activities of al-Qaeda. Six people tell MASON they are interested in what he has to say and so MASON arranges a meeting with the six people at his private house. MASON will address the meeting.

At what point, if at all, does MASON commit an offence contrary to the Terrorism Act 2000?

A When he puts on the armband stating that he is a member of al-Qaeda.
B When he invites people to support the activities of al-Qaeda.
C When he arranges the meeting at his house.
D No offence is committed by MASON.

Question 23.3

PARDEW manages investment funds for a number of organisations and individuals. One of the accounts he manages belongs to MASTERSON. While PARDEW is at work and administering the funds in MASTERSON's account, he becomes aware of certain irregularities in the way in which the money for the account is obtained. PARDEW makes several enquiries about the fund and is provided with information by CRAY which suggests that the funds in the MASTERSON account are funding terrorist activity. This causes PARDEW to suspect that the funds in the account are connected to terrorism.

According to s. 19 of the Terrorism Act 2000, what, if anything at all, must PARDEW do?

A There is no obligation on PARDEW to do anything unless he believes the money he administers is connected to terrorism.
B PARDEW must make further enquiries in relation to the funds to establish if they are legitimate before making contact with a law enforcement agency.
C PARDEW must, as soon as is reasonably practicable, disclose the suspicion and the information on which it is based to a constable.
D PARDEW must inform his company director who, in turn, must contact the police within 7 days of being notified by PARDEW about the suspicions relating to the MASTERSON account.

Question 23.4

WATTS (a British citizen who lives in Birmingham) is on holiday in Spain and on the last night of his holiday he strikes up a conversation with NUMAN (who is also a British citizen living in Birmingham) in a bar. The two men get very drunk and begin to talk about politics. NUMAN expresses extremist right-wing views about immigration and tells WATTS that he despises Muslims. He informs WATTS that he has had enough and is going to attack a mosque with a machine gun he has purchased when he returns to Birmingham the following week. WATTS believes NUMAN is serious; the fact is that NUMAN is not serious at all and is merely ranting in a drunken conversation. WATTS returns to Birmingham the following day, landing at Birmingham airport, but does not tell anyone about the conversation with NUMAN.

Considering the offence relating to information about acts of terrorism (contrary to s. 38B of the Terrorism Act 2000), which of the following comments is correct?

A When WATTS arrives in Birmingham he must disclose the information regarding NUMAN to a constable as soon as reasonably practicable.

B WATTS has not committed the offence as he came by the information when he was outside the United Kingdom.

C When WATTS arrives in Birmingham he must disclose the information regarding NUMAN to any person in authority.

D WATTS has not committed the offence as the offence relating to information about acts of terrorism can only be committed by a person coming by the information in a professional capacity.

Question 23.5

LEEMAN has extremist far-right political views and agrees with the actions of anyone who kills Muslims in order to continue what he describes as 'the fight against Islam'. He creates and activates a website on the Internet which glorifies the killing of Muslims and states that true English patriots should emulate such examples and kill Muslims using firearms and explosives. The website is seen by a number of people before it is quickly closed down.

Considering the offence under s. 1(2) of the Terrorism Act 2006 (publishing a statement to encourage the commission, preparation or instigation of acts of terrorism), which of the following comments is correct?

A LEEMAN has not committed the offence because electronic publications are not covered by the legislation.

B LEEMAN has committed the offence in these circumstances.

C The offence has not been committed as LEEMAN has not engaged in the dissemination of terrorist publications.

D The offence has been committed but only because LEEMAN used words to glorify the killings and encouraged others to emulate them; it cannot be committed by the use of sounds and images alone.

Question 23.6

SMALL is an extremely wealthy businessman who is strongly opposed to animal experimentation. He donates significant amounts of money to animal charities and because of his known views he is contacted by BOSTAN who is a member of an animal rights extremist group. BOSTAN is looking for funding from SMALL and after telling SMALL that he is an animal rights extremist, he invites SMALL to attend a camp and tells SMALL that at the camp members of the extremist group are receiving weapons training in order to carry out violent terrorist attacks on staff at various animal experimentation centres. SMALL visits two camps run by BOSTAN, one situated just outside Norwich (in England) and the other situated near to Calais (in France). SMALL watches members of the extremist group carrying out weapons training but decides that they are too extreme in their views and declines to offer the group any funding.

Has SMALL committed an offence in relation to the attendance at a place used for terrorist training (contrary to s. 8(1) of the Terrorism Act 2006)?

A Yes, but only in relation to the visit to the camp outside Norwich.
B No, as a person needs to take an active part in the training to commit the offence.
C Yes, in respect of both locations (the one just outside Norwich and the one near to Calais).
D No, because he did not provide any instruction to persons attending the terrorist training centre.

Question 23.7

Section 41 of the Terrorism Act 2000 provides a power of arrest without warrant in relation to 'terrorism'.

Which of the following comments is correct in relation to that power?

A A constable may arrest a person without warrant for being 'a terrorist' but the officer must reasonably believe the person is a terrorist.
B If a constable reasonably suspects a person of being 'a terrorist' then the constable may arrest that person without warrant, but the person arrested must have committed a specific offence relating to terrorism.
C A constable may arrest without warrant a person whom the constable reasonably suspects to be a terrorist.
D A police constable may arrest a person without warrant for being 'a terrorist' if the constable knows that the person is a terrorist.

Question 23.8

Due to a terrorist incident taking place in Manchester, it is considered expedient to set up a cordon (as per s. 33 of the Terrorism Act 2000) in a small area of the city centre for the purposes of a terrorist investigation.

In ordinary circumstances, who would authorise such a process?

A The chief constable or his/her designated deputy.

B An officer of the rank of assistant chief constable or above.

C An officer of the rank of superintendent or above.

D An officer of the rank of inspector or above.

Question 23.9

DCs ADEMAYO and TOWELL are posted to a Counter-Terrorism Unit and are receiving training regarding the powers available to the police under the Terrorism Act 2000. One of the powers discussed by the officers relates to cordons (available under s. 33 of the Terrorism Act 2000). In particular, the officers are discussing issues relating to the timing of such cordons and the authorisation process for them.

Which one of the following comments by the officers shows a correct understanding of the law?

A DC ADEMAYO states that the period for which a cordon can be authorised can begin after the order to set up the cordon is given, i.e. the cordon can begin at some time in the future.

B DC TOWELL states that the initial period to which the cordon can extend cannot extend beyond 7 days from the time the order is made.

C DC ADEMAYO states that the overall time limit for which a cordon can exist is 28 days.

D DC TOWELL states that an authorisation for a cordon could not be given by anyone below the rank of inspector.

Question 23.10

As a consequence of a terrorist investigation, a cordon designation has been provided (under s. 33 of the Terrorism Act 2000). PC JESSOP (who is wearing police uniform) and TI PANARKAR (who is wearing plain clothes) visit the area where the cordon has been established. The officers become involved with the policing of the cordon and carry out several activities within and near to the cordoned area.

Considering the powers of police officers under s. 36 of the Terrorism Act 2000 relating to cordons, which one of the following comments is correct?

A TI PANARKAR can arrange for the removal of a vehicle from the cordoned area.

B PC JESSOP can order a person immediately to leave premises which are partly in the cordoned area.

C TI PANARKAR can order a person in charge of a vehicle in a cordoned area to move it from the area immediately.

D PC JESSOP can arrange for the movement of a vehicle adjacent to a cordoned area.

Question 23.11

INNES (a citizen of the United Kingdom) has strong family connections in the Republic of Ireland and has many relatives living in Dublin. His relatives in Dublin have suffered financially as a consequence of several budget decisions made by the Republic's government and INNES is extremely angry at their predicament. INNES travels to Dublin and hides several large fireworks inside a lectern that will be used by several politicians to make speeches regarding budget cuts. INNES plans to remotely detonate the fireworks and intends to endanger the life of one or more of the politicians. CREENEY, a politician due to make a speech, begins to make his way towards the lectern but before he reaches it, INNES nervously detonates the fireworks too soon. A large explosion occurs and the lectern and part of the stage it stands on are completely destroyed; if CREENEY had been standing at the lectern he would have been killed, but fortunately neither CREENEY nor any other person is injured.

Considering the offence of causing an explosion likely to endanger life or property (contrary to s. 2 of the Explosives Substances Act 1883), which of the following statements is correct?

A INNES has not committed the offence as the action took place in the Republic of Ireland.

B INNES has not committed the offence as fireworks are not 'explosives' for the purposes of this offence.

C INNES has not committed the offence as no life was endangered.

D INNES has committed the offence in these circumstances.

Question 23.12

DUNLOP is extremely interested in explosive devices and finds an Internet site that explains how to make a pipe bomb using explosives drained from fireworks. Out of pure curiosity DUNLOP purchases a number of fireworks, drains the explosives from them and makes a pipe bomb. He tells ROPER what he has done as ROPER is also interested in explosives. ROPER asks if he can have the pipe bomb to examine it and potentially make one himself, again out of pure curiosity. DUNLOP agrees and gives the pipe bomb to ROPER who stores it in a storage facility several miles away from his home. A member of staff at the storage facility finds the pipe bomb and informs the police.

Which of the following comments is correct when considering the behaviour of DUNLOP and ROPER and the offence of making or possessing explosives under suspicious circumstances (contrary to s. 4 of the Explosive Substances Act 1883)?

A No offence has been committed by either DUNLOP or ROPER as there is an absence of criminal purpose in their activities.

B DUNLOP has committed the offence but ROPER has not as he does not have the pipe bomb in his possession.

C DUNLOP and ROPER commit the offence.

D No offence has been committed as neither DUNLOP nor ROPER intended to injure or kill any person with the explosive.

Question 23.13

SYLVIAN is strongly opposed to any form of testing via animal research. He has been monitoring the activities of Marston Bio Ltd and knows that they are carrying out experimentation on animals within their company premises. He waits outside the company premises and sees GREER (an employee of Marston Bio Ltd) leaving the premises in her car. SYLVIAN believes GREER works in the laboratories in the premises and follows her to her home. When GREER arrives at her home SYLVIAN approaches her and asks her to stop working for the company; GREER tells SYLVIAN to go away and enters her house. Moments later, HUBBARD, a friend of GREER, arrives at GREER's house. SYLVIAN tells HUBBARD that unless GREER stops working for the company all of the windows in GREER's home will be smashed. HUBBARD ignores SYLVIAN but tells GREER what was said. GREER confronts SYLVIAN outside her house and at this stage SYLVIAN tells GREER to stop working for the company or he will assault her.

At what stage is an offence of intimidation of persons connected with animal research organisations (contrary to s. 146(1) of the Serious Organised Crime and Police Act 2005) first committed?

A When SYLVIAN follows GREER to her home.

B When SYLVIAN confronts GREER outside her house and asks her not to work for the company.

C When SYLVIAN tells HUBBARD that GREER's windows will be smashed.

D When SYLVIAN threatens to assault GREER.

Question 23.14

Intelligence of high quality is received from a reliable source to the effect that there is going to be a terrorist attack in the city centre of Birmingham. It is decided that it is appropriate to authorise the power of stop and search under s. 47A of the Terrorism Act 2000.

In respect of such an authorisation, which of the following comments is correct?

A The authorisation allows a police officer, in or out of uniform, to stop pedestrians and/or vehicles in a certain area and search the pedestrian, vehicle and/or occupants of the vehicle.

B The authorising officer in respect of this power is a police officer for the area who is of at least the rank of assistant chief constable (or commander).

C An authorisation under s. 47A may last for a period no longer than 48 hours.

D A pedestrian, vehicle and/or occupants can only be searched by a police officer exercising the power under s. 47A if the officer reasonably believes the person is involved in terrorist activities and/or the vehicle is being used for the purposes of terrorism.

Question 23.15

ALTAR is subject to a terrorism prevention and investigation measures order (under the Terrorism Prevention and Investigative Measures Act 2011).

What is the maximum time period that such measures may last for?

A One year.

B Two years.

C Three years.

D Four years.

ANSWERS

Answer 23.1

Answer **D** — Terrorism (under s. 1 of the Terrorism Act 2000) is defined as:

(1) the use or threat of action where—
 (a) the action falls within subsection (2),
 (b) the use or threat is designed to influence the government or an international governmental organisation, or to intimidate the public or a section of the public, and
 (c) the use or threat is made for the purpose of advancing a political, religious, racial or ideological cause.
(2) Action falls within this subsection if it—
 (a) involves serious violence against a person,
 (b) involves serious damage to property,
 (c) endangers a person's life, other than the person committing the action,
 (d) creates a serious risk to the health or safety of the public or a section of the public, or
 (e) is designed to seriously interfere with or seriously disrupt an electronic system.
(3) The use or threat of action falling within subsection (2) which involves the use of firearms or explosives is terrorism whether or not subsection (1)(b) is satisfied.

The reference to 'action' here includes action outside the United Kingdom, making answer A incorrect. Answer B is incorrect as terrorism is not limited to the endangering of life (subsection (2)(c)) alone. Subsection (2)(e) includes action against electronic systems, making answer C incorrect. The purpose of advancing a 'racial' cause (correct answer D) was inserted into the definition by s. 75 of the Counter-Terrorism Act 2008.

Investigators' Manual, para. 3.10.2

Answer 23.2

Answer **A** — It is a summary offence to wear an item of clothing, or wear or carry or display an article in such a way or in such circumstances as to arouse reasonable suspicion that the defendant is a member or supporter of a proscribed organisation (s. 13). Inviting people to support al-Qaeda and arranging a meeting are also offences (s. 12(1) and s. 12(2) respectively).

Investigators' Manual, para. 3.10.2.1

Answer 23.3

Answer **C** — Section 19 states that where a person believes or suspects that another person has committed an offence under ss. 15 to 18 of the Terrorism Act 2000 and bases that belief or suspicion on information which comes to his attention in the course of a trade, profession or business or in the course of his employment (whether or not in the course of a trade, profession or business), he must disclose to a constable as soon as is reasonably practicable that belief or suspicion, and the information on which it is based, otherwise he commits an offence punishable with five years' imprisonment.

Investigators' Manual, para. 3.10.4.1

Answer 23.4

Answer **A** — The offence is committed where a person has information which he knows or believes might be of material assistance in preventing the commission by another person of an act of terrorism or in securing the apprehension, prosecution or conviction of another person, in the United Kingdom, for an offence involving the commission, preparation or instigation of an act of terrorism. This offence relates to any person who has information which he knows or believes might help prevent an act of terrorism or help bring terrorists to justice, making answer D incorrect. Section 38B(6) of the Terrorism Act 2000 has the effect that a person resident in the United Kingdom could be charged with the offence even if he was outside the country when he became aware of the information, making answer B incorrect. Disclosure in England and Wales is made to a constable, making answer C incorrect.

Investigators' Manual, para. 3.10.4.3

Answer 23.5

Answer **B** — Section 1(2) of the Terrorism Act 2006 creates an offence of publishing a statement to encourage the commission, preparation or instigation of acts of terrorism or Convention offences. Section 3(1) provides that this offence can be committed by publishing a statement electronically, i.e. via the Internet, making answer A incorrect. 'Statement' includes a communication of any description, including a communication without words consisting of sounds or images or both (s. 20(6)), making answer D incorrect. Therefore, LEEMAN has committed the offence (answer B). LEEMAN does not need to engage in the dissemination of terrorist publications (this is a separate offence under s. 2(1) of the Act), which makes answer C incorrect.

Investigators' Manual, para. 3.10.6.1

Answer 23.6

Answer **C** — It is an offence to attend at a place used for terrorist training. It does not matter that SMALL does not provide training or take an active part in the training, making answers B and D incorrect. The offence may be committed either in the United Kingdom or elsewhere, making answer A incorrect.

Investigators' Manual, para. 3.10.6.2

Answer 23.7

Answer **C** — Section 41 of the Terrorism Act 2000 gives a constable a power to arrest without warrant a person whom the constable reasonably suspects to be 'a terrorist', making answers A and D incorrect (and answer C correct). One of the benefits of the power under s. 41 is the requirement that the officer reasonably suspects the person of being a terrorist rather than suspecting his involvement in a specific offence, making answer B incorrect.

Investigators' Manual, para. 3.10.7.1

Answer 23.8

Answer **C** — Section 34 of the Terrorism Act 2000 states that a cordon authorisation may only be made by an officer for the police area who is of at least the rank of superintendent.

Investigators' Manual, para. 3.10.7.6

Answer 23.9

Answer **C** — The period of designation for the cordon begins at the time the order is made (i.e. it cannot be made to begin at some time in the future), making answer A incorrect. Answer B is incorrect as the initial authorisation period cannot extend beyond 14 days from the time the order is made (s. 35(2)). Answer D is incorrect as an authorisation can be given by an officer below the rank of superintendent in an urgent situation (s. 34(3)).

Investigators' Manual, para. 3.10.7.6

Answer 23.10

Answer **B** — The powers under s. 36 are only available if the officer is in uniform, making answers A and C incorrect. The officer in uniform has a number of powers, one of which (under s. 36(1)(e)) is to arrange for the movement of a vehicle within a cordoned area—not adjacent, making answer D incorrect.

Investigators' Manual, para. 3.10.7.7

Answer 23.11

Answer **D** — This offence is committed when a person who in the United Kingdom or (being a citizen of the United Kingdom and Colonies) in the Republic of Ireland unlawfully and maliciously causes by any explosive substance an explosion of a nature likely to endanger life or cause serious injury to property, whether or not any injury to person or property has been actually caused. Activity by a United Kingdom citizen in the Republic of Ireland would be covered, making answer A incorrect. The definition of 'explosive' under the Explosives Act 1875 applies to this offence and therefore fireworks are covered (*R* v *Bouch* [1983] QB 246), making answer B incorrect. It does not matter whether a life is actually endangered—it is the potential of the explosion that matters, so answer C is incorrect.

Investigators' Manual, para. 3.10.9

Answer 23.12

Answer **C** — Section 4 of the Explosive Substances Act 1883 states that any person who makes (DUNLOP) or knowingly has in his possession or under his control (ROPER) any explosive substance under such circumstances as to give rise to a reasonable suspicion that he is not making it or does not have it in his possession or under his control for a lawful object, shall, unless he can show that he made it or had it in his possession or under his control for a lawful object, be guilty of an offence. In *R* v *Riding* [2009] EWCA Crim 892, the defendant alleged that he had made a pipe bomb out of mere curiosity, using explosives drained from a number of fireworks. The defence contended that a 'lawful object' meant an absence of a criminal purpose rather than a positive object that was lawful. However, the court was satisfied that it meant the latter and mere curiosity could not be a 'lawful object' in making a lethal pipe bomb, making answer A incorrect. There is no requirement for an intention to kill or injure by making, possessing or controlling the explosive, making answer D incorrect. The offence includes the word 'control', which is far wider than mere possession, so 'control' over the pipe bomb in the storage facility would be covered, making answer B incorrect.

Investigators' Manual, para. 3.10.9

Answer 23.13

Answer **C** — Section 146 of the Serious Organised Crime and Police Act 2005 states that a person (A) commits an offence if, with the intention of causing a second person (B) to abstain from doing something which they are entitled to do (or abstain from doing) and A threatens B that A or somebody else will do a relevant act, and A does so wholly or mainly because B is a person falling within subsection (2). Persons covered by subsection 2 are numerous but include employees of an animal research organisation. It also covers spouses, civil partners, friends or relatives of such people, so a threat to HUBBARD would count. A 'relevant act' is any criminal or tortuous act. Following GREER home and peacefully asking her to stop work would not be covered (answers A and B).

Investigators' Manual, para. 3.10.11.2

Answer 23.14

Answer **B** — The power is available to officers in uniform only, making answer A incorrect. Answer C is incorrect as although no actual time limit in respect of the use of the power is stated in the legislation, it does state (at s. 47A(1)(iii)) that the duration of the authorisation should be no longer than is necessary to prevent an act of terrorism. Once the power has been authorised, a constable in uniform can stop and search pedestrians, vehicles and their occupants. There is no requirement that the searching officer 'reasonably believes' the vehicle/person(s) subject to the search are involved in terrorist activities; therefore answer D is incorrect.

Investigators' Manual, para. 3.10.7.4

Answer 23.15

Answer **B** — The measures that may be imposed under a TPIM are set out in sch.1 to the Act and have a time limit of two years.

Investigators' Manual, para. 3.10.8

24 Cybercrime

QUESTIONS

Question 24.1

The police in the United Kingdom have provided a definition as to what 'cybercrime' actually is.

What is that definition?

A Cybercrime is defined as the use of any computer network for criminal activity.

B Cybercrime is defined as the use of the Internet for criminal activity.

C Cybercrime is defined as the use of any computer to assist in the commission of fiduciary crimes.

D Cybercrime is defined as the use of any computer network for any criminal activity excluding those relating to sexual offences.

Question 24.2

BRIDGE works as a cleaner in the control room of a police force. As the control room is in operation 24 hours a day, BRIDGE must access the control room when resources are being despatched to incidents and also when computers are being used for a variety of police related issues. BRIDGE is vacuuming the floor of the control room when he hears one of the operators mention the name 'John HOBB' and also mentions HOBB's home address. HOBB is BRIDGE's best friend and intending to see why his friend has come to the attention of the police, BRIDGE looks over the shoulder of the operator and examines data which is displayed on the computer screen. BRIDGE intends to tell HOBB anything that he sees on the screen that he thinks will be of assistance to HOBB.

Considering the offence of unauthorised access to computer materials (contrary to s. 1 of the Computer Misuse Act 1990), which of the following comments is correct?

A BRIDGE has not committed the offence as he has not had any physical contact with the computer hardware.

B BRIDGE has committed the offence as he has secured access to restricted data.

C BRIDGE has not committed the offence as simply looking over a computer operator's shoulder to read what is on the screen would not be covered.

D BRIDGE has committed the offence which is triable on indictment only and punishable with five years' imprisonment.

Question 24.3

TIs DRAPER and EDGE are discussing the offence under s. 1 of the Computer Misuse Act 1990 and also the definition of a number of the Act's terms. The officers make a number of statements in relation to this legislation but only one is correct.

Which one is it?

A TI DRAPER states that erasing computer data would not constitute an offence under s. 1 of the Act.

B TI EDGE states that attempting to log on to a computer, even if it were unsuccessful, would still involve getting a computer to perform a function.

C TI DRAPER states that the only way a person can secure access to any program or data for the purpose of committing an offence under s. 1 is by using or copying data.

D TI EDGE states that this offence can only be committed by accessing a computer via the Internet.

Question 24.4

THOMPSON commits an offence under s. 1 of the Computer Misuse Act 1990 (unauthorised access to computer materials). The information he accesses provides bank account details of several hundred customers of the bank he works for. It is THOMPSON's intention to allow ISMAY to use the bank account details sometime in the following week in order to commit offences of fraud. What THOMPSON does not know is that he has accessed the bank account details of old customers of the bank; all of the account information he accesses is useless because the accounts no longer exist.

Considering the offence of unauthorised access with intent to commit further offences (contrary to s. 2 of the Computer Misuse Act 1990), which of the following comments is correct?

A THOMPSON has not committed the offence as he intends that the information concerned will facilitate the commission of an offence by another person.

B THOMPSON has not committed the offence because he intends the information to be used in the future and not on the same occasion as the unauthorised access offence was committed.

C THOMPSON has not committed the offence as the data he has accessed is useless and makes the commission of the future offence of fraud impossible.

D THOMPSON has committed the offence in these circumstances.

Question 24.5

MAYHEW works for NOSWORTHY who provides financial advice to thousands of her customers via the Internet. After a dispute, NOSWORTHY sacks MAYHEW. MAYHEW is outraged by NOSWORTHY's behaviour and wants revenge on his ex-employer. At home, MAYHEW develops a program that he intends will cause a series of problems for the computers at NOSWORTHY's business premises and impair their use. On the pretext of collecting some personal items, MAYHEW returns to the company premises and whilst in his old office he makes an unauthorised access to NOSWORTHY's computer system and runs the program he has developed. The program causes NOSWORTHY's computer system to record that information that came from one source actually came from another entirely different source. The program then generates millions of e-mails and sends them to NOSWORTHY's account, clogging up and impairing the use of the computer system. All of these effects are of a temporary nature and cease to operate one week after MAYHEW's visit to the company.

In relation to the offence of unauthorised acts to impair the operation of computers (contrary to s. 3 of the Computer Misuse Act 1990), at what point is the offence first committed by MAYHEW?

A When he creates the program at his home.

B When he makes the unauthorised access to NOSWORTHY's computer and runs the program.

C When the program causes NOSWORTHY's computer to incorrectly record information.

D When the program generates millions of e-mails.

Question 24.6

SABLE is extremely annoyed with KELLY (a neighbour of SABLE's who lives in a house opposite to SABLE) as KELLY allows his dog to foul on the footpath outside SABLE's house. SABLE picks up some of the faeces left by KELLY's dog and puts it through KELLY's letterbox. SABLE intends that KELLY should suffer distress as a consequence.

Considering the offence of sending a malicious communication (contrary to s. 1(1) of the Malicious Communications Act 1988), which of the following comments is correct?

A The offence has not been committed by SABLE as this is not a 'communication'.

B The offence has been committed by SABLE in these circumstances.

C The offence has not been committed by SABLE as the communication was not delivered in the form of a letter or electronic communication.

D The offence has not been committed as this is not a communication involving information which is false and known or believed to be false by the sender.

ANSWERS

Answer 24.1

Answer **A** — Cybercrime is defined as the use of any computer network for criminal activity. The Internet could well form a part of that network but it is not so limited, making answer B incorrect. Cybercrime is not limited to the commission of fiduciary (financial) crimes, eliminating answer C. Sexual offences are one of the main areas for concern when considering computer crime and are certainly not excluded, making answer D incorrect.

Investigators' Manual, para. 3.11.1

Answer 24.2

Answer **C** — This offence involves 'causing a computer to perform any function'. This means more than simply looking at material on a computer screen or having any physical contact with the computer hardware. The case of *R* v *Bow Street Metropolitan Stipendiary Magistrate, ex parte Government of the USA* [2000] 2 AC 216 is illustrative that the purpose of the Act is to address unauthorised access as opposed to unauthorised use of data, so behaviour such as looking over a computer operator's shoulder to read what is on the screen would not be covered, making answer B incorrect. Physical contact with the hardware is not required, making answer A incorrect. The offence is triable either way and punishable with a maximum term of imprisonment of two years, making answer D incorrect.

Investigators' Manual, para. 3.11.2.1

Answer 24.3

Answer **B** — Section 17 of the Computer Misuse Act 1990 defines a number of terms used in the Act. Section 17(2) starts that a person secures access to any program or data held in a computer if by causing a computer to perform any function he (a) alters or erases the program or data, (b) copies or moves it to any storage medium other than that in which it is held or to a different location in the storage medium in which it is held, (c) uses it or (d) has it output from the computer in which it is held (whether by having it displayed or in any other manner). This makes answers A and C incorrect. The offence does not require that the computer concerned needs to be connected to the Internet, making answer D incorrect. Any attempt to log on to a computer would involve getting a computer to perform a function.

Investigators' Manual, paras 3.11.2, 3.11.2.1, 3.11.2.2

Answer 24.4

Answer **D** — A person is guilty of an offence under s. 2 of the Computer Misuse Act 1990 if he commits an offence under s. 1 of the Act (as THOMPSON has done) with (a) the intention of committing another offence or (b) facilitating the commission of another offence (whether by himself or another). This makes answer A incorrect. Section 2(3) states that it is immaterial whether the further offence is to be committed on the same occasion as the unauthorised access offence, making answer B incorrect. Answer C is incorrect as s. 2(4) states that a person may be guilty of an offence under s. 2 even though the facts are such that the commission of the further offence is impossible.

Investigators' Manual, para. 3.11.2.3

Answer 24.5

Answer **B** — The offence is committed when a person does any unauthorised act in relation to a computer intending thereby to (a) impair the operation of any computer, (b) prevent or hinder access to any program or data held on any computer or (c) to impair the operation of any such program or the reliability of any such data. Therefore, the offence is committed when the unauthorised act is carried out with the requisite intention on the part of the offender (point B).

Investigators' Manual, para. 3.11.2.4

Answer 24.6

Answer **B** — The offence is not restricted to the sending of threatening or indecent communications and, in addition to sending letters, the offence covers sending any article when the sender's purpose is to cause anxiety or distress to the recipient. This will cover occasions where the article itself is indecent or grossly offensive (such as putting dog faeces through someone's letterbox).

Investigators' Manual, para. 3.11.4

PART FOUR

Sexual Offences

25 Sexual Offences, Rape and Sexual Assault

QUESTIONS

Question 25.1

WRIGHT works with LAKER and during an office party he suggests to LAKER that they have sex together; LAKER refuses. This annoys WRIGHT and later on he follows LAKER into the female toilets. WRIGHT demands that LAKER talk with him in one of the toilet cubicles and, once inside, WRIGHT locks the door. WRIGHT demands to know why LAKER refused to have sex with him and when LAKER begins to cry, WRIGHT tells her he would be happy if she took part in oral sex with him. LAKER asks to be let out of the cubicle but WRIGHT refuses. LAKER realises that WRIGHT will not let her out, so agrees to have oral sex with him and allows WRIGHT to put his penis in her mouth.

Considering the offence of rape only (contrary to s. 1 of the Sexual Offences Act 2003), which of the following statements is correct?

A No offence of rape has been committed because LAKER consented to the act of oral sex.

B Rape can only be committed if WRIGHT penetrates the vagina or anus of LAKER.

C WRIGHT commits rape, as LAKER was unlawfully detained at the time of the relevant act.

D WRIGHT has not committed rape because he has not used violence or caused LAKER to believe immediate violence would be used against her.

Question 25.2

DUPONT approaches THOMPSON in the street. He shows her a photograph of her three-year-old son and says, *'Me and my mate have been watching you and your boy, my mate's watching him now. Unless you do as I say, my mate will hurt your kid.'*

THOMPSON believes that her son is in immediate danger and that DUPONT's associate will harm him. DUPONT demands that THOMPSON follow him into a nearby alleyway where he puts his fingers into DUPONT's vagina. DUPONT does not have a friend watching THOMPSON's child, who is in no actual danger at the time of the act.

Has DUPONT committed an offence of rape?

A Yes, because at the time of the relevant act he has caused THOMPSON to believe that immediate violence would be used against another person.

B No, because he did not use violence against THOMPSON or cause her to believe that immediate violence would be used against her.

C Yes, because he has intentionally deceived THOMPSON into taking part in the relevant act.

D No, because intentionally penetrating THOMPSON's vagina with his fingers is not the *actus reus* of rape.

Question 25.3

SALHAN goes to a house party but because she is taking medication she only drinks orange juice. Her friend, CROSS, thinks it will be funny to spike SALHAN's drinks and without SALHAN's knowledge adds several vodkas to SALHAN's orange juice, causing SALHAN to become disorientated and drowsy. SALHAN goes to a bedroom in the house and lies down to get some rest. ALLEN walks into the room and seeing SALHAN on the bed he suggests that they have sexual intercourse. ALLEN has no idea that SALHAN is suffering from the combined effects of the medication and the vodka. SALHAN agrees and the two have sexual intercourse. The next day, SALHAN realises what has happened and accuses ALLEN of rape.

Which of the following statements is true?

A ALLEN is not guilty of rape, as he did not know that SALHAN had had her drinks spiked.

B The offence could only be committed if ALLEN was the person who had spiked SALHAN's drinks.

C ALLEN is guilty of rape, as at the time the sexual intercourse took place, a substance had been administered to SALHAN that was capable of causing her to be stupefied.

D Administering a substance capable of causing the complainant to be stupefied or overpowered would not constitute an offence of rape.

Question 25.4

ALLDAY and MASSEY (both males) have consensual anal intercourse. Immediately after the act, ALLDAY feels extremely guilty and begs MASSEY not to tell either of their wives what they have done. MASSEY punches ALLDAY in the face and tells him he will do what he likes. MASSEY then demands that ALLDAY place his penis in MASSEY's mouth or he will beat ALLDAY up. Compelled under the threat of violence, ALLDAY does so. Several minutes later, MASSEY demands anal intercourse. ALLDAY refuses but MASSEY tells him that he will tell their wives of their activities and as a result (in fear of MASSEY exposing what has taken place between the two men), ALLDAY allows MASSEY to have anal sexual intercourse with him.

At what stage, if at all, is the offence of rape committed?

A When MASSEY punches ALLDAY in the face immediately after the act of anal sexual intercourse.

B When ALLDAY is compelled to put his penis into MASSEY's mouth.

C When ALLDAY, out of fear, allows MASSEY to have anal sexual intercourse for a second time.

D The offence of rape is not committed.

Question 25.5

HARRISON has recently had gender reassignment surgery where the penis was removed and replaced with a surgically constructed vagina. HARRISON attends a party and flirts with DARVEL, suggesting that the two of them should have sexual intercourse, to which DARVEL agrees. The two go to a bedroom and begin to have sexual intercourse (penis to surgically constructed vagina). Several minutes into the act, HARRISON feels sick and asks DARVEL to stop. DARVEL takes no notice of HARRISON and continues to have sexual intercourse with HARRISON for several minutes despite HARRISON's protests. DARVEL then penetrates HARRISON's anus with his penis against HARRISON's wishes.

Which of the following statements is correct?

A A surgically constructed vagina would not be classed as part of the body for the purposes of rape.

B DARVEL commits rape when, after HARRISON asks him to stop, he continues to penetrate HARRISON's surgically constructed vagina.

C No offence of rape is committed because HARRISON initially consented to sexual intercourse with DARVEL.

D DARVEL only commits rape when he penetrates HARRISON's anus.

Question 25.6

CLAY goes to a party held at PIKE's house. During the evening of the party he goes into the bathroom where he sees WEBSTER lying on the floor having passed out from drinking too much. CLAY locks the bathroom door and removes all of WEBSTER's clothes. CLAY lies next to WEBSTER and kisses her, putting his tongue into WEBSTER's mouth in the process. Several minutes later he places his tongue into WEBSTER's vagina. CLAY then puts his penis inside WEBSTER's mouth before he puts a finger into WEBSTER's vagina.

At what point does CLAY commit an offence of assault by penetration (contrary to s. 2 of the Sexual Offences Act 2003)?

A When he puts his tongue into WEBSTER's mouth.
B When he puts his tongue into WEBSTER's vagina.
C When he puts his penis into WEBSTER's mouth.
D When he puts his finger into WEBSTER's vagina.

Question 25.7

HUNN and her common-law husband, DARROW, kidnap POOLE in a bid to extort a cash ransom from POOLE's husband. The two blindfold and handcuff POOLE and keep her in a basement flat for several days before the ransom is paid. During this time POOLE is subject to abuse by HUNN and DARROW. HUNN forces a candle into POOLE's vagina and while HUNN carries out this act, DARROW pushes a candle into POOLE's anus.

Considering the offence of assault by penetration (s. 2 of the Sexual Offences Act 2003) only, which of the following statements is correct?

A Only DARROW is guilty of this offence as it can only be committed by a male.
B Only DARROW commits the offence as assault by penetration only relates to the penetration of the vagina.
C Both HUNN and DARROW commit the offence.
D Neither HUNN nor DARROW commit the offence because POOLE was not penetrated with a part of the body.

Question 25.8

BEDDOW is at a nightclub and approaches GRAINGER and tries to talk to her as he finds her sexually attractive. GRAINGER is not interested in BEDDOW and tells him to go away. Later in the evening, GRAINGER is standing at the bar waiting to be served when BEDDOW approaches her from behind. To obtain sexual gratification, he takes out his penis and lightly touches GRAINGER's buttocks (through her clothing) with the tip of his penis. BEDDOW is aroused by this contact and ejaculates onto GRAINGER's skirt while he is touching her. GRAINGER is completely unaware that BEDDOW has behaved in this way.

Considering the offence of sexual assault (contrary to s. 3 of the Sexual Offences Act 2003), which of the following comments is correct?

A The offence has not been committed as no violence was used by BEDDOW.

B The offence has not been committed as BEDDOW has not touched GRAINGER's sexual organs.

C The offence has not been committed as GRAINGER is unaware that she has been touched.

D BEDDOW commits the offence in these circumstances.

Question 25.9

LAND is arrested on suspicion of a triple murder. She tells DC MOULT, the female arresting officer, that she has hidden a knife inside her vagina and the police will never get hold of it. She tells DC MOULT that at the first opportunity she will use the knife to kill a police officer in the custody area. As a result, inspector FOWLER authorises an intimate search of LAND to recover the knife. Because of the urgency of the situation, the intimate search takes place at the police station. LAND does not consent to the search and, against LAND's wishes, DC MOULT inserts her finger into LAND's vagina and recovers the knife.

Which of the following statements is correct?

A DC MOULT commits an offence of rape (contrary to s. 1 of the Sexual Offences Act 2003).

B DC MOULT commits an offence of assault by penetration (contrary to s. 2 of the Sexual Offences Act 2003).

C DC MOULT commits an offence of sexual assault (contrary to s. 3 of the Sexual Offences Act 2003).

D DC MOULT commits no offence in these circumstances.

Question 25.10

SPENCER is standing at a bus stop directly behind TUCKETT, who is holding an umbrella in his hand. TUCKETT is aware that SPENCER is relatively close to him and deliberately moves his umbrella so that the tip moves between SPENCER's legs and touches her vagina through her trousers. TUCKETT obtains sexual gratification from the act.

Considering only s. 3 of the Sexual Offences Act 2003, which of the following statements is correct?

A TUCKETT commits the offence because 'touching' includes touching with anything, in this case the umbrella.

B The offence has not been committed because TUCKETT must touch SPENCER with a part of his body.

C For the offence to be committed, the touching must amount to penetration.

D As the touching was carried out through SPENCER's trousers, the offence is incomplete.

Question 25.11

YARDLEY, MAJOR and LOCKHART (all females) are drinking together at LOCKHART's house. YARDLEY and LOCKHART take off all their clothes and begin to kiss and touch each other while MAJOR watches. LOCKHART asks MAJOR to kiss YARDLEY's breasts, to which MAJOR refuses. LOCKHART tells MAJOR that unless she does as she demands she will be assaulted. Because of the threat and against her will, MAJOR does as LOCKHART demands. YARDLEY consents to the act.

What is LOCKHART's liability in relation to the offence of causing a person to engage in sexual activity without consent (s. 4 of the Sexual Offences Act 2003)?

A LOCKHART does not commit the offence, as it must involve penetration.

B Because YARDLEY consented to the act, LOCKHART does not commit the offence.

C LOCKHART has committed the offence in these circumstances.

D As LOCKHART is a female, she cannot commit this offence.

Question 25.12

NAZIR and BOSWELL are walking down an alleyway when DEVILLE approaches them. DEVILLE produces a handgun and demands that BOSWELL kneel on the ground while NAZIR places his penis in BOSWELL's mouth. Fearing that they will be harmed NAZIR and BOSWELL do as they have been told to.

Considering these circumstances in light of s. 4 of the Sexual Offences Act 2003 only, which of the following statements is correct?

A This offence is punishable with a maximum sentence of five years' imprisonment.

B This offence is punishable with a maximum sentence of 10 years' imprisonment.

C This offence is punishable with a maximum sentence of 15 years' imprisonment.
D This offence is punishable with a maximum sentence of life imprisonment.

Question 25.13

ABLITT is in a nightclub where he begins talking to RICHARDS, who is an actress. ABLITT tells RICHARDS that he is only in the country for a week, after which he will fly out to America where he will be directing a film starring a major Hollywood actor; this is a lie as ABLITT is in fact a plumber. ABLITT tells RICHARDS that he can get her a part in the film but he will only do so if she has sexual intercourse with him. To further her acting career, RICHARDS goes to ABLITT's house, where she has sexual intercourse with him.

What effect will s. 76 of the Sexual Offences Act 2003 have on ABLITT's actions?

A As ABLITT has deceived RICHARDS regarding the nature of the act, RICHARDS will be presumed not to consent to it.
B RICHARDS will be presumed not to have consented to the act as ABLITT has intentionally deceived her by impersonating a film director.
C It will have no effect as ABLITT has not impersonated a person known personally to RICHARDS.
D It will have no effect as this section relates to the use of violence to obtain consent from the victim.

Question 25.14

CHANNON (aged 35 years) kidnaps ILIFF (aged 12 years) and forces ILIFF to have sexual intercourse with him (penis to vagina). CHANNON is later arrested for an offence of rape (s. 1 of the Sexual Offences Act 2003).

Which of the following statements is correct?

A The prosecution will have to prove intentional penetration alone.
B The prosecution will have to prove the child's age alone.
C The prosecution will have to prove intentional penetration and the child's age.
D The prosecution will have to prove intentional penetration, the child's age and the fact that ILIFF did not consent to the act.

Question 25.15

SHARPE kidnaps YOUNG and locks her in the basement of his house for several days. During this time SHARPE compels YOUNG to put a vibrator into her mouth. SHARPE tells his friend, HEMMING, about YOUNG and invites HEMMING to watch him abuse her. HEMMING enters the basement and watches YOUNG being abused. HEMMING asks YOUNG if she will have sexual intercourse with him. YOUNG does not reply so HEMMING has sexual intercourse with her (penis to vagina).

Which of the following statements is correct with regard to the Sexual Offences Act 2003?

A HEMMING commits the offence of rape (contrary to s. 1 of the Sexual Offences Act 2003).

B Both SHARPE and HEMMING commit the offence of rape (contrary to s. 1 of the Sexual Offences Act 2003).

C SHARPE commits the offence of assault by penetration (contrary to s. 2 of the Sexual Offences Act 2003).

D Both SHARPE and HEMMING commit the offence of assault by penetration (contrary to s. 2 of the Sexual Offences Act 2003).

Question 25.16

STARREN meets PORTER in a pub and the two get on very well with each other. STARREN invites PORTER back to her house for a drink. At STARREN's house the couple begin to kiss and touch each other and PORTER asks STARREN if she will have sexual intercourse with him. STARREN replies that she will but because this is a 'one-night-stand' she will only do so if PORTER wears a condom on his penis while they are having sexual intercourse; PORTER agrees to do so. While PORTER is trying to place the condom on his penis he accidentally rips it so that it is useless. He wants to have sexual intercourse with STARREN so he tells her that he has put a condom on and as a consequence she allows him to have sexual intercourse (penis to vagina) with her.

Considering the issues surrounding the offence of rape (contrary to s. 1 of the Sexual Offences Act 2003), which of the following statements is correct?

A This is not an offence of rape as STARREN has not been deceived as to the nature of the act.

B This is an offence of rape and the evidential presumptions in respect of consent under s. 75 of the Sexual Offences Act 2003 would be applicable in these circumstances.

C This is not an offence of rape as STARREN has consented to sexual intercourse with PORTER.

D This is an offence of rape as STARREN would only consent to sexual intercourse if PORTER was wearing a condom at the time and he was not.

Question 25.17

LAMBERT (aged 15 years) is the victim of an offence of sexual activity with a child (contrary to s. 9 of the Sexual Offences Act 2003). She speaks to DC SALK (the officer in the case), as she is concerned that her identity will be disclosed during the forthcoming trial.

What advice should DC SALK offer?

A LAMBERT is entitled to anonymity throughout her lifetime.

B Only rape victims are entitled to anonymity.

C LAMBERT's identity will be protected until she is 18 years old.

D Anonymity is only provided to victims where violence has formed part of the offence.

Question 25.18

DEAR breaks into a house owned by HESSION. DEAR enters HESSION's bedroom and wakes her up by placing his hand over her mouth. HESSION can see that DEAR is holding a gun to her head and is terrified. DEAR tells HESSION to be quiet and do what he tells her to do or he will kill her; he then removes his hand. He tells HESSION he wants her to '*talk dirty to him*' and tell him how she would have sexual intercourse with him. As HESSION is graphically describing what she would do, DEAR takes out his penis and begins to masturbate. DEAR then tells HESSION that if she masturbates herself he will go away. HESSION does as DEAR demands and shortly afterwards DEAR ejaculates and then leaves.

At what point, if at all, does DEAR first commit an offence contrary to s. 4 of the Sexual Offences Act 2003 (causing sexual activity without consent)?

A When he forces HESSION to engage in a conversation of a sexual nature.

B When he masturbates himself.

C When he forces HESSION to masturbate herself.

D DEAR does not commit the offence in this situation.

ANSWERS

Answer 25.1

Answer **C** — Rape can be committed if a male penetrates the vagina, anus or mouth of his victim, making answer B incorrect. Although the use of or threat to use violence would negate consent (s. 72(2)(a) and (b)), this is not the only way that a complainant can be deemed to have refused consent to the relevant act, making answer D incorrect. Consent will only be true consent if the person agrees by choice and has the freedom and capacity to make that choice. Under s. 75(2)(c) of the Act, the complainant is taken not to have consented to the relevant act if the complainant was, and the defendant was not, unlawfully detained at the time of the relevant act, making answer A incorrect.

Investigators' Manual, paras 4.2.1 to 4.2.6

Answer 25.2

Answer **D** — Although answer A is correct insofar as the consent obtained from THOMPSON is not true consent as it is obtained by threatening immediate violence against another person, the *actus reus* of rape is the penetration of the vagina, anus or mouth of another person with the penis, making this answer incorrect. Answer B is incorrect as had DUPONT used violence, this would still not be rape. The deception in rape must be as to the nature or purpose of the relevant act, not the circumstances leading up to the act, making answer C incorrect.

Investigators' Manual, paras 4.2.1 to 4.2.6

Answer 25.3

Answer **A** — Answer D is incorrect as these circumstances are catered for in s. 75(2)(f) of the Act. *Any person* can administer or cause the substance to be taken, making answer B incorrect. Under s. 75 (evidential presumptions about consent), it must be proved that the defendant (i) did the relevant act, (ii) that any of the circumstances specified in subsection (2) existed and (iii) that the defendant *knew* that those circumstances existed. In these circumstances, ALLEN does not know that SALHAN has had her drinks spiked and therefore is not guilty of the offence of rape, making answer C incorrect.

Investigators' Manual, paras 4.2.1 to 4.2.6

Answer 25.4

Answer **C** — Rape is committed when a person (A) intentionally penetrates the vagina, anus or mouth of another person (B) with his penis and that other person (B) does not consent to the penetration and A does not reasonably believe that B consents. The first act of anal sexual intercourse was consensual and although violence was used by MASSEY after this act, that will not alter the true consent given to anal intercourse on the first occasion, making answer A incorrect. Answer B is incorrect as rape is committed when the defendant intentionally penetrates the vagina, anus or mouth of the complainant with his penis—it is not committed when the defendant (A) forces the complainant (B) to penetrate A's mouth with B's penis. The offence is committed at point C as at this point although ALLDAY allows the penetration to take place, it is only allowed because of ALLDAY's fear that his activities will be exposed to his wife. As a result, this is not 'true' consent. 'True' consent is given by a person who agrees by choice and has the freedom and capacity to make that choice. Therefore, if a person does not have any choice in the matter, or their choice is not a genuine exercise of their free will (and ALLDAY's choice is not), they will not have consented, making answer D incorrect in the process.

Investigators' Manual, paras 4.2.1 to 4.2.6

Answer 25.5

Answer **B** — Answer A is incorrect as s. 79(3) of the Act states that references to the body include references to a part surgically constructed (in particular, through gender reassignment surgery). Answer C is incorrect because although HARRISON initially agreed to sexual intercourse with DARVEL, s. 79(2) of the Act states that penetration is a continuing act from entry to withdrawal so that where a person consents at the time of entry to penetration, but then withdraws consent and the penetration continues, the person penetrating is guilty of rape. This section makes answer D incorrect, as the offence of rape is complete when HARRISON continues penetration of DARVEL's vagina.

Investigators' Manual, paras 4.2.1 to 4.2.6

Answer 25.6

Answer **B** — The offence under s. 2 of the Act is committed when a person intentionally penetrates the vagina or anus of another person with a part of his body or anything else. The offence is not committed by penetration of the mouth of the victim, making answers A and C incorrect. The offence is committed at point B as at this point, CLAY penetrates WEBSTER's vagina with his tongue (a part of his body), making answer D incorrect.

Investigators' Manual, para. 4.3.1

Answer 25.7

Answer **C** — This offence can be committed by a male or female against a male or female, making answer A incorrect. The offence is committed when the vagina or anus of the victim is penetrated by the offender, making answer B incorrect. The penetration can be with a part of his/her body or anything else, making answer D incorrect.

Investigators' Manual, para. 4.3.1

Answer 25.8

Answer **D** — There is no requirement for force or violence for the offence to be committed, making answer A incorrect. Answer B is incorrect as the part of the body touched does not have to be a sexual organ. Answer C is incorrect as the victim need not be aware of being touched, so the offence was committed when the accused secretly took his penis out of his trousers and ejaculated onto a woman's clothing when pressed up against her dancing at a nightclub (*R* v *Bounekhla* [2006] EWCA Crim 1217).

Investigators' Manual, paras 4.3.3, 4.3.4

Answer 25.9

Answer **D** — Rape can only be committed by a male, making answer A incorrect. An intimate search carried out in these circumstances is legal and so the central issue in relation to these circumstances is whether the activity is 'sexual'. Section 78 of the Act defines the word 'sexual' so that it excludes medical procedures and intimate searches where (in this case) LAND does not consent to the penetration and DC MOULT does not reasonably believe that LAND consents. As the activity would not be considered 'sexual', answers B and C are incorrect.

Investigators' Manual, paras 4.3.1 to 4.3.4

Answer 25.10

Answer **A** — A sexual assault under s. 3 of the Act is committed when a person intentionally touches another person, the touching is sexual and the victim does not consent to the touching and the offender does not reasonably believe that the victim consents. Section 79(8) defines 'touching' for the purposes of the act as including touching with (a) any part of the body, (b) with anything else or (c) through anything and in particular includes touching amounting to penetration. The definition of 'touching' therefore includes the use of the umbrella to commit the offence as it falls under s. 79(8)(b) of the Act, making answers B, C and D incorrect.

Investigators' Manual, paras 4.3.3 to 4.3.4

Answer 25.11

Answer **C** — Answer A is incorrect as the offence involves any activity that is 'sexual' as opposed to acts involving penetration only. The fact that YARDLEY consented to the act is immaterial as MAJOR (the victim) did not consent, making answer B incorrect. Answer D is incorrect as this offence can be committed by a male or female.

Investigators' Manual, para. 4.3.5

Answer 25.12

Answer **D** — The sentencing provisions of this offence make it punishable with life imprisonment. These circumstances arise when the offence involves penetration, in particular: of the victim's anus or vagina, *of the victim's mouth with a penis* (BOSWELL), of any other person's anus or vagina with a part of the victim's body or *of any person's mouth by the victim's penis* (NAZIR).

Investigators' Manual, para. 4.3.5

Answer 25.13

Answer **C** — This section of the Act relates to the use of some form of deception in order to obtain consent from the victim and not the use of violence to obtain consent (covered by s. 75 of the Act), making answer D incorrect. Answer A is incorrect as RICHARDS has not been deceived into the act by a misrepresentation as to the nature of the act; RICHARDS knew that what she was doing was sexual intercourse. Answer B is incorrect as the person impersonated must be known *personally* to the victim.

Investigators' Manual, paras 4.2.5 to 4.2.6

Answer 25.14

Answer **C** — If the victim of the offence is under the age of 13, the prosecution simply have to prove intentional penetration and the child's age. No issue of 'consent' arises.

Investigators' Manual, para. 4.2.1

Answer 25.15

Answer **A** — Rape can only be committed by a male intentionally penetrating the vagina, anus or mouth of the victim with his penis. This makes answer B incorrect. Assault by penetration does not include penetration of the victim's mouth, making answers C and D incorrect. Where the complainant was, and the defendant was not, unlawfully detained at the time of the relevant act and the defendant knew that fact existed, it will be presumed that the victim did not consent.

Investigators' Manual, paras 4.2.1 to 4.2.5

Answer 25.16

Answer **D** — Answer B is incorrect as the presumptions under s. 75 would not be applicable to a case of this nature. Answer A is incorrect as although STARREN knows that she is having sexual intercourse, misrepresentation in relation to the nature of the act is not the only way that rape can be committed (deception in relation to the nature of the act is important when considering the presumptions under s. 76 of the Act). Answer C is incorrect as although STARREN has consented to sexual intercourse with PORTER this is conditional on the fact that he wears a condom; he is not doing so. In *Assange* v *Swedish Prosecution Authority* [2011] EWHC 2489 (Admin), the Divisional Court held that it would be open to a jury to hold that, if a complainant had made it clear that she would consent to sexual intercourse only if the appellant used a condom, then there would be no consent if, without her consent, he did not use a condom, or removed or tore the condom without her consent.

Investigators' Manual, paras 4.2.1 to 4.2.4

Answer 25.17

Answer **A** — Under the Sexual Offences (Amendment) Acts 1976 and 1992, victims of most sexual offences, including rape and indecency with children, are entitled to anonymity throughout their lifetime.

Investigators' Manual, para. 4.1.3

Answer 25.18

Answer **A** — This offence can involve a number of permutations, for example a woman making a man penetrate her, a man forcing someone else to masturbate him, or a woman making another woman masturbate a third person or even an animal. The term 'activity' is not defined and can include engaging someone in a conversation of a sexual nature (*R* v *Grout* [2011] EWCA Crim 299), meaning that the offence is committed at point A.

Investigators' Manual, para. 4.3.5

26 Child Sex Offences

QUESTIONS

Question 26.1

STEADMAN (aged 17 years) is approached by KEANE (aged 14 years). KEANE has a 'crush' on STEADMAN and she asks STEADMAN if he will have sexual intercourse with her. STEADMAN refuses but states that he will take part in oral sex with KEANE. The two meet a few hours later, when STEADMAN places his penis into KEANE's mouth.

In relation to s. 9 of the Sexual Offences Act 2003 (sexual activity with a child), which of the following statements is correct?

A No offence is committed by STEADMAN as he is under 18 years of age.

B No offence is committed by STEADMAN as KEANE has consented to the act.

C No offence is committed by STEADMAN as KEANE is over 13 years of age.

D No offence is committed by STEADMAN as the sexual activity does not involve penetration of the vagina or the anus.

Question 26.2

CASE and her boyfriend PRIZEMAN (both aged 25 years) are babysitting SHIPMAN (aged 12 years). CASE and PRIZEMAN are watching television in the downstairs lounge when PRIZEMAN sees SHIPMAN looking through an open doorway into the lounge and watching the television. CASE is unaware of the presence of SHIPMAN. PRIZEMAN undresses CASE and begins to have sexual intercourse with her. He intends that SHIPMAN should see the act and wishes to obtain sexual gratification from that fact. Unknown to PRIZEMAN, who believes SHIPMAN is watching, SHIPMAN has in fact returned to her bedroom on the first floor and does not see PRIZEMAN undress CASE and have sexual intercourse with her.

Is PRIZEMAN guilty of an offence of engaging in sexual activity in the presence of a child (contrary to s. 11 of the Sexual Offences Act 2003)?

A Yes, even though SHIPMAN is not present PRIZEMAN intended the act to be viewed by her.

B No, because SHIPMAN is not present or in a place where she can observe the act.

C Yes, because PRIZEMAN believes that SHIPMAN is watching the sexual activity.

D No, because CASE was never aware of SHIPMAN's presence.

Question 26.3

An offence under s. 11 of the Sexual Offences Act 2003 is committed when a person engages in sexual activity in the presence of a child.

Which of the following statements is correct with regard to this offence?

A The person committing this offence must be at least 16 years old.

B The activity need not be carried out in order to obtain sexual gratification.

C There must be a person under 16 years old present or in a place from which the defendant can be observed.

D It is necessary to show that the child was aware of the activity.

Question 26.4

LANDEN (aged 20 years) approaches EIFION (aged 12 years) in a park. LANDEN persuades EIFION to accompany him back to his house, where LANDEN plays a DVD to EIFION that contains animated cartoon images of sexual activity. LANDEN obtains sexual gratification from this activity.

Has LANDEN committed an offence under s. 12 of the Sexual Offences Act 2003 (causing a child to watch a sexual act)?

A Yes, the images that EIFION sees can be images of imaginary persons so an animated cartoon image would be covered by the offence.

B No, the sexual act must be performed by LANDEN.

C Yes, but only because EIFION is under 13 years of age; if he were over 13, then the offence would not be committed.

D No, the image must be that of a 'person' engaged in sexual activity and not of a cartoon.

Question 26.5

HUGHES (aged 45 years) holds a barbeque at his house and invites a large number of guests and their children. Several hours after the barbeque has started, HUGHES goes into his house and into his study where he turns on his computer and goes on to the Internet. While he is on the Internet he visits several pornographic sites that show pictures of adults taking part in explicit sexual activity. HUGHES has left the door to his study open because he believes all of his guests are outside and nobody will see what he is doing. HUGHES's purpose when he is looking at the pictures is to obtain sexual gratification. Unknown to HUGHES, FORREST (aged 15 years) is looking at the same pictures because HUGHES has left the door to his study open.

Considering the offence of causing a child to watch a sexual act (contrary to s. 12 of the Sexual Offences Act 2003), which of the following statements is correct?

A As there are children at the party HUGHES would know of the likelihood of a child seeing the images and therefore commits an offence.

B As HUGHES has acted for the purposes of sexual gratification, the offence is complete.

C HUGHES does not commit the offence as still images are not included in this section of the legislation.

D HUGHES does not commit an offence under this section as he must intentionally cause another person to watch the activity.

Question 26.6

If a child or young person under the age of 18 years does anything that would be an offence under ss. 9 to 12 of the Sexual Offences Act 2003, s. 13 of the Act makes that activity an offence.

What is the purpose of this section of the Act?

A The purpose of this section is to provide a lower penalty of one year's imprisonment where the offender is aged under 18 years.

B The purpose of this section is to provide a lower penalty of three years' imprisonment where the offender is aged under 18 years.

C The purpose of this section is to provide a lower penalty of five years' imprisonment where the offender is aged under 18 years.

D The purpose of this section is to provide a lower penalty of seven years' imprisonment where the offender is aged under 18 years.

Question 26.7

DEVILLE has been on holiday to Thailand on several occasions. During his holidays he had sexual intercourse with girls under 13 years old. He tells his friend, HALLBROOK, about his holiday experiences. HALLBROOK asks DEVILLE if he will arrange flights, hotel accommodation and personal contacts for him so that he can visit Thailand for the same reason. HALLBROOK tells DEVILLE that he has never done anything like this before and so when he goes to Thailand he may not actually have sexual intercourse with girls under the age of 13. DEVILLE makes the necessary arrangements for HALLBROOK in the belief that HALLBROOK will have sexual intercourse with girls under the age of 13 once he arrives in Thailand.

With regard to s. 14 of the Sexual Offences Act 2003 (arranging or facilitating the commission of a child sex offence), which of the following statements is true?

A DEVILLE does not commit the offence as he has arranged for the activities to take place outside the United Kingdom.

B DEVILLE commits the offence as he believes that HALLBROOK will have sexual intercourse with girls under 13 years of age.

C DEVILLE will commit the offence if HALLBROOK actually has sexual intercourse with girls under the age of 13; if he does not then DEVILLE does not commit the offence.

D DEVILLE does not commit the offence as he only believes rather than intends that HALLBROOK will have sexual intercourse with girls under the age of 13.

Question 26.8

EVERLY is a predatory paedophile and wishes to rape a girl under the age of 13 (contrary to s. 5 of the Sexual Offences Act 2003). He befriends CLAMP (a girl aged nine years) using an Internet 'chat room' and arranges to meet her outside her school the next day in order to commit the offence. Unknown to EVERLY, CLAMP is not a nine-year-old child but is in fact a police officer using the Internet to track and arrest paedophiles.

Why is no offence of arranging or facilitating the commission of a child sex offence (contrary to s. 14 of the Sexual Offences Act 2003) committed by EVERLY?

A Because this offence is only committed when a person arranges or facilitates something that he intends another person to do or believes that another person will do.

B Because rape of a child under 13 (contrary to s. 5 of the Sexual Offences Act 2003) is not an offence that is covered by this section.

C Because the offence could never be committed. The person that EVERLY had arranged to meet is a police officer and not a nine-year-old child.

D Because the arrangements were made using the Internet and not face to face.

Question 26.9

BALLARD (aged 20 years) attends his cousin's 18th birthday party. During the evening of the party he speaks to GALBRAITH, who tells BALLARD that she is only 14 years old. GALBRAITH tells BALLARD that she would like to see a tennis match at Wimbledon but cannot afford a ticket. BALLARD asks GALBRAITH to meet him in a week's time as he has a contact at Wimbledon and can obtain free tickets; GALBRAITH agrees. One week later, BALLARD travels to meet GALBRAITH as he has obtained a ticket for Wimbledon for her. However, on the journey to meet her, BALLARD decides to sexually assault GALBRAITH after their meeting and travels to meet her with that intent.

With regard to the offence of meeting a child following sexual grooming (s. 15 of the Sexual Offences Act 2003), which of the following statements is correct?

A The offence is not committed as BALLARD did not intend to sexually assault GALBRAITH when they first met.

B BALLARD commits the offence as he is travelling to meet GALBRAITH with the intention to commit a relevant offence.

C BALLARD will only commit the offence when he actually meets with GALBRAITH.

D BALLARD does not commit the offence as he has not met or communicated with GALBRAITH on at least two earlier occasions.

Question 26.10

HARVEY (aged 45 years) is on holiday in Cyprus. He goes to an Internet café where he communicates with PREECE in an Internet 'chat room'. PREECE tells HARVEY that she is 15 years old and lives in the United States. During the course of his holiday, HARVEY communicates with PREECE on another five occasions, during which the two exchange home addresses. In their last communication, PREECE tells HARVEY that she would like to have sexual intercourse when she visits the United Kingdom in a week's time, an offer that HARVEY accepts (intending to have sexual intercourse with PREECE). HARVEY returns home to the United Kingdom and, one week after his return, PREECE visits HARVEY's home address. PREECE tells HARVEY that she would like to make good on her promise and have sexual intercourse with him.

Has HARVEY committed an offence contrary to s. 15 of the Sexual Offences Act 2003 (meeting a child following sexual grooming)?

A No, because the original communications took place in Cyprus and not in the United Kingdom.

B Yes, the offence is complete when PREECE travels to meet HARVEY.

C No, because the previous meeting between the two was via an Internet 'chat room' rather than a face-to-face meeting.

D Yes, the offence is complete but only when PREECE arrives at HARVEY's home address.

Question 26.11

SHARRAT (aged 36 years) has a son (aged two years). While SHARRAT's wife is out working, SHARRAT enters his son's nursery and puts his penis inside his son's mouth.

In relation to s. 25 of the Sexual Offences Act 2003 (sexual activity with a child family member), which of the following statements is correct?

A SHARRAT is not liable for this offence as it does not include penetration of the victim's mouth.

B SHARRAT has committed the offence and because his victim is under 16 years of age the punishment is life imprisonment.

C SHARRAT has committed the offence, which is triable on indictment and punishable with 14 years' imprisonment.

D SHARRAT has committed the offence, which is triable either way and punishable with five years' imprisonment.

Question 26.12

POWELL (aged 26 years) drives to a family wedding reception where he speaks to his first cousin, IMBER (aged 17 years). IMBER has lived in Australia all her life and this is the first time the two have ever met so they are totally unaware that they are cousins. The two talk to each other all night and as the evening draws to a close, IMBER tells POWELL that she wants to have sexual intercourse with him. They go outside the wedding venue, get into POWELL's car and have sexual intercourse (penis to vagina).

Considering ss. 25 and 27 of the Sexual Offences Act 2003, has POWELL committed an offence?

A No, because the relationship between the two is not known to either party.

B Yes, because IMBER is under 18 years of age.

C No, because IMBER is over 16 years of age.

D Yes, sexual intercourse with a first cousin would constitute an offence in these circumstances.

Question 26.13

Under s. 25 of the Sexual Offences Act 2003 (sexual activity with a child family member), the prosecution will have to prove that the defendant 'touched' the victim and that the touching was 'sexual'. However, other evidence must be proved in order for a defendant to be found guilty of such an offence.

Which of the following is correct with regard to the other evidence?

A The age of the victim must be proved and the defendant will have an evidential burden to discharge in that regard.

B The existence of the relevant family relationship between the defendant and the victim and the age of the victim must be proved and the defendant will have an evidential burden to discharge in that regard.

C The existence of the relevant family relationship between the defendant and the victim must be proved and the prosecution will have an evidential burden to discharge in that regard.

D The age of the victim must be proved and the prosecution will have an evidential burden to discharge in that regard.

Question 26.14

JARVIS (aged 15 years) is the half-brother of LYONS (aged 15 years). The two attend the same school and go on a school trip to Wales, where they share a tent. One evening, LYONS takes off all of his clothes and approaches JARVIS, suggesting that they should have anal sexual intercourse together. JARVIS is offended and flatly refuses.

With regard to ss. 25, 26 and 27 of the Sexual Offences Act 2003, which of the following statements is correct?

A LYONS does not commit an offence under either section as a half-brother is not a relevant family relationship (s. 27 of the Act).

B LYONS is guilty of an offence of sexual activity with a child member (s. 25 of the Act).

C LYONS does not commit an offence under either section as he is under 18 years of age.

D LYONS is guilty of an offence of inciting sexual activity with a child member (s. 26 of the Act).

Question 26.15

RENTON (aged 25 years) visits his old foster parent, STRAKER. While visiting STRAKER, RENTON is introduced to THAWLEY (aged 16 years), who has been living with STRAKER for the past two years. Prior to this meeting, RENTON and THAWLEY have never met each other. RENTON and THAWLEY get on extremely well and begin to see each other on a regular basis as boyfriend and girlfriend. One month after their initial meeting, RENTON and THAWLEY have consensual sexual intercourse.

Has RENTON committed an offence contrary to s. 25 of the Sexual Offences Act 2003?

A Yes, as RENTON and THAWLEY have the same foster parent.

B No, because sexual intercourse between the two is consensual.

C Yes, because THAWLEY is under 18 years of age.

D No, because RENTON and THAWLEY have never lived in the same household.

Question 26.16

WOOD (aged 17 years) and PERCIVAL (aged 17 years) have been going out together for six months and have had sexual intercourse on a number of occasions. Their respective parents have met each other several times and they begin a relationship together that leads to their marriage. This results in both parents, WOOD and PERCIVAL moving into the same house.

If WOOD and PERCIVAL now have sexual intercourse, which of the following will be true with regard to s. 25 of the Sexual Offences Act 2003 (sexual activity with a child family member)?

A WOOD and PERCIVAL are now stepsister and stepbrother and they cannot have sexual intercourse without committing an offence.

B The only way that WOOD and PERCIVAL would not commit an offence would be if they were lawfully married at the time.

C WOOD and PERCIVAL will not commit an offence as their sexual relationship predates the newly created family relationship.

D WOOD and PERCIVAL are both under the age of 18 and cannot commit the offence.

Question 26.17

ARCHER (aged 25 years) meets BARNARD (aged 23 years) in a bar. The two go on to a nightclub together and then go back to ARCHER's home address. ARCHER masturbates BARNARD's penis before putting her forefinger into BARNARD's anus. The two then have consensual sexual intercourse (penis to vagina). Unknown to either ARCHER or BARNARD, they are in fact brother and sister.

At what point, if at all, does the offence of sex with an adult relative (s. 64 of the Sexual Offences Act 2003) take place?

A When ARCHER masturbates BARNARD.

B When ARCHER puts her forefinger into BARNARD's anus.

C When ARCHER and BARNARD have consensual sexual intercourse.

D The offence under s. 64 is not committed in these circumstances.

Question 26.18

CANNON (aged 19 years) has consensual anal intercourse with DARROCH (aged 40 years), who is CANNON's uncle. This is an offence contrary to s. 64 of the Sexual Offences Act 2003 (sex with an adult relative).

If the two men were to be prosecuted for this offence, what is the maximum sentence that can be imposed on them?

A The maximum sentence for this offence is two years' imprisonment.

B The maximum sentence for this offence is three years' imprisonment.

C The maximum sentence for this offence is four years' imprisonment.

D The maximum sentence for this offence is five years' imprisonment.

Question 26.19

GATRELL (aged 21 years) is living with his partner HADLOW (aged 17 years) in an enduring family relationship. GATRELL takes a dozen photographs of HADLOW taking part in simulated sex acts with INGLEY (aged 25 years). HADLOW and INGLEY are both naked in the photographs and both consent to the photographs being taken by GATRELL. GATRELL wishes to keep the photographs for his own pleasure and does not intend to distribute them in any way.

With regard to the taking of indecent photographs (contrary to s. 1 of the Protection of Children Act 1978 (as amended by s. 45 of the Sexual Offences Act 2003)), has GATRELL committed an offence?

A Yes, as the photographs show a person other than GATRELL and HADLOW.

B No, because GATRELL and HADLOW were living together in an enduring family relationship.

C Yes, because indecent photographs of a child under 18 years of age cannot be taken in any circumstances.

D No, because HADLOW consented to the photographs being taken and she is over 16 years of age.

Question 26.20

JOHNSON (aged 20 years) takes indecent photographs of LAWFORD (aged 16 years). At the time the photographs are taken by JOHNSON, all the requirements of s. 45 of the Sexual Offences Act 2003 (providing a defence to the taking of indecent photographs) are satisfied so that the actual taking of the photographs is not in itself illegal.

Considering only s. 1 of the Protection of Children Act 1978 (indecent photographs of children), at what stage, if at all, would JOHNSON commit an offence?

A When he has the indecent photographs in his possession to view them for his own personal pleasure.

B When he has the indecent photographs in his possession with a view to showing them to his friend, MANNING (aged 23 years).

C When he has the indecent photographs in his possession and shows them to his friend, NEWPORT (aged 23 years).

D JOHNSON does not commit an offence in these circumstances.

Question 26.21

ROLFE is a local councillor who is running an anti-child pornography campaign. Because of ROLFE's campaign, PARNELL (a paedophile) decides to send ROLFE a large number of indecent photographs of children in order to offend him. PARNELL contacts OXLEY, a delivery van driver, to deliver a parcel containing hundreds of indecent photographs of children under the age of ten to ROLFE's home address. OXLEY (unaware of the contents) collects the parcel from PARNELL and places it on the front seat of his van and sets off. Several miles later, OXLEY has to brake sharply to avoid an accident and the parcel slips off the front seat and hits the dashboard of his van. In the process, the packaging is damaged and OXLEY sees the contents. OXLEY needs the money for delivering the parcel and so continues to his destination, where he delivers the parcel to ROLFE. The photographs outrage ROLFE and, believing he has a legitimate reason to show the photographs, he shows them to a local newspaper editor as evidence to highlight his anti-child pornography campaign.

Who has committed an offence contrary to s. 1 of the Protection of Children Act 1978?

A PARNELL only.

B PARNELL and OXLEY.

C PARNELL and ROLFE.

D PARNELL, OXLEY and ROLFE (although ROLFE would have a defence if charged with the offence).

Question 26.22

Section 1 of the Protection of Children Act 1978 and s. 160 of the Criminal Justice Act 1988 both deal with indecent photographs and 'pseudo-photographs' of children. These images can be obtained, in many cases, via the use of the Internet. There has been a significant amount of authoritative case law in this area that investigators ought to be aware of when gathering evidence of these offences.

With regard to the authoritative case law, which of the following statements is correct?

A 'Making' a pseudo-photograph does not include voluntarily browsing through indecent images of children on and from the Internet.

B Evidence showing how a computer had been used to access paedophile news groups, chat-lines and websites would not be relevant to a case relating to the creation of an indecent image of a child.

C An image consisting of two parts of two different photographs taped together (the naked body of a woman taped to the head of a child) would not be a 'pseudo-photograph'.

D Downloading images from the Internet will not amount to 'making' a photograph.

Question 26.23

SANDBROOK (aged 25 years) has several indecent photographs of TAFANO (aged 14 years) posted through his front door. SANDBROOK had not made any prior request for these photographs to be delivered. SANDBROOK opens the envelope containing the photographs and, having examined them, he leaves them on a shelf in his flat. Six months later, SANDBROOK's flat is raided by the police and the photographs of TAFANO are discovered. SANDBROOK states that he has not shown or distributed the photographs of TAFANO to anyone else, nor did he intend to do so.

With regard to s. 160 of the Criminal Justice Act 1988, which of the following statements is correct?

A SANDBROOK does not commit the offence as the photographs are of a child aged over 13 years of age.

B SANDBROOK has committed the offence but would have a defence because the photographs were sent to him without any prior request.

C As SANDBROOK has not shown or distributed the photographs to anyone else, he has not committed an offence under this Act.

D SANDBROOK has committed the offence, which is punishable with up to five years' imprisonment.

Question 26.24

The police carry out a raid on a house belonging to CHAPMAN in connection with sexual offences against children. During the course of the search of the premises, a number of images are recovered. One set of images are in the form of a short video clip recovered from a mobile phone. They illustrate HARPER (a 17-year-old-female) standing next to CHAPMAN who is naked and masturbating. In a video clip recovered from CHAPMAN's computer, CHAPMAN can be seen placing his penis in the anus of a cartoon (imaginary) child.

Considering the offence of possession of prohibited images of children (contrary to s. 62 of the Coroners and Justice Act 2009), which of the following statements is correct?

A The image of HARPER and the imaginary child are prohibited images.

B Only the image of HARPER is a prohibited image.

C Only the image of the imaginary child is a prohibited image.

D These images are not prohibited images under s. 62 of the Act.

ANSWERS

Answer 26.1

Answer **A** — The offence under s. 9 of the Act can only be committed where the defendant is aged 18 years or over. Answer B is incorrect as whether KEANE consented to the act or not is irrelevant. Answer C is incorrect as this offence applies to a person aged under 16 years of age. Answer D is incorrect as this section covers the sexual activity that takes place between the two.

Investigators' Manual, para. 4.4.2

Answer 26.2

Answer **B** — This offence is committed if a person aged 18 or over (A) engages in sexual activity, for the purpose of obtaining sexual gratification and the activity is engaged in *when another person is present or is in a place from which (A) can be observed.* The fact that PRIZEMAN intended SHIPMAN to view the act (answer A) or the fact that he believed her to be watching the activity (answer C) are both immaterial if SHIPMAN is not present or in a place from which PRIZEMAN can be observed. Answer D is incorrect, as the fact that CASE was unaware of SHIPMAN's presence would not preclude PRIZEMAN committing the offence if SHIPMAN was present when the activity took place.

Investigators' Manual, para. 4.4.3

Answer 26.3

Answer **C** — Answer A is incorrect as the person committing this offence must be at least 18 years old. Answer B is incorrect as not only must the activity carried out be 'sexual', but also it must be carried out in order to obtain sexual gratification. Answer D is incorrect as it is not necessary to show that the child was in fact aware of the activity in every case.

Investigators' Manual, para. 4.4.3

Answer 26.4

Answer **A** — This offence relates to causing a child to watch a third person engage in sexual activity or to look at an image of any person engaging in an activity. Answer B is incorrect on that basis. Answer C is incorrect because the offence can be committed against a child aged under 16 years of age. Answer D is incorrect as s. 79(5) of the Act states that an 'image' includes images of an imaginary person and, as such, animated cartoon images would be covered by the legislation.

Investigators' Manual, para. 4.4.4

Answer 26.5

Answer **D** — The offence of causing a child to watch a sexual act under s. 12 of the Act must be committed *intentionally*. Answer A is incorrect as although there might be a chance that children would see the images, unless HUGHES has carried out the activity with the intention that a child will observe it then the offence is not committed. Answer B is incorrect as although HUGHES has carried out the act for the purposes of sexual gratification, the sexual gratification aspect of the offence is incomplete. Sexual gratification for the purposes of this section must be gained by watching the child watching the activity of a third person or an image and not by watching an image for oneself. Answer C is incorrect as the term 'image' includes a moving or a still image.

Investigators' Manual, para. 4.4.4

Answer 26.6

Answer **C** — The purpose of s. 13 of the Sexual Offences Act 2003 is to provide a lower penalty of five years' imprisonment where the offender is aged under 18 years.

Investigators' Manual, paras 4.4.2 to 4.4.4

Answer 26.7

Answer **B** — The offence of arranging or facilitating the commission of a child sex offence can be committed if the arranging or facilitating is for an offence to be committed in any part of the world, making answer A incorrect. Answer C is incorrect as the offence is complete whether or not the sexual activity takes place. Answer D is incorrect as the offence is complete if the defendant arranges or facilitates something that he intends to do, intends another person to do, *or believes that another person will do*.

Investigators' Manual, para. 4.4.5

Answer 26.8

Answer **B** — A person can only commit an offence under s. 14 of the Act if he arranges or facilitates an offence that would be an offence under ss. 9 to 13 of the Act. The offence under s. 14 of the Act can be committed if the defendant arranges or facilitates something *that he intends to do*, as well as arranging or facilitating the acts of others, making answer A incorrect. Answer C is incorrect as this offence is complete whether sexual activity takes place or not. Whether the person contacted is a police officer makes no difference as it is the arranging or facilitating that is the crux of the offence. Answer D is incorrect as there are no limitations as to the nature or type of contact. The arrangements or facilitation can be made by any means whatsoever, the Internet being a prime example.

Investigators' Manual, para. 4.4.5

Answer 26.9

Answer **B** — Answer A is incorrect as the intentions of the defendant at the time of the first meeting with a potential victim are immaterial; it is the defendant's intentions at the time of either meeting with or travelling to meet the victim after one or more previous communications or meetings that is relevant. Answer C is incorrect as the offence can be committed when travelling to meet the victim with the requisite intent. Section 36 of the Criminal Justice and Courts Act 2015 (in force from 13th April 2015) makes a small but significant change to the offence of 'grooming', changing the 'two occasions' required to one occasion and making answer D incorrect.

Investigators' Manual, para. 4.4.5

Answer 26.10

Answer **B** — The offence is committed in several different ways. One of those is when a person who is 18 or over (HARVEY) has met or communicated with another person (in this case PREECE) on one or more occasions and, subsequently (under s. 15(1)(a) (iii)), PREECE travels with the intention of meeting HARVEY anywhere in the world and HARVEY intends to do anything to PREECE that would amount to a relevant offence (relevant offences being offences under ss. 9 to 13 of the Sexual Offences Act 2003). This means that an offence has been committed by HARVEY at point B (meaning that answer D is incorrect). The meetings or communication, for the purposes of this section, can have taken place in any part of the world (s. 15(2)), making answer A incorrect. Answer C is incorrect as the communication can include text messaging or interactions via Internet 'chat rooms'.

Investigators' Manual, para. 4.4.5

Answer 26.11

Answer **C** — Answer A is incorrect as the *actus reus* of this offence includes penetration of the victim's mouth with the defendant's penis. Answer B is incorrect as the law makes no distinction in sentence with regard to the age of the victim. Answer D is incorrect as when the offence involves penetration, it is indictable only and the maximum sentence is 14 years' imprisonment.

Investigators' Manual, para. 4.4.5

Answer 26.12

Answer **A** — The offence can only be committed if the relationship between the parties concerned is known or could reasonably be expected to be known by the offender—this is not the case in this scenario, making answers B, C and D incorrect.

Investigators' Manual, para. 4.4.6

Answer 26.13

Answer **B** — Apart from 'touching' and 'sexual', there are two further elements that must be proved in relation to s. 25 of the Act. The first is the existence of the relevant family relationship and the second is the age of the victim (making answers A, C and D incorrect). In addition, answers C and D are incorrect in respect of both the relationship and the age of the victim; the *defendant* will have an evidential burden to discharge in that regard (s. 25(2) and (3)).

Investigators' Manual, para. 4.4.6

Answer 26.14

Answer **D** — Answer A is incorrect as the relationship of half-brother is covered by s. 27 of the Act. Answer B is incorrect as LYONS has not actually touched JARVIS and so the offence under s. 25 is incomplete. Answer C is incorrect as a person under 18 years of age can commit this offence but the maximum penalty is less in such circumstances.

Investigators' Manual, para. 4.4.6

Answer 26.15

Answer **D** — This question revolves around the issue of whether there is a relevant family relationship between RENTON and THAWLEY. Section 27 of the Act defines core family relationships and also provides additional categories where a relationship will be deemed to exist. One of those categories is when the defendant and the victim *live or have lived* in the same household and they have the same parent or foster parent. Although RENTON and THAWLEY have the same foster parent (STRAKER) they do not live and never have lived in the same household. In other words, there is no family relationship between the two. This fact makes answers A and C incorrect. Answer B is incorrect as whether the sexual intercourse was consensual or not is immaterial for the purposes of an offence under s. 25 of the Act.

Investigators' Manual, para. 4.4.6

Answer 26.16

Answer **C** — Section 29 of the Act caters for sexual relationships which pre-date family relationships. A person is not liable for a familial child sex offence under s. 25 where a lawful sexual relationship existed between the parties immediately before the onset of the circumstances giving rise to the familial relationship. Although WOOD and PERCIVAL are now stepsister and stepbrother they do not commit the offence because of s. 29, making answer A incorrect. A further exception (under s. 28 of the Act) relates to marriage exceptions; however, this is not the only exception and therefore answer B is incorrect. Answer D is incorrect as persons under the age of 18 can commit this offence.

Investigators' Manual, para. 4.4.6

Answer 26.17

Answer **D** — Although ARCHER and BARNARD are brother and sister and are therefore 'relatives' for the purposes of s. 64 of the Act, the offence under s. 64 can only be committed when the relative knows (or could reasonably be expected to know) that he/she is related to the other. If this knowledge is not present then the offence cannot be committed, making answers A, B and C incorrect. If the two were knowingly related then the offence would take place at point B as masturbation is not included in the *actus reus* of the offence.

Investigators' Manual, para. 4.4.7

Answer 26.18

Answer **A** — The offence under s. 64 of the Act is triable either way and is punishable by up to two years' imprisonment, making answers B, C and D incorrect.

Investigators' Manual, para. 4.4.7

Answer 26.19

Answer **A** — Section 1(1)(a) of the Protection of Children Act 1978 makes it an offence for a person to take, or permit to be taken or to make, any indecent photograph or pseudo-photograph of a child. Section 45 of the Sexual Offences Act 2003 amends the Protection of Children Act so that where photographs are concerned a person will be considered a 'child' if they are 16 or 17 years of age. However, photographs taken and used within an established relationship will not be criminalised if: (i) the defendant proves that the photograph in question was of a child aged 16 or over and at the time of the taking or making, he and the child were married or living together as partners in an enduring family relationship; (ii) the child consented to the photograph being taken or the defendant reasonably believed that the child consented; and (iii) the photograph must not be one that shows a person other than the child and the defendant. If *any* of these conditions is not satisfied then the prosecution need only prove the offence as set out in s. 1(1)(a) of the 1978 Act. Answers B and D are incorrect as they only form part of the potential defence available to GATRELL. In addition, answer D is incorrect as it asserts that taking photographs of a child over the age of 16 is permissible with the consent of the child. Answer C is incorrect as this defence exists if all three elements are present.

Investigators' Manual, para. 4.4.8

Answer 26.20

Answer **B** — If all the requirements of s. 45 of the Sexual Offences Act 2003 are met this will mean that at the time the photographs were taken (i) LAWFORD was at least 16 years of age and JOHNSON and LAWFORD were either married or living together in an enduring family relationship; (ii) there is enough evidence to show that LAWFORD consented to the photograph being taken; and (iii) the photograph does not show any person other than the child and the defendant. This will provide an exception to offences under s. 1(1)(a), (b) and (c) of the Protection of Children Act 1978. However, just because the photographs are 'legitimate' the showing or distribution offence under s. 1(1)(b) *will be committed* if that showing or distribution is to a person other than the child, so the offence would be complete at B when JOHNSON possesses the photographs with a view to show them to MANNING.

Investigators' Manual, para. 4.4.8

Answer 26.21

Answer **D** — Under s. 1(1)(b) of the Act it is an offence to distribute or show indecent photographs or pseudo-photographs. PARNELL is guilty of this offence by sending the package containing the indecent photographs, via OXLEY, to ROLFE. OXLEY is also guilty of this offence. It would be a defence for a person charged with such an offence under s. 1(4)(b) of the Act to prove that he had not himself seen the photographs or pseudo-photographs and did not know, nor had any cause to suspect, them to be indecent. OXLEY would have been able to avail himself of this defence up until the point when he realised what the contents of the package were, meaning that answers A and C are incorrect. Answer B is incorrect as ROLFE has committed the offence. He does have a defence in this situation under s. 1(4)(b) of the Act, which states that he will have a defence if he had a legitimate reason for distributing or showing the photographs or pseudo-photographs.

Investigators' Manual, para. 4.4.8

Answer 26.22

Answer **C** — Answer A is incorrect as 'making' a pseudo-photograph *does* include voluntarily browsing through indecent images of children on and from the Internet (*R* v *Smith and Jayson* [2002] EWCA Crim 683). Answer B is incorrect as evidence showing how a computer had been used to access paedophile news groups, chatlines and websites *would* be relevant to a case relating to the creation of an indecent image of a child (*R* v *Mould* (2001) 2 Cr App R(S) 8). Answer D is incorrect as downloading images from the Internet *will* amount to 'making' a photograph (*R* v *Bowden* [2000] 2 WLR 1083). An image consisting of two parts of two different photographs taped together (the naked body of a woman taped to the head of a child) is not a pseudo-photograph. If such an image were copied, it could be (*R* v *Dooley* [2005] EWCA Crim 3093).

Investigators' Manual, para. 4.4.8

Answer 26.23

Answer **D** — Answer A is incorrect as a 'child' is a person under the age of 18 years of age at the material time. Answer B is incorrect as although the photographs were sent to SANDBROOK without any prior request being made by him for such material (the first part of the defence under s. 160(2)(c)), he has kept them for an unreasonable time, thereby defeating the defence. Answer C is incorrect as showing or distributing the indecent photographs relates to an offence under s. 1 of the Protection of Children Act 1978 and not to the offence of possessing indecent photographs under this Act.

Investigators' Manual, para. 4.4.8

Answer 26.24

Answer **A** — The Coroners and Justice Act 2009, s. 62 states:

(1) It is an offence for a person to be in possession of a prohibited image of a child.
(2) A prohibited image is an image which—
    (a) is pornographic,
    (b) falls within subsection (6), and
    (c) is grossly offensive, disgusting or otherwise of an obscene character.

An image falls within subs. (6) if it is an image which focuses solely or principally on a child's genitals or anal region, or portrays any of the acts mentioned below. Amongst other acts they include:

- the performance by a person of an act of intercourse or oral sex with or in the presence of a child;
- an act of masturbation by, of, involving or in the presence of a child.

Section 65 states that an 'image' includes a moving or still image (produced by any means) such as a photograph or film, or data (stored by any means) which is capable of conversion into a moveable or still image such as data stored electronically (as on a computer disk), which is capable of conversion into an image. This covers material available on computers, mobile phones or any other electronic device. A 'child' means a person under the age of 18 (s. 65(5)). References to an image of a person include references to an image of an imaginary person. References to an image of a child include references to an image of an imaginary child. So the behaviour in both images is captured, making answers B, C and D incorrect.

Investigators' Manual, para. 4.4.9

27 Protection of Children

QUESTIONS

Question 27.1

DC WELL receives information that PORT has physically abused her children and visits PORT, who lets the officer into her house. DC WELL speaks to JANE PORT (aged 16 years) and ALEX PORT (aged 12 years). JANE PORT has several cuts and bruises to her face; ALEX PORT shows no signs of being physically abused. JANE PORT tells the officer that her mother is responsible for her injuries and that this is not the first time she has been assaulted by her. ALEX PORT tells the officer that he has heard his mother beating his sister and it frightens him and he cannot eat as a result. Because of what he has seen and heard, DC WELL is considering taking both children into 'Police Protection' (under s. 46 of the Children Act 1989).

Which of the following statements is correct?

A DC WELL can take ALEX PORT into 'Police Protection' but cannot take JANE PORT into 'Police Protection' because she is not a 'child' for the purposes of the Act.

B DC WELL can take JANE PORT into 'Police Protection' if he has reasonable cause to believe that she will suffer significant harm and ALEX PORT because of any impairment he may suffer from hearing his sister being ill-treated.

C DC WELL can take JANE PORT into 'Police Protection' but cannot take ALEX PORT into 'Police Protection' because he has not suffered any physical abuse.

D DC WELL cannot take either of the children into police protection in these circumstances.

Question 27.2

DC HAMBLING has taken JEPHCOTT into 'Police Protection' (under s. 46 of the Children Act 1989).

What is the maximum period that JEPHCOTT can spend in 'Police Protection'?

A 24 hours.

B 48 hours.

C 72 hours.

D 96 hours.

Question 27.3

MILBURN (aged 13 years) is subject to an emergency protection order and is in the care of his social worker, PRINCE. MILBURN's stepfather, HOLT, rings MILBURN on his mobile phone and tells him that life would be far better for him if he ran away from PRINCE's care and came back to his family. HOLT tells MILBURN that if he does run away from PRINCE he will take him to Disneyland in Florida.

Has HOLT committed an offence of acting in contravention of a protection order (contrary to s. 49 of the Children Act 1989)?

A Yes, he has induced and incited MILBURN to run away from a responsible person.

B No, this offence can only be committed by taking MILBURN away from the responsible person.

C Yes, but only if MILBURN actually runs away from the responsible person.

D No, this offence relates to children who are in care or in police protection and not to those subject to an emergency protection order.

Question 27.4

JUDSON leaves FOXLEY, her common-law husband, after their relationship breaks down and takes their three-year-old child with her. FOXLEY contacts DC BANHAM and reports the child's absence. DC BANHAM later locates JUDSON, who is staying in a women's refuge with her three-year-old child. At the request of JUDSON, DC BANHAM tells FOXLEY that the child is safe but refuses to tell him where the child is. FOXLEY hires a solicitor and *ex parte* (i.e. without telling the police) applies for an order from the County Court under s. 33 of the Family Law Act 1986, requiring the police to disclose the information.

Considering the law with regard to the disclosure of a child's whereabouts, which of the following statements is correct?

A If FOXLEY obtains such an order then DC BANHAM will have to provide him with details of the child's whereabouts.

B An order under s. 33 in respect of the police will be made without their presence (*ex parte*) in all cases.

C If FOXLEY's application is successful then DC BANHAM will have to tell FOXLEY's solicitor of the child's whereabouts.

D It has been held that only in exceptional circumstances will the police be asked to divulge the whereabouts of a child under a s. 33 order.

ANSWERS

Answer 27.1

Answer **B** — Section 46 of the Act states that where a constable has reasonable cause to believe that a child would otherwise be likely to suffer significant harm, he may remove the child to suitable accommodation. Answer A is incorrect as a 'child' is someone who is under 18 years old (s. 105). Answer C is incorrect as the definition of 'harm' is very broad and includes forms of ill-treatment that are not 'physical'. It also covers the impairment of health (physical or mental) and also physical, intellectual, emotional, social or behavioural development. The definition also extends to impairment suffered from seeing or hearing the ill-treatment of *any other person*. Answer D is incorrect for these reasons.

Investigators' Manual, para. 4.5.3

Answer 27.2

Answer **C** — The longest period that a child can spend in 'Police Protection' is 72 hours (s. 46(6)).

Investigators' Manual, para. 4.5.3

Answer 27.3

Answer **A** — Answer D is incorrect as s. 49(2) states that this offence applies to a child who is in care, subject of an emergency protection order or in police protection (s. 46). A 'responsible person' is any person who at the time has care of the child by virtue of a care order, an emergency protection order or by s. 46 of the Act, i.e. PRINCE. The offence can be committed by (a) taking a child to whom this section applies away from a responsible person, or (b) keeping such a child away from a responsible person or (c) inducing, assisting or inciting such a child to run away from or stay away from the responsible person. Therefore, answers B and C are incorrect.

Investigators' Manual, para. 4.5.5

Answer 27.4

Answer **D** — This question relates to the circumstances in *S* v *S (Chief Constable of West Yorkshire Intervening)* [1998] 1 WLR 1716. In this case, Butler-Sloss LJ stated that an order under s. 33 provides for the information to be disclosed to the court and not to any other party or his/her solicitor, making answers A and C incorrect. She also stated that an order made under s. 33 should not normally be made in respect of the police without their being present, making answer B incorrect.

Investigators' Manual, para. 4.5.6

28 Sexual Offences against People with a Mental Disorder and Offences Relating to Prostitution

QUESTIONS

Question 28.1

ULLESTHORPE sneaks into a care home which specifically caters for people with mental illnesses who are unable to look after themselves. ORTON is a patient at the home and is in a constant vegetative state, unable to speak or move. ULLESTHORPE is fully aware of the nature of the home and the condition of the people who are in it and creeps into ORTON's room where he fondles ORTON's breasts to obtain sexual gratification. ULLESTHORPE becomes sexually aroused and places his erect penis in ORTON's hand. He then uses ORTON's hand to masturbate himself.

At what point, if at all, does ULLESTHORPE first commit an offence of sexual activity with a person with a mental disorder (contrary to s. 30 of the Sexual Offences Act 2003)?

A When he fondles ORTON's breasts.
B When he places his erect penis in ORTON's hand.
C When he uses ORTON's hand to masturbate himself.
D The offence has not been committed by ORTON.

Question 28.2

CORRIN is 27 years old and suffers from cerebral palsy meaning that she has an IQ of 50. CORRIN is able to speak but because of her condition, she is unable to communicate her choice in a way that other women, not suffering from such disabilities, would be able to. A further effect of the condition is that she cannot walk and is in a wheelchair. CORRIN's friend, MUXLOE, often takes her to a nearby park where GRAY (a 73-year-old man who is aware of CORRIN's condition) has befriended CORRIN and speaks to her. One afternoon MUXLOE leaves CORRIN and GRAY in the park while she visits a newsagents. GRAY moves CORRIN behind a shed and asks CORRIN if he can kiss her breasts; CORRIN says *'Yes'*. GRAY kisses her breasts and then asks if he can digitally penetrate her vagina and again CORRIN says *'Yes'* and GRAY penetrates CORRIN's vagina with one of his fingers.

Considering the offence under s. 30 of the Sexual Offences Act 2003 (sexual activity with a person with a mental disorder) only, which of the following comments is correct?

A The offence has not been committed as CORRIN is able to refuse to be touched by GRAY.

B The offence has been committed but only when GRAY kisses CORRIN's breasts.

C The offence has been committed but only when GRAY digitally penetrates CORRIN's vagina.

D The offence has been committed by GRAY and this will encompass him kissing CORRIN's breasts and digitally penetrating her vagina.

Question 28.3

SHAMBER is a sexual predator and has been watching the front entrance of a mental health care home for several days, waiting for an opportunity to sexually assault one or more of the residents of the care home. He watches as two female residents of the home, EDGEWARE (aged 14) and BOSS (aged 18) are escorted into a waiting minibus by JAKEMAN who sits inside the bus with them; the bus is driven by FROST. Just as the engine starts, SHAMBER runs over to the side of the minibus and jumps inside. He produces a gun and points it at FROST and tells him to drive away from the home. Due to their mental disability, EDGEWARE and BOSS are oblivious to the threat that SHAMBER poses. Two miles along the road, SHAMBER orders FROST to stop the minibus. He tells JAKEMAN and FROST to get out of the minibus and then sexually assaults EDGEWARE and BOSS by squeezing their breasts.

Has an offence under s. 30 of the Sexual Offences Act 2003 (sexual activity with a person with a mental disorder) been committed in these circumstances?

A No, as the activity did not take place in a care home for persons suffering from a mental disorder.

B Yes, but only in relation to EDGEWARE.

C No, as the activity did not involve penetration.

D Yes, the offence has been committed against EDGEWARE and BOSS.

Question 28.4

VENNING is suffering from a schizo-affective disorder and has a low IQ and a history of alcohol abuse. She is sitting in a pub and engages in conversation with GARDNER who has no ideas of VENNING's mental disorder. GARDNER buys VENNING a number of drinks and then asks VENNING if she wants to have sexual intercourse with him; VENNING replies that she does. The only reason VENNING consents is because of her schizo-affective disorder causing her to become panicked and afraid of GARDNER, thereby unable to refuse GARDNER's request. The two leave the pub and go to GARDNER's house where they have oral sex (GARDNER's penis to VENNING's mouth).

Has GARDNER committed an offence of sexual activity with a person with a mental disorder (contrary to s. 30 of the Sexual Offences Act 2003)?

A No, GARDNER did not know about VENNING's mental disorder.

B Yes, and because VENNING was given alcohol by GARDNER, the presumptions under s. 75 of the Act will be applicable.

C No, as the sexual act did not involve penetration of VENNING's vagina or anus.

D Yes, but permission to prosecute the offence will be required from the Director of Public Prosecutions.

Question 28.5

STRAND and HARPER commit an offence under s. 30 of the Sexual Offences Act 2003 against MAY who is a 20-year-old woman with Down's Syndrome. The behaviour of the two offenders consists of STRAND putting his penis in MAY's mouth and MAY masturbating HARPER's penis.

What is the maximum term of imprisonment the two offenders could face if they were tried on indictment?

A STRAND 10 years' imprisonment; HARPER seven years' imprisonment.

B STRAND 14 years' imprisonment; HARPER 10 years' imprisonment.

C STRAND life imprisonment; HARPER 14 years' imprisonment.

D STRAND and HARPER could both face life imprisonment.

Question 28.6

McAVOY regularly visits a bingo hall with her mother. During the course of the visits McAVOY has become very friendly with TURVEY who works at the bingo hall. McAVOY's mother has told TURVEY that her daughter has a mental disorder which makes her very vulnerable to suggestion and unable to refuse anything. During one visit to the bingo hall, TURVEY tells McAVOY that he wants to have sexual intercourse with her. McAVOY replies that she has heard that people need to be married before they can have sexual intercourse and asks if TURVEY will marry her. To get McAVOY's agreement to have sexual intercourse with him, TURVEY tells McAVOY that they will get married. The two have sexual intercourse in a broom cupboard at the bingo hall but after the sexual intercourse has taken place, TURVEY tells McAVOY that he will never marry her and only said he would to make sure that she had sex with him.

Has TURVEY committed an offence under s. 34 of the Sexual Offences Act 2003 (procuring sexual activity with a person with a mental disorder)?

A No, as the nature of the act was sexual intercourse and that has not been misrepresented in any way by TURVEY.

B Yes, as TURVEY has obtained McAVOY's agreement to sexual intercourse by an inducement (the promise to marry her).

C No, as McAVOY's agreement to sexual intercourse was not obtained by a threat.

D Yes, but the prosecution must prove that the victim of the offence was unable to refuse as a consequence of her mental disorder.

Question 28.7

CLEMENT (aged 17 years) is accompanying his parents on a visit to see his grandmother who is 72 years old and suffering from advanced senile dementia, leaving her bedridden as a resident in a mental care home. CLEMENT's parents leave the room his grandmother is in leaving CLEMENT and his grandmother alone. CLEMENT deeply resents spending time visiting his grandmother and out of spite and maliciousness he takes out his penis and waves it in front of his grandmother's face and then begins to masturbate in front of her saying, *'You can't do anything like this any more, can you old bag!'* CLEMENT is fully aware of his grandmother's condition and of the fact that she can do nothing about his behaviour.

CLEMENT has not committed the offence under s. 32 of the Sexual Offences Act 2003 (sexual activity in the presence of a mentally disordered person) but why not?

A CLEMENT has not committed this offence as he did not engage in sexual activity with another person in the presence of his grandmother.

B CLEMENT has not committed the offence because he is under 18 years of age.

C CLEMENT has not committed the offence because no inducement was offered to his grandmother to watch the sexual act.

D CLEMENT has not committed the offence because he did not act for the purpose of obtaining sexual gratification.

Question 28.8

The Sexual Offences Act 2003 provides a definition of the term 'prostitution' which is important when considering offences under the Act that deal with such behaviour and associated behaviour.

In respect of that definition, which of the following comments is true?

A The definition applies to women only.

B The definition would not apply to a person who has been compelled to offer or provide sexual services to another person.

C To be classed as a 'prostitute' a person must, on at least two occasions, offer sexual services to another person.

D The offer or provision of sexual services to another person could be made in return for a promise of payment to a third person.

Question 28.9

PARSON is a cocaine addict and is finding it hard to maintain his lifestyle as he is spending all of his income on the drug. PARSON's partner, MACE, is speaking to KELLY about the problem and KELLY offers MACE a solution. KELLY tells MACE that he will supply PARSON with all the cocaine he wants if MACE is willing to have sex with other men at a holiday cottage in France on weekends. KELLY states that he will organise the trips so MACE will have nothing to worry about. MACE agrees and travels to France where he has sexual intercourse with several men and PARSON is supplied with a large amount of cocaine as a reward. KELLY does not gain anything for himself from this arrangement, he is just trying to help MACE in his relationship with PARSON.

Thinking about the offence of causing, inciting or controlling prostitution (under s. 52 of the Sexual Offences Act 2003), which of the following statements is correct?

A KELLY has not committed the offence because MACE provides the sexual services outside the United Kingdom (in France).

B KELLY commits the offence when he suggests that MACE becomes a prostitute.

C KELLY has not committed the offence because he does not gain anything for himself as a result of this arrangement.

D KELLY commits the offence but only when MACE has sex and PARSON is rewarded with cocaine.

Question 28.10

Section 53A of the Sexual Offences Act 2003 creates an offence which is committed if someone pays or promises payment for the sexual services of a prostitute who has been subject to exploitative conduct of a kind likely to induce or encourage the provision of a sexual service.

In relation to that offence, which of the following statements is true?

A 'Exploitative conduct' only relates to the use of violence or the threat to use violence.

B It does not matter where in the world the sexual services are provided.

C To be guilty of the offence the defendant must know or ought to have known that the prostitute has been subject to 'exploitative conduct'.

D There is a defence to the offence if the defendant can prove that he/she was unaware that the prostitute providing the sexual services had been subjected to 'exploitative conduct'.

Question 28.11

HAYE owns and runs a massage parlour where ILLTEN and STONELEIGH (both female) provide massage for customers. HAYE knows that ILLTEN and STONELEIGH regularly provide 'extras' for their male customers; this takes the form of oral sex with the customers. ILLTEN and STONELEIGH charge £50 for the 'extra' service but HAYE does not take a cut of the money as he is just happy that people are using the massage parlour.

Considering the offence of keeping a brothel used for prostitution (contrary to s. 33A of the Sexual Offences Act 1956) only, which of the following comments is true?

A No offence has been committed by HAYE as he does not take any payment for the sexual services offered by ILLTEN and STONELEIGH.

B For HAYE to be convicted of the offence, the prosecution would need to prove that persons resorted to the 'brothel' on more than one occasion.

C No offence has been committed as a 'brothel' is a place to which people resort for the purposes of unlawful sexual intercourse and in this situation full sexual intercourse does not take place.

D HAYE has committed the offence in this situation.

Question 28.12

MILL has an argument with his neighbour (NEWBOLD) who strongly disapproves of MILL as he knows that MILL is a prostitute. MILL wants to upset NEWBOLD so he persuades DEESLEY (one of MILL's regular customers) to come to his house and have sexual intercourse with him in the front room of his house in front of the window so that NEWBOLD can see what they are doing when he is tending his garden. MILL tells DEESLEY that for the favour he will only charge 50% of his usual fee and DEESLEY agrees. When NEWBOLD is tending his garden, MILL begins to have sexual intercourse with DEESLEY and MILL bangs on the front window to attract NEWBOLD's attention. NEWBOLD sees what the pair are doing and is outraged by their conduct and calls the police.

With regard to the common law offence of keeping a disorderly house, which of the following is correct?

A The offence requires a degree of persistence so a single instance (such as an indecent performance) would not amount to an offence.

B The offence has been committed and is punishable (on indictment only) by a term of imprisonment of 10 years.

C The offence has been committed by MILL as the house is 'open' (i.e. to a customer or customers).

D The offence has not been committed as this behaviour takes place in a dwelling house.

Question 28.13

KORIE (who is 19 years old) is a prostitute and works from her home where she has sexual intercourse with customers she picks up outside a local pub. She injures her knee meaning that she has trouble walking so she stands in the doorway of her house (which abuts the street she lives on) and offers her services to men who walk past the front door of her house.

If KORIE is to commit an offence of soliciting (under s. 1 of the Street Offences Act 1959), which of the following requirements must be met?

A Her conduct must take place on three or more occasions in any period of one month.

B Her conduct must take place on two or more occasions in any period of three months.

C Her conduct must take place on three or more occasions in any period of six months.

D Her conduct must take place on two occasions or more in any period of 12 months.

Question 28.14

MONTIGUE is searching for a prostitute to have sexual intercourse with. He is driving his vehicle along a street when he slows down and stops next to BRYSON who is standing on the street corner waiting to be picked up by her boyfriend. MONTIGUE winds the window of his car down and shouts out to BRYSON, *'You look like you need a fuck—how much for a quickie?'* BRYSON ignores MONTIGUE who then shouts out *'C'mon, don't be shy. I'll pay you good money for a shag'*. BRYSON continues to ignore MONTIGUE who steps out of his car onto the street and approaches BRYSON saying, *'Playing hard to get, eh? OK, then, I'll give you £100 for a hand-job'*. BRYSON slaps MONTIGUE in the face and walks away from him.

At what point, if at all, does MONTIGUE first commit an offence contrary to s. 51A of the Sexual Offences Act 2003 (soliciting by 'kerb-crawling')?

A When he winds the window of his car down and first speaks to BRYSON saying, *'You look like you need a fuck—how much for a quickie?'*

B On the second occasion he speaks to BRYSON and says, *'C'mon, don't be shy. I'll pay you good money for a shag'*.

C When he is on the street and speaks to BRYSON on the third occasion saying, *'Playing hard to get, eh? OK, then, I'll give you £100 for a hand-job'*.

D MONTIGUE does not commit the offence in these circumstances.

ANSWERS

Answer 28.1

Answer **A** — A person commits an offence under s. 30(1) if:

(a) he intentionally touches another person (B),
(b) the touching is sexual,
(c) B is unable to refuse because of or for a reason related to a mental disorder, and
(d) A knows or could reasonably be expected to know that B has a mental disorder and that because of it or for a reason related to it B is unlikely to refuse.

ULLESTHORPE clearly commits the offence when he fondles ORTON's breasts, making answers B, C and D incorrect.

Investigators' Manual, para. 4.6.3

Answer 28.2

Answer **D** — A person commits an offence under s. 30(1) if:

(a) he intentionally touches another person (B),
(b) the touching is sexual,
(c) B is unable to refuse because of or for a reason related to a mental disorder, and
(d) A knows or could reasonably be expected to know that B has a mental disorder and that because of it or for a reason related to it B is unlikely to refuse.

Answer A is incorrect as CORRIN is unable to refuse to be touched by GRAY. In *Hulme* v *DPP* [2006] EWHC 1347 (Admin), the Divisional Court examined a decision reached by a magistrates' court in relation to a complainant who was a cerebral palsy sufferer with a low IQ (aged 27). The magistrates' court had decided that the complainant was unable to refuse to be sexually touched; the Divisional Court agreed and the conviction against the defendant (who was 73) was upheld. The touching can involve penetration meaning answer B is incorrect and answer C is incorrect as the kissing of CORRIN's breasts is certainly sexual.

Investigators' Manual, para. 4.6.3

Answer 28.3

Answer **D** — A person commits an offence under s. 30(1) if:

(a) he intentionally touches another person (B),
(b) the touching is sexual,
(c) B is unable to refuse because of or for a reason related to a mental disorder, and
(d) A knows or could reasonably be expected to know that B has a mental disorder and that because of it or for a reason related to it B is unlikely to refuse.

The offence could be carried out at any location, making answer A incorrect. It can involve sexual touching and/or penetration, making answer C incorrect. There are no age restrictions in respect of the offence under s. 30, so the offence is committed against both females, making B incorrect.

Investigators' Manual, para. 4.6.3

Answer 28.4

Answer **A** — The offence under s. 30(1) can be committed by penetration or by sexual touching, making answer C incorrect. Answers B and D are incorrect as the offence has not been committed. Section 30(1)(d) states that the defendant must know or could reasonably be expected to know that the victim has a mental disorder and that because of it or for a reason related to it the victim is likely to be unable to refuse. B is further incorrect as the presumptions under ss. 74 to 76 do not apply to this offence; that is the purpose of s. 30(1)(c) and (d), and D is further incorrect as no special permission is required to prosecute the offence.

Investigators' Manual, para. 4.6.3

Answer 28.5

Answer **C** — If the offence under s. 30 involves penetration of the victim's anus or vagina, or of the victim's mouth with the defendant's penis (STRAND), or of the defendant's mouth by the victim's penis, then the offence is punishable by a maximum term of life imprisonment. Otherwise it is 14 years' imprisonment (HARPER).

Investigators' Manual, para. 4.6.3

Answer 28.6

Answer **B** — If the defendant obtains the victim's agreement to sexual touching/activity by means of any inducement (offered or given), or a threat or deception *for that purpose*, the defendant commits a specific offence under s. 34 of the Sexual Offences Act 2003 (punishable in the same way as an offence under s. 30). An example of such an offence would be where the defendant (TURVEY) promises to give the victim (McAVOY) some reward in exchange for allowing sexual touching/activity (the promise of marriage for sex). No 'threat' is required, making answer C incorrect. In specific cases of inducements, threats or deception, there is still a need to prove that the defendant knew (or could reasonably have been expected to know) of the victim's mental disorder but *no need to prove that the victim was unable to refuse*, making answer D incorrect.

Investigators' Manual, para. 4.6.3

Answer 28.7

Answer **D** — The sexual activity carried out must be for the purpose of obtaining sexual gratification—if it is for *any other reason* no offence under s. 32 is committed.

Investigators' Manual, para. 4.6.4

Answer 28.8

Answer **D** — A prostitute is a person (A) who:

- on at least one occasion (making answer C incorrect); and
- whether or not compelled to do so (making answer B incorrect);
- offers or provides sexual services to another person;
- in return for payment or a promise of payment to A or a third person (answer D).

Section 51(2) of the Sexual Offences Act 2003 states that the definition applies to both men and women (making answer A incorrect).

Investigators' Manual, para. 4.7.2

Answer 28.9

Answer **B** — Section 52(1) of the Sexual Offences Act 2003 states that a person commits an offence if:

(a) he intentionally causes or incites another person to become a prostitute in any part of the world, and
(b) he does so for or in the expectation of gain for himself or a third person.

Gain means any financial advantage, including the discharge of an obligation to pay or the provision of goods or services (including sexual services) gratuitously or at a discount or the goodwill of any person which is or appears likely, in time, to bring financial advantage (s. 54). So the 'gain' here is for PARSON (a third person), making C incorrect. It does not matter that the behaviour takes place in France, making answer A incorrect. The offence is committed when KELLY 'incites' MACE to become a prostitute (remembering that incitement is a form of encouragement to do something).

Investigators' Manual, para. 4.7.3

Answer 28.10

Answer **B** — Section 53A(3) states that a person engages in exploitative conduct if he/she uses force, threats (whether or not relating to violence) or any other form of coercion or practises any form of deception, making answer A incorrect. An offence is committed regardless of whether the person paying or promising payment for sexual services knows or ought to know or be aware that the prostitute has been subject to exploitative conduct, making answer C incorrect. This means that this offence is one of strict liability and no mental element is required in respect of the offender's knowledge that the prostitute was forced, threatened, coerced or deceived. There is no defence of the type mentioned in answer D.

Investigators' Manual, para. 4.7.4

Answer 28.11

Answer **D** — A brothel is a place to which people resort for the purposes of unlawful sexual intercourse with more than one prostitute. However, it is not necessary that full sexual intercourse takes place or is even offered—a massage parlour where other acts of lewdness or indecency for sexual gratification are offered may be a brothel, making answer C incorrect. Section 33A(1) states that it is an offence for a person to keep, or to manage, or act or assist in the management of, a brothel to which people resort for practices involving prostitution (whether or not also for other practices). Prostitution means offering or providing sexual services, whether under compulsion or not, to another in return for payment or a promise of payment to the prostitute or a third person, so it does not matter that HAYE does not receive a 'cut' of the money ILLTEN and STONELEIGH make, making answer A incorrect. There is no requirement for the prosecution to prove that the premises were resorted to on more than one occasion, making answer B incorrect.

Investigators' Manual, para. 4.7.5

Answer 28.12

Answer **A** — The offence is punishable with an unlimited sentence, making answer B incorrect. It makes no difference whatsoever whether the premises concerned are a dwelling house, making answer D incorrect. The house may be classed as 'open' to customers but the offence requires a degree of persistence so a single incident such as an indecent performance would not satisfy the requirements of the offence, making C incorrect.

Investigators' Manual, para. 4.7.5

Answer 28.13

Answer **B** — Conduct is 'persistent' for the purposes of this offence if it takes place on two or more occasions in any period of three months (s. 1(4)(a)), making answers A, C and D incorrect.

Investigators' Manual, para. 4.7.6

Answer 28.14

Answer **A** — Section 51A(1) of the Sexual Offences Act 2003 states that it is an offence for a person in a street or public place to solicit another (B) for the purpose of obtaining B's sexual services as a prostitute. Section 51A(2) states that the reference to a person in a street or public place includes a person in a vehicle in a street or public place. The offence is punishable on the first occasion the activity takes place, meaning the offence takes place at point A and that answers B, C and D are therefore incorrect.

Investigators' Manual, para. 4.7.6

29 Preparatory Offences

QUESTIONS

Question 29.1

FEARING applies for a job as a lifeguard at his local swimming pool. Part of his prospective duties will include giving swimming lessons to children between the ages of five and 12 years old. FEARING's ulterior motive is to gain employment at the swimming pool and then take indecent photographs of the children (contrary to s. 1 of the Protection of Children Act 1978). To help him get the job, he forges several certificates that state he has passed examinations as a lifeguard. As a result, FEARING is given the job as a lifeguard.

Considering the offence of committing a criminal offence with intent to commit a sexual offence (s. 62 of the Sexual Offences Act 2003), which of the following statements is right?

A FEARING does not commit the offence as taking indecent photographs of children under s. 1 of the Protection of Children Act 1978 is not a 'relevant sexual offence'.

B This offence can only be committed if the criminal offence is one of kidnapping or false imprisonment, therefore FEARING has not committed the offence.

C Until FEARING commits a sexual assault on one of the children he cannot be arrested for committing this offence.

D FEARING has initially committed an offence of obtaining a pecuniary advantage by deception (s. 16 of the Theft Act 1968) and therefore commits this offence.

Question 29.2

HALLAM's car breaks down in a country lane late one night. Rather than risk getting lost, she decides to sleep in her car and seek assistance in the morning. Several hours later, MILLENSTED walks past HALLAM's car and sees her sleeping inside. He decides to sexually touch HALLAM (an activity that would constitute an offence under s. 3 of the Sexual Offences Act 2003). MILLENSTED smashes the front window of the car and crawls inside. HALLAM, who is woken by the noise, manages to open one of the car doors and gets away from MILLENSTED.

With regard to the offence of trespass with intent to commit a sexual offence (s. 63 of the Sexual Offences Act 2003), which of the following statements is correct?

A The only intention that would make MILLENSTED guilty of this offence would be an intention to rape HALLAM.

B MILLENSTED has not committed the offence as a car would not be classed as a structure or part of a structure for the purposes of this offence.

C MILLENSTED has committed the offence as the term 'premises' for the purpose of s. 62 will include a vehicle.

D As HALLAM escaped before MILLENSTED committed the relevant sexual offence, he does not commit the offence.

Question 29.3

DIX decides that he is going to break into a house owned by AVERLEY. His intention is to commit an offence of rape (contrary to s. 1 of the Sexual Offences Act 2003) against AVERLEY and so he equips himself with a rope to tie her up with, condoms to minimise any DNA evidence he may leave and a bayonet to threaten her with. When DIX arrives at AVERLEY's house he sees her next-door neighbour, LAMBURN, leaving for an evening out. DIX decides that he will break into LAMBURN's house first and steal anything of value before he breaks into AVERLEY's house to rape her. He breaks into LAMBURN's house and steals property before breaking into AVERLEY's house.

At what point, if at all, does DIX commit an offence of trespass with intent to commit a sexual offence (contrary to s. 63 of the Sexual Offences Act 2003)?

A When he decides to break into AVERLEY's house and equips himself with the rope, condoms and bayonet.

B When he breaks into LAMBURN's house.

C When he breaks into AVERLEY's house.

D DIX does not commit the offence.

Question 29.4

JORDAN commits an offence of administering a substance with intent (contrary to s. 61 of the Sexual Offences Act 2003).

Which of the following statements is correct with regard to this offence?

A This offence carries a maximum sentence of two years' imprisonment.

B This offence carries a maximum sentence of three years' imprisonment.

C This offence carries a maximum sentence of 10 years' imprisonment.

D This offence carries a maximum sentence of 15 years' imprisonment.

Question 29.5

PEACH is drinking in a bar with McMANUS and WRIGHT. PEACH decides that he wants to have sexual intercourse with WRIGHT but knows that she is married and will never consent. He mentions this to McMANUS and gives McMANUS some Rohypnol (a 'date-rape' drug) to place in WRIGHT's drink. When WRIGHT is not looking, McMANUS puts the drug into WRIGHT's lager, intending to stupefy WRIGHT so as to enable PEACH to have sexual intercourse with her. WRIGHT drinks her drugged lager and quickly becomes ill. Before anything else happens, one of WRIGHT's friends appears and takes her home.

Which of the following statements is correct with regard to the offence of administering a substance with intent (contrary to s. 61 of the Sexual Offences Act 2003)?

A McMANUS has not committed the offence because he did not administer the drug with the intention of engaging in sexual activity with WRIGHT.

B No offence has been committed in these circumstances because no sexual activity took place.

C Only McMANUS has committed the offence in these circumstances.

D PEACH and McMANUS commit the offence in these circumstances.

Question 29.6

CHRISTON is in a nightclub and starts to chat to TRUELOCK. The two are getting on well and CHRISTON decides that he wants to have a sexual encounter with TRUELOCK. TRUELOCK is drinking triple vodka drinks and CHRISTON buys her a number of these, encouraging her to get drunk; TRUELOCK is aware that she is drinking alcohol. CHRISTON thinks that if TRUELOCK becomes drunk she will agree to masturbate him in the toilets of the nightclub.

Thinking about the offence under s. 61 of the Sexual Offences Act 2003 (administering a substance with intent) only, which of the following comments is correct?

A CHRISTON has not committed the offence because he did not intend to commit a sexual offence involving penetration.

B CHRISTON has committed the offence as he intends to stupefy TRUELOCK.

C CHRISTON has not committed the offence because TRUELOCK knew she was consuming alcohol.

D CHRISTON has committed the offence but the prosecution would have to show that a sexual act took place to prove the offence.

Question 29.7

SAMSON is a burglar and intends to steal property from a house belonging to DACE. He is watching the rear of DACE's house when he sees DACE putting some clothes on a line and decides that she is sexually attractive and that when he commits the burglary he will also rape her. A few minutes later, he enters the garden of the house by climbing over a back garden fence and then breaks into the house via the kitchen door and enters the kitchen. He hears some noise from upstairs and runs up the stairs and into a bedroom where he sees DACE trying to hide from him. He grabs her and tries to rape her but she fights him off and manages to escape by running into the street.

At what stage does SAMSON first commit the offence of trespass with intent to commit a sexual offence?

A When he enters the back garden of the house.

B When he breaks into the kitchen.

C When he runs into the upstairs bedroom.

D When he tries to rape DACE.

ANSWERS

Answer 29.1

Answer **A** — Section 62 of the Sexual Offences Act 2003 states that a person commits an offence under this section if he commits any offence with the intention of committing a relevant sexual offence. There are no restrictions on the nature or type of offence committed as long as it can be shown that there was an intention, when committing the original offence, to commit a relevant sexual offence. This makes answer B incorrect. Answer C is incorrect as the offence under s. 62 is committed when the first offence is committed with the required intention. Answer D is incorrect as although FEARING has committed an offence, taking photographs of children (contrary to s. 1 of the Protection of Children Act 1978) is not a 'relevant offence' for the purposes of s. 62. A 'relevant offence' means a sexual offence under Part 1 of the Sexual Offences Act 2003.

Investigators' Manual, para. 4.8.2

Answer 29.2

Answer **C** — Answer A is incorrect as MILLENSTED intends to commit a 'relevant sexual offence' (i.e. an offence under Part 1 of the Sexual Offences Act 2003). Answer D is incorrect as this is an offence of intention rather than consequence, therefore there is no need to prove that the substantive sexual offence took place. The term 'premises' for the purposes of this offence is far wider than that which relates to burglary under the Theft Act 1968. Section 63(2) of the Sexual Offences Act 2003 defines 'premises' as including a structure or part of a structure and this will include a tent, a vehicle or vessel or other temporary or moveable structure. This makes answer B incorrect.

Investigators' Manual, para. 4.8.3

Answer 29.3

Answer **C** — Answer A is incorrect as at this stage, DIX has not trespassed on any premises even though he has the intention of doing so. Answer B is incorrect as the defendant must intend to commit the relevant sexual offence on the premises where he/she is a trespasser. Unless DIX intends to commit a relevant sexual offence in LAMBURN's house he does not commit the offence (although he would be guilty of aggravated burglary at this stage). The offence is therefore committed at point C (making answer D incorrect).

Investigators' Manual, para. 4.8.3

Answer 29.4

Answer **C** — This offence is punishable with a maximum sentence of 10 years' imprisonment (under s. 4 of the Sexual Offences Act 1956 the equivalent offence carried a term of two years' imprisonment and had no specific power of arrest).

Investigators' Manual, para. 4.8.1

Answer 29.5

Answer **D** — Section 61(1) of the Act states that a person is guilty of an offence if he administers a substance to, or causes a substance to be taken by, another person (B), knowing that (B) does not consent and with the intention of stupefying or overpowering (B) so as to enable *any person* to engage in sexual activity that involves (B). Answer A is incorrect as it does not matter that McMANUS is not the person who will engage in sexual activity if he is administering the substance. Answer B is incorrect as the fact that sexual activity did not take place is immaterial if the substance is administered with that intent. 'Administering' or 'causing to be taken by' cover a broad range of conduct and would include a set of circumstances where PEACH persuades McMANUS to administer a drug to WRIGHT so that PEACH could have sex with WRIGHT, making answer C incorrect.

Investigators' Manual, para. 4.8.1

Answer 29.6

Answer **C** — This offence is aimed at the use of 'date rape' drugs administered without the victim's knowledge or consent, but would also cover the use of any other substance with the relevant intention. It would cover A spiking B's soft drink with alcohol where B did not know he/she was consuming alcohol, *but it would not cover A encouraging B to get drunk so that A could have sex with B, where B knew he/she was consuming alcohol* so CHRISTON would not commit the offence in these circumstances (making answers B and D incorrect). Answer A is incorrect as the offence requires an intention to enable any person to engage in sexual activity with the victim which may or may not involve penetration.

Investigators' Manual, para. 4.8.1

Answer 29.7

Answer **A** — The Sexual Offences Act 2003, s. 63 states:

(1) A person commits an offence if—
 (a) he is a trespasser on any premises,
 (b) he intends to commit a relevant sexual offence on the premises, and
 (c) he knows that, or is reckless as to whether, he is a trespasser.

A person is a trespasser if they are on the premises without the owner's or occupier's consent, whether express or implied, or they are there without a power at law to be there. Generally, defendants ought to know whether or not they are trespassing and recklessness will be enough in that regard. Premises here will include a structure or part of a structure (including a tent, vehicle or vessel or other temporary or moveable structure (s. 63(2))). This offence is intended to capture, for example, the situation where A enters a building owned by B, or goes into *B's garden* or garage without B's consent, and he/she intends to commit a relevant sexual offence against the occupier or other person on the premises. So as soon as SAMSON enters the garden the offence is complete, making answers B, C and D incorrect.

Investigators' Manual, para. 4.8.3

Question Checklist

The following checklist is designed to help you keep track of your progress when answering the multiple-choice questions. If you fill this in after one attempt at each question, you will be able to check how many you have got right and which questions you need to revisit a second time.

	First attempt Correct (✓)	Second attempt Correct (✓)
1 State of Mind, Criminal Conduct and Incomplete Offences		
1.1		
1.2		
1.3		
1.4		
1.5		
1.6		
1.7		
1.8		
1.9		
1.10		
1.11		
1.12		
1.13		
1.14		
1.15		
1.16		
1.17		
1.18		
1.19		
1.20		
1.21		

	First attempt Correct (✓)	Second attempt Correct (✓)
1.22		
1.23		
1.24		
2 Regulation of Investigatory Powers Act 2000		
2.1		
2.2		
2.3		
2.4		
2.5		
2.6		
2.7		
2.8		
2.9		
3 Entry, Search and Seizure/Code B		
3.1		
3.2		
3.3		
3.4		
3.5		
3.6		
3.7		

	First attempt Correct (✓)	Second attempt Correct (✓)
3.8		
3.9		
3.10		
3.11		
3.12		
3.13		
4 Detention and Treatment of Persons by Police Officers/Code C		
4.1		
4.2		
4.3		
4.4		
4.5		
4.6		
4.7		
4.8		
4.9		
4.10		
4.11		
4.12		
4.13		
4.14		
4.15		
4.16		
4.17		
4.18		
4.19		
4.20		
4.21		
4.22		
4.23		
4.24		
4.25		
4.26		
4.27		
4.28		
4.29		
4.30		

	First attempt Correct (✓)	Second attempt Correct (✓)
5 Interviews/Code C/Code E/Code F		
5.1		
5.2		
5.3		
5.4		
5.5		
5.6		
5.7		
5.8		
5.9		
5.10		
5.11		
5.12		
5.13		
6 Identification/Code D		
6.1		
6.2		
6.3		
6.4		
6.5		
6.6		
6.7		
6.8		
6.9		
6.10		
6.11		
6.12		
6.13		
6.14		
6.15		
7 Bail		
7.1		
7.2		
7.3		
7.4		
7.5		

	First attempt Correct (✓)	Second attempt Correct (✓)
7.6		
7.7		
7.8		
7.9		
7.10		
8 Disclosure of Evidence		
8.1		
8.2		
8.3		
8.4		
8.5		
8.6		
8.7		
8.8		
8.9		
9 Issues in Evidence and Offences against the Administration of Justice and Public Interest		
9.1		
9.2		
9.3		
9.4		
9.5		
9.6		
9.7		
9.8		
9.9		
9.10		
9.11		
9.12		
9.13		
10 Theft		
10.1		
10.2		
10.3		
10.4		
10.5		

	First attempt Correct (✓)	Second attempt Correct (✓)
10.6		
10.7		
10.8		
10.9		
10.10		
10.11		
10.12		
10.13		
10.14		
10.15		
10.16		
11 Burglary		
11.1		
11.2		
11.3		
11.4		
11.5		
11.6		
11.7		
11.8		
11.9		
11.10		
11.11		
11.12		
11.13		
11.14		
11.15		
11.16		
11.17		
11.18		
11.19		
11.20		
11.21		
11.22		
12 Robbery		
12.1		
12.2		

	First attempt Correct (✓)	Second attempt Correct (✓)
12.3		
12.4		
12.5		
12.6		
12.7		
12.8		
13 Blackmail		
13.1		
13.2		
13.3		
13.4		
13.5		
13.6		
14 Fraud		
14.1		
14.2		
14.3		
14.4		
14.5		
14.6		
14.7		
14.8		
14.9		
14.10		
14.11		
14.12		
15 Handling, Buying Scrap Metal for Cash and the Proceeds of Crime Act 2002		
15.1		
15.2		
15.3		
15.4		
15.5		
15.6		
15.7		

	First attempt Correct (✓)	Second attempt Correct (✓)
15.8		
15.9		
15.10		
15.11		
15.12		
15.13		
16 Criminal Damage		
16.1		
16.2		
16.3		
16.4		
16.5		
16.6		
17 Homicide		
17.1		
17.2		
17.3		
17.4		
17.5		
17.6		
17.7		
17.8		
18 Non-fatal Offences against the Person		
18.1		
18.2		
18.3		
18.4		
18.5		
18.6		
18.7		
18.8		
18.9		
18.10		
18.11		
18.12		

	First attempt Correct (✓)	Second attempt Correct (✓)
19 Child Abduction, False Imprisonment and Kidnap		
19.1		
19.2		
19.3		
19.4		
19.5		
19.6		
20 Public Order and Racially, Religiously Aggravated and Homophobic Offences		
20.1		
20.2		
20.3		
20.4		
20.5		
21 Misuse of Drugs		
21.1		
21.2		
21.3		
21.4		
21.5		
21.6		
21.7		
21.8		
21.9		
21.10		
21.11		
21.12		
21.13		
21.14		
22 Firearms and Gun Crime		
22.1		
22.2		
22.3		
22.4		

	First attempt Correct (✓)	Second attempt Correct (✓)
22.5		
22.6		
22.7		
22.8		
23 Terrorism and Associated Offences		
23.1		
23.2		
23.3		
23.4		
23.5		
23.6		
23.7		
23.8		
23.9		
23.10		
23.11		
23.12		
23.13		
23.14		
23.15		
24 Cybercrime		
24.1		
24.2		
24.3		
24.4		
24.5		
24.6		
25 Sexual Offences, Rape and Sexual Assault		
25.1		
25.2		
25.3		
25.4		
25.5		
25.6		
25.7		
25.8		

	First attempt Correct (✓)	Second attempt Correct (✓)
25.9		
25.10		
25.11		
25.12		
25.13		
25.14		
25.15		
25.16		
25.17		
25.18		
26 Child Sex Offences		
26.1		
26.2		
26.3		
26.4		
26.5		
26.6		
26.7		
26.8		
26.9		
26.10		
26.11		
26.12		
26.13		
26.14		
26.15		
26.16		
26.17		
26.18		
26.19		
26.20		
26.21		
26.22		

	First attempt Correct (✓)	Second attempt Correct (✓)
26.23		
26.24		
27 Protection of Children		
27.1		
27.2		
27.3		
27.4		
28 Sexual Offences against People with a Mental Disorder and Offences Relating to Prostitution		
28.1		
28.2		
28.3		
28.4		
28.5		
28.6		
28.7		
28.8		
28.9		
28.10		
28.11		
28.12		
28.13		
28.14		
29 Preparatory Offences		
29.1		
29.2		
29.3		
29.4		
29.5		
29.6		
29.7		